INFANTRYMAN
P·E·T·T·I·T

INFANTRYMAN
P · E · T · T · I · T

THE CIVIL WAR LETTERS OF CORPORAL FREDERICK PETTIT

EDITED BY

WILLIAM GILFILLAN GAVIN

AVON BOOKS ◆ NEW YORK

Dedicated to the memory of
Corporal Frederick Pettit
Who gave the last full measure of devotion

AVON BOOKS
A division of
The Hearst Corporation
1350 Avenue of the Americas
New York, New York 10019

Copyright © 1990 by William G. Gavin
Cover photograph courtesy of Massachusetts Commandery, Military Order of the Loyan Legion and the U.S. Army Military History Institute
Published by arrangement with White Mane Publishing Company, Inc.
Library of Congress Catalog Card Number: 90-43561
ISBN: 0-380-71437-X

The White Mane Publishing Company edition contains the following Library of Congress Cataloging in Publication Data:
Pettit, Frederick, 1842-1864.
     Infantryman Pettit : the Civil War letters of Corporal Frederick Pettit,
late of Company C, 100th Pennsylvania Veteran Volunteer Infantry Regiment,
"The Roundheads," 1862-1864 / edited by William Gilfillan Gavin.
     p.   cm.   Includes bibliographical references and index.
1. Pettit, Frederick, 1842-1864—Correspondence.   2. United States. Army.
Pennsylvania Infantry Regiment, 100th (1862-1865)—Biography.   3. United
States—History—Civil War, 1861-1865—Personal narratives.   4. Pennsylvania—
History—Civil War, 1861-1865—Personal narratives.   5. Soldiers—Pennsylvania—
Correspondence.   I. Gavin, William Gilfillan, 1924-   II. Title.
E527.5   100th .P47   1990   90-43561
973.7′448′092—dc20   CIP

First Avon Books Trade Printing: September 1991

AVON TRADEMARK REG. U.S. PAT. OFF. AND IN OTHER COUNTRIES, MARCA REGISTRADA,
HECHO EN U.S.A.

Printed in the U.S.A.

OPM   10   9   8   7   6   5   4   3   2   1

TABLE OF CONTENTS

INTRODUCTION

During research work in preparation for the 100th Pennsylvania's regimental history, *Campaigning With The Roundheads*, the author was introduced by Dr. Richard J. Sommers, Archivist-Historian, of the U.S. Army Military Institute, Carlisle Barracks, Pennsylvania to a collection of letters written during the Civil War by a soldier of Company C of the 100th Pennsylvania. There were approximately 125 letters in the collection written between July 1862 and July 1864. Additionally, there are a limited number of letters sent to Pettit by members of his immediate family. The letters had been transcribed and were in the collection of the *Civil War Times Illustrated Collection* and were in turn made available to the Archives of the USAMHI at Carlisle Barracks. A brief description from the files of the Archives describe these letters:

"His [Pettit's] letters vividly describe all operations in which he participated and also reflect the intense religious, moral, and political sentiments of the famous "Roundhead Regiment."

The present location of the original letters is unknown and only the typescript copies are found in the USAMHI collection along with typescript copy of a diary kept by Pettit in 1863-1864 contained in this volume as Appendix A. Some member of the Pettit family, probably one of his sisters, Mary Ann or Margaret, carefully preserved most of the letters written home regardless of which member of the family originally received them. Unfortunately, Pettit's diaries were apparently not saved as only the one covering September 1863 to January 1864 is in the collection. Efforts to identify the person or persons who originally donated the transcript copies of the letters to *Civil War Times Illustrated* several years ago have been unsuccessful.

Upon reading the Pettit letters, the author readily concluded that they were invaluable in the preparation of the definitive history of the 100th Pennsylvania Regiment.[1] Pettit was a faithful diarist and makes many references to his diaries in the letters to his family. In fact, upon his death, his company commander, Captain David Critchlow, lists a diary as being among the effects being sent home to the deceased soldier's next of kin. The sole surviving diary as far as is known is the one mentioned above and is found in Appendix A.

Pettit's goal was to write home to his family on a roughly once a week basis. He adhered to this plan when possible, but when in active field campaigning such as during the Jackson, Mississippi campaign, and the Virginia battles of May and June, 1864, it was impossible to write home. With these few exceptions,

---

[1] William G. Gavin, *Campaigning With The Roundheads, History of the 100th Pennsylvania Veteran Volunteer Infantry*, Morningside Press, Dayton, Ohio, 1989.

however, Pettit's letters generally flowed weekly through the mails to his family for two years until his death in front of Petersburg on July 9, 1864.

In many of his longer letters, Pettit consulted his diary continuously and many of his writings contain an almost day by day account of the location and the activities of his regiment. It was unique information because of its continuity in describing the operations of the 100th Pennsylvania regiment for 22 months of their service. Had Pettit survived the war, his letters undoubtedly would have continued and been the source of much additional information concerning the history of the regiment. His writings are sorely missed as a source because of his sudden death in action in July 1864.

Pettit obviously possessed a good basic education. His grammar and vocabulary are exceptionally good. He writes and expresses himself well. Pettit was a close observer of his surroundings and was always interested in describing the camp locations, routes of march, and battlefield positions to his family. His interest and concern for his fellowman is seen in the details written regarding sickness and lack of proper food supplies.

Although he was raised on a farm in rural Pennsylvania and undoubtedly had done extensive farming until he enlisted at age 20, his primary interest appears to have been in attending college and pursuing a teaching career. Shortly after enlisting, he writes his sister, Mary Ann, and expresses his interest in attending a college, such as Edinboro [Edinsboro State College, Pennsylvania] where she was at the time.

An analysis of the Pettit letters provides an interesting analysis of his character and personality. Above all, Fred Pettit was an intensely religious person, devoted to God, who often quoted scriptures toward the close of his letters. He exhorts his younger brothers and sisters to follow his religious beliefs. He possessed a strong faith in Eternal life and mentions this subject often. There are always words of encouragement to the younger brothers and sisters to do their best in their elementary schooling as well. His religious devotion enhanced his love of his family greatly and increased his concern for their welfare at all times. Among his personal effects sent home after his death were his Bible and hymn book.

In addition, he was devoted to duty, honor, and country. His last letters, written when he was wounded and in the hospital, verify his devotion to his country and his regiment. His patriotism was of the highest order. He spurned an opportunity for a furlough home and a hospital staff position after his wounding at Cold Harbor on June 2nd. He felt it was the duty of every soldier to be at the front if at all physically possible. Typically, Pettit pressured his surgeons to release him so he could return to Petersburg, even though his arm wound was not completely healed. Such devotion to duty following his sacrifices in May and June of 1864 is most exemplary. His patriotism was of the highest order. He despised the so called "copperheads" [anti-war movement] and in discussing them displays a degree of temper which seldom surfaces on any other subject. The "copperheads" were, in his opinion, traitors, and should be dealt with in the severest manner, lest they generate uprisings to endanger the war effort.

His pride of being in the army and of his regiment and its distinguished record are attitudes well reflected throughout the letters.

Pettit was a contented person. There are few complaints about army life, army rations, and the difficulties of life in the field during the Civil War — he is always in "my usual good health." He adapted well to army life and tolerated many unpleasant and unnecessary inconveniences without protest. He regarded army life as something to be endured without criticism of superiors or fellow soldiers.

With his meager army pay, Pettit was still concerned about his father's ability to pay off certain financial obligations. He often writes of sending money home to assist his family.

In editing the letters, the only compromise made was in the paragraphing. Pettit wrote long paragraphs which included many diversified subjects. In the interest of easier reading, the paragraphs have been broken up into smaller ones, with each one containing a single thought or subject. Pettit's words appear exactly as he wrote them, however minor spelling corrections, especially in place names, have been made as well as some punctuation corrections. Many details of the Pettit family and concern over matters at home in Pennsylvania have been retained so as to preserve the flavor of that period in the homesteads as well as the battlefields. Occasionally, when two or more letters were written in a short time span to different members of the family, there is repetition, but the letters have been presented as written so as not to interfere with their historical integrity. (Pettit used the colloquial nineteenth century word "nigger" in some of his letters. The editor has changed this to "Negro," the polite form used at the time.)

Hazel Dell, Pennsylvania, was the site of Pettit's home and of the Pettit farm. Hazel Dell is now included within the Borough of Ellwood City called the Fourth Ward. It is in Wayne Township, Lawrence County, Pennsylvania. Wayne Township was created from a part of North Sewickly Township, [which is mentioned in many of Pettit's letters] Beaver County, at the time Lawrence County was founded. [March 20, 1849] Wayne Township, then, is one of the original townships of Lawrence County. Through it flows Connoqugenessing Creek. There were originally three villages in the township, Chewton, Staylesville, and Wurtemburg.[2] The first post office in Hazel Dell was not established until 1872 and was near the creek bank located on what is now Wampum Avenue.

Fred Pettit's maternal grandparents were named Grieb. His maternal grandmother was a Quaker from Loudon County, Virginia, probably in area of the village of Waterford. After their marriage, the Griebs established their farm in Hazel Dell, Pennsylvania, next to a farm owned by the Pettit family. Eventually, Barbara Grieb, their daughter [born 1821] married one of the Pettit sons, Nathaniel [born 1813]. From this union, Frederick Pettit, the first child,

2 Dr. A. E. Whitaker, Editor, *History of Ellwood City, Pennsylvania*, Ellwood City Historical Association, Ellwood City, Pennsylvania [1932 - 1942], Page 27 and 28.

was born on April 21, 1842. The Pettits raised a large family. There were 11 children, born between 1842 and 1858. There were six daughters, Mary Ann, Margaret, Amelia, Ruth, Harriet, and Alice. Including Fred, there were five sons, Evan, Cyrus, Joseph, and Albert. In many of the letters sent home, Pettit mentions his brothers and sisters. Mary Ann and Margaret [Maggie] actively corresponded with him. They were just one and two years younger, and obviously were very close to their brother. Brother Evan, born in 1846, is likewise frequently mentioned. There is also one brief letter from Cyrus, fifteen years old at the time, written to his brother Fred in 1864. A great many of Pettit's letters were addressed to the family and directed to "Dear parents, brothers, and sisters" in order that the entire family could enjoy the news from the war.

Fred made a conscientious effort to write as often as possible, to keep his close knit family appraised of his activities and of the progress of the war.[3] Though conjecture, it is believed one of Fred's older sisters, Mary Ann or Margaret, was mostly likely the family member who gathered and carefully preserved the bulk of his wartime letters. Perhaps at some future date, we will have an answer to this question.

Fortunately, we have photographs of Pettit, preserved by Mr. Albert Pettit. Fred Pettit mentions in one of his early letters shortly after joining the 100th Pennsylvania that he was sending two photographs home along with his carpetsack. Shortly after the Jackson, Mississippi, battle he wrote on July 24, 1863: "Maggie and Mary wish me to send them a photograph. We do not have the luxury of such an institution away down south here!" One period carte de visite album containing photographs of members of Company C appeared on the market several years ago, but none of Pettit was included in that collection.

Pettit's official service record in the National Archives shows that he enlisted August 19, 1862, at age 20, in New Castle, Pennsylvania, under the certification of Captain Thomas J. Hamilton, of the 100th Pennsylvania, who was recruiting officer. His occupation is listed as a farmer, and he was 6 feet, ¼ inches tall, had blue eyes, dark hair, and fair complexion. A second Volunteer Enlistment covers Pettit's reenlistment at Blaine's Cross Roads, Tennessee, on December 28, 1863. A "Discharge" document date August 14, 1864, signed by Pettit's company commander, Captain David Critchlow, certified the discharge "by reason of Death, killed by a rifle shot near Petersburg, Va., whilst in line of duty July 9th, 1864."[4]

Fred's regiment, the 100th Pennsylvania, well known as the "Roundheads", was organized in August 1861, and early in the war was assigned to the

---

[3] The brief Pettit family genealogy is found in the Pettit Civil War letters collection, File 76.140, The *Civil War Times Illustrated* Collection of Civil War Papers. "Pettit, Frederick, 1862-1864. Private and Corporal, 100th Pennsylvania Infantry Regiment." These papers are located in the Archives Branch, at the United States Army Military History Institute, Carlisle Barracks, Pennsylvania.

[4] U.S. National Archives, Military Reference Branch, Military Archives Division, Washington, D.C. Veterans Records, Corporal Frederick Pettit, Company C, 100th Pennsylvania Veteran Volunteer Infantry Regiment, 1862-1864.

Department of the South and served in South Carolina under Generals Thomas W. Sherman and Isaac I. Stevens. They participated in the Federal capture of Hilton Head Island and then garrisoned in the nearby town of Beaufort, South Carolina. The Roundheads moved north against Charleston, South Carolina, in June 1862, and were in the fruitless attack against Battery Lamar, [Battle of Secessionville] on June 16 of that year. This was their first real battle and resulted in heavy casualties.

The 100th then moved back to Virginia, joined Pope's army of Virginia, and were in the battles of 2nd Manassas and Chantilly in August and September 1862. Here again, they suffered substantial losses in both officers and men killed and wounded.

Recruit Pettit joined the Roundheads as they moved toward Frederick, Maryland, on September 10, 1862. His letters give excellent details of the battles and campaigns in which he was involved until his death before Petersburg in July, 1864.

The Roundheads suffered heavy losses, three weeks after Pettit's death in the Battle of the Crater. Later, they won victories in the Battle of the Weldon Railroad and at Pegram's Farm. Their last battle, Fort Stedman, was fought March 25, 1865, in front of Petersburg, and was a substantial victory for the Union forces. For a detailed background study of the 100th Pennsylvania through their 47 months of service, *Campaigning With The Roundheads*, the regimental history, is recommended. Additional sources are listed in the Bibliography in this work.

Pettit could well be proud of his regiment. They did not win all of their battles, but always behaved with steadiness and courage. They were considered a "Fighting Regiment" and ranked near the top in total casualties suffered by all Pennsylvania regiments during the war. Appendix C is an extract from Fox's *Regimental Losses in the American Civil War*[5] and lists 224 killed and mortally wounded and 183 deaths from disease, accidents, and prisons from a total enrollment of 2,014 officers and men.

Corporal Fred Pettit did not survive the war but he is an outstanding example of the devoted and patriotic young Americans of his time, both north and south, who suffered much and willingly gave their lives for the principles in which they believed. Fred Pettit was a great American, one of which we may all be proud.

Although unknown by most, he is renowned in morality and high principles by the greatest unknown. He is representative of the devoted and dedicated volunteer soldier who sacrificed his life that the United States would remain undivided.

---

5 Lt. Col. William F. Fox, *Regimental Losses in the American Civil War*, Albany, New York, 1889, Page 288.

ACKNOWLEDGEMENTS

The editor is indebted to Dr. Richard J. Sommers, Archivist Historian, Archives Branch, United States Army Military History Institute, Carlisle Barracks, Pennsylvania. Dr. Sommers and his staff have been most helpful on all occasions. It was in 1979 that Dr. Sommers first wrote the editor about material on the 100th Pennsylvania Regiment in the archives at USAMHI. The Fred Pettit Collection of Civil War Letters was a part of the *Civil War Times Illustrated* collection which was given to USAMHI several years ago. The author is grateful to both *CWTI* and USAMHI for their cooperation with the Pettit collection.

Messrs. Michael Winey and Randolph Hackenburg, at USAMHI cooperated in providing copies of the majority of photographs of members of Company C of the 100th regiment which appear in the book.

My thanks to Mrs. Harriette McGrath, editor, who carefully edited the entire book and made many helpful changes.

CHAPTER ONE

FRED PETTIT JOINS THE ARMY

"I suppose you are wondering what has become of me!"

It is July 1862 and Fred Pettit, age 20, is giving strong consideration to joining the army. However, he is a farmer on his father's farm in the community of Hazel Dell, Lawrence County, Pennsylvania, and there is concern on his part regarding the pending harvest. His first letter, one written to his sister who is enrolled at Edinboro State Normal School,[1] Edinboro, Pennsylvania, comments on the situation and reveals his intentions.

Written to:
Miss M.A. Pettit
Edinboro State Normal School
Edinboro, Pa.

Hazel Dell
Lawrence County, Pa.
July 14th, 1862

"Dear Sister:

I received yours of the 4th inst. last Friday and was very much pleased to hear from you. The same mail also brought a catalogue of the school which looks very nice. You spoke of the examination of the

---

[1] Now Edinboro State College, Edinboro, Pennsylvania, founded in 1859.

graduates but did not tell me who they were. I wish you would write me their names. I spent my 4th at home hauling timber. The boys went to Mr. Dobbs' for cherries. They got as many as they could carry. Cherries are quite plentiful here.

We have not done much at our harvest yet. We cut some grass last week but it was so wet that we have not got it in yet. We commenced cutting wheat this morning but it has rained and we can do no more at it today.

Our Sunday School at Centre is going on nicely. Alice and Albert go this summer. The prayer meeting at Hazel Dell still goes on. There is preaching there occasionally by Messrs. Travet, Ploughman, and Boots. Eld. Gill talks of leaving us. He will let us know in August. He is going west but has promised to get another man to fill his place.

I received a letter from J.W. Gallagher written June 23rd. He was then 4½ miles from Richmond near Mechanicsville. I have since learned through the papers that he and Stilly Nye were both wounded and taken prisoners. John J. Butler of Hope Dale notoriety was killed. It now appears James McHaskey who was reported killed at the battle new Charleston[2] was only wounded and taken prisoner. No person has received any letters from the army yet since the "six days battle".

You need not expect me at Edinboro next fall. I *intent to enlist in the army* [emphasis added] as soon as we get through harvesting if not drafted sooner.

Grandfathers are all well and Hazen's folks are the same. We are all well at present and hope you are the same.

> Your brother,
> F. Pettit"

Another month passed before Pettit actually was sworn into the army on August 19, 1862. Nathaniel and Barbara Pettit, his parents, gave written permission for him to enter the service:

> Wayne Tp., Lawrence
> County, Pa.
> August 19th, 1862

"To all whom it may concern: this certifieth that we the undersigned have given our son Frederick Pettit permission to enlist and serve as a soldier in the army of the United States of America.

> Nathaniel Pettit
> Barbara Pettit"

---

[2] Battle of Secessionville, South Carolina, June 16, 1862. The 100th Pennsylvania was heavily engaged here.

Through the efforts of Captain Thomas J. Hamilton, veteran officer of the 100th Pennsylvania Regiment home from the field on recruiting service, Pettit and eight other recruits enlisted with the regiment and left New Castle on August 26 for Camp Curtin in Harrisburg.[3]

The 100th had been ordered to Newport News from South Carolina and by July 16th had arrived in Virginia. Shortly thereafter, they joined Pope's campaign and participated in the battles of 2nd Manassas and Chantilly in late August and early September.

Pettit wrote his first letter home as a soldier in Pittsburgh.

Written to:
Mr. N. Pettit
North Sewickley, Beaver Co., Pa.

Pittsburgh, Pa.
August 27th '62

"Dear parents, brothers, and sisters:

For the first time I write you from this smoky city. I did not expect to write you a letter from here but such are the fortunes of war. We left New Castle about 2 o'clock yesterday and had a very pleasant ride to Enon Station, 13 miles. We passed through Mahoningtown and Mt. Jackson. At Enon we took the 6 o'clock train for Pittsburgh. It was the express and we only stopped at each station about 3 minutes. We ran 44 miles in 2 hours. I saw no one that I knew on the route. There are 9 men of us, but I am not acquainted with any of them. But I am rambling.

We arrived at this place about 8 o'clock last night. After marching about for some time we obtained lodging at the Red Lion Hotel. Today Capt. Hamilton[4] turned us over to the recruiting authorities of this place. They have furnished us quarters at a Dutch tavern. All I can say about it is that "grub" is plenty. Grub means food mind that.

We will leave for Harrisburg tomorrow evening and will arrive Friday morning.

I have just returned from Allegheny City. I think I shall soon become acquainted with the city. I saw A.V. Cunningham today. He boards close by us.

You should see the Pittsburgh market. There is no end to the fruit and vegetables. Apples, pears, plums, peaches and all I ever thought of. Watermelons are here by the wagonload and almost so large as a 5 gallon key.

---

3 Official correspondence in the McDowell Collection, Historical Collections and Labor Archives, Pennsylvania State University, indicates Hamilton was ordered to New Castle, Lawrence County, on July 20, 1862, to "establish a recruiting station".

4 Captain Thomas J. Hamilton, Company D, 100th Pennsylvania Volunteers. Hamilton was mortally wounded while leading the regiment during the Battle of the Crater on July 30, 1864, and died in Petersburg after being captured.

I cannot write you anything of importance. I am well and well contented. I have made up my mind to take things as they come without grumbling. I never felt better contented than when I enlisted in the army.

Yours truly,
F. Pettit

[P.S.] Thursday Morning, August 28. I am still well and hearty. Spent last evening with Mr. Cunningham. We leave tonight at half past 8 for Harrisburg. We will not get to the Regiment before next week.

F.P.''

Written to:
Mr. N. Pettit
North Sewickly
Beaver County, Pa.

Camp Curtin, Pa.
August 31st 1862

"Dear parents, brothers, and sisters:

Having nothing to do today but to read, write, and think I will write you a letter. We left Pittsburgh Thursday night at 8½ o'clock and arrived at Harrisburg at 5½ o'clock Friday morning. Distance about 230 miles. It was very tiresome traveling but I managed to sleep some. From the cars we marched to the [Provost] Marshal's in town but he was not at home. We were then marched to Camp Curtin about 1 mile from town. We were halted in front of the cook shop where we remained 2 or 3 hours in the dusty street when an officer came and ordered our breakfasts. Our rations were crackers, beef, and coffee. Their crackers are as much as I can eat at one time. Rations 4. We get crackers and meat twice and bread one daily. Coffee morning and evening, beans for dinner. Our tin cups hold 1½ pints and we get them full of coffee or beans at a meal. Grub is good and plenty.

We are quartered in the "Barricks" [Sic]. They are large board shanties with tight floors and will hold about 100 men each. There are 50 or 60 in ours now. The 1st night we had no blankets and we had to lie on the floor. It was so cold we could not sleep longer than 1 o'clock. But there was a stove in one end of the barricks and we soon had a fire and got warm.

Yesterday we passed the Surgeon's examination and received our blankets and tin cups. Last night we slept first rate on the floor with our carpetsacks for pillows.

Mr. Bradford from New Brighton was here just now. He belongs to the Sanitary Commission. He spoke some words of encouragement. There are 2000 or 3000 men in camp here now. 5000 have left since we came here. The new regiments are in tents and the old Reg. recruits are in the barricks. All the drilling we do now is to appear at dress parade at 5 o'clock in the evening.

We expect to be mustered in and equipped on Monday. This is Sunday and I suppose you are all at Camp Meeting. But there is no Sunday here. Things go on much as usual. In our barricks some are sleeping, some lounging, some playing cards, some reading their Bibles, and many writing letters. I am well and well contented with my lot. Camp life tries the moral character severely and no one can remain without help.

F. Pettit

[P.S.] September 3rd, 1862

We have gotten our uniforms and were mustered in yesterday and have got orders to move today. I received a U. S. bond for twenty nine dollars ($29) which I think I will send in this letter. I am well. I saw Thamer and Wright this morning. I have sent my things to Mag. I will write as soon as I get to the Regiment and then you can to me.

F. Pettit
100 Reg. P.V."

Written to: [Either Mary Ann or Margaret, sisters]

Camp Curtin
September 3rd, 1862

"Dear Sister:

I suppose you are wondering what has become of me. A soldier meets with many disappointments and must learn to put up with them. I passed through New Brighton on Tuesday, August 26th on the 6 o'clock train. Stated in Pittsburgh 2 days when I came to Harrisburg where we are now encamped. Soldiers are coming and going every day. All the new companies are encamped in tents but the recruits for the old Regiments are in the barracks. The barracks are large board buildings. Ours contains about 50 men. We have got our uniform, 1 blanket, 1 dress coat, 1 pair pants and drawers, shoes, cap, knapsack, haversack, canteen, etc.

We get plenty to eat and have nothing to do but go about on dress parade and mount guard. Dress parade is at five in the evening. I was on guard yesterday and last night. From 12 to 2, from 6 to 8, from 12 to 2, and 6 to 8 this morning. The health of this camp is middling good. Diarrhea is the prevailing disease.

I have been middling well since I came here. We intend to be mustered in today and get our bounty. I think I will send my carpetsack to you. You will find my likeness in it.

I do not know when we will go to the Regiment. We heard last night that a number had been wounded and killed amongst the former is the colonel.[5]

Mr. Bradford was here last Sunday. He spoke very encouragingly to us. Sunday here is not much like Sunday at home. The wickedness of persons here who at home are decent and respectable quite surprises me.

[P.S.] Wednesday Sept. 4-1862.

We were mustered in yesterday and we leave today. I will send my carpetsack to you with my likeness and two army crackers. I have not much time to write.

> F. Pettit, 100 Reg't
> P.V."

Written to: [Parents]
Mr. N. Pettit
North Sewickley, Beaver Co., Pa.

> Washington,
> September 4th, 1862

"Dear Parents:

I arrived at this city this evening at dark. We left Harrisburg yesterday about 1 o'clock and arrived in Baltimore at dark. We were marched about half a mile and halted near the place where the Massachusetts men were fired on April 19, 1861. Here we waited about one hour when we were marched to the rooms of the Soldiers Relief Association where we received a splendid supper of cheese, ham, bread, and coffee, but the joke of it was I had the headache so I could not eat much.

After supper we marched into the street and [were] ordered to make ourselves comfortable. There was a large pile of cooper stuff by the side of the street and we threw down our blankets, wrapped ourselves up, and slept so soundly as you could wish, although the cars and wagons and thieves were running at our feet.

This morning we got our breakfast and lounged about one place and another until noon or after when we went on board the cars, arrived at this place at dark.

---

[5] This is undoubtedly in reference to the regimental commander of the 100th Pennsylvania Volunteers, Colonel Daniel Leasure, who was wounded at the battle of 2nd Manassas on 29 August 1862. The regiment suffered severe casualties during their assault against the Confederate main line along the unfinished railroad cut.

The first thing we saw here was a long train of cars containing our paroled prisoners taken by the rebels last Friday and Saturday.[6] Report says there were a number of the Roundheads amongst them. But we cannot ascertain whether is it true as the train has left.[7]

We got a very good supper here of beef, bread, and coffee. We have good quarters in the barracks for tonight. A great many rumors are going here tonight, we do not know exactly the state of affairs but one thing is certain the enemy are not far off. You should hear the returned soldiers tell their stories. They are enough to scare any coward.

While marching through Baltimore we passed many fine residences of 3 to 5 stories but afterward found they were all occupied as hospitals.

Last night we slept near where the troops were fired on last spring a year. About 800 men came from Baltimore for the old Regiment in the train in which we came. They were a wild set I can assure you. We received $49 bounty in Harrisburg and most of them spent the greater part of it in Baltimore. I sent you 25 dollars in my last letter in bank bills as I needed part of it. It is getting late and I must close. I am in good health.

F. Pettit

[P.S.] Thursday Morning, September 5th.

I am still well. We can still hear the cannon booming. Chain Bridge is 7 miles from here. I am well prepared for a march in wet weather having purchased a gum blanket and oil cloth havelock. The government supplies neither. We do not know where we will go next. Do not write until I get to the regiment. Do not be surprised if you get no letter for some time. The government stops the letters here until it sees fit to send them. Some say they have gotten no letters since July.

Your son,
F. Pettit"

Written to:
Mr. N. Pettit
North Sewickly
Beaver County, Pa.

Camp near Long Bridge, Va.
Sept. 8th, 1862.

"Dear parents, brothers, and sisters:

Once more I commence to write to you. The last time I wrote we were in Washington. We left it on the 5th inst. and took the steamer

---

6 This refers to the Battle of Second Manassas, August 29 and 30, 1862.

7 *Official Records* [*War of the Rebellion*] Series 1, Volume 12, Part 2, Page 261, lists total casualties of the 100th Pennsylvania Roundheads as being 140 including 8 prisoners for the battles of 2nd Manassas and Chantilly.

for Alexandria where we arrived about 10 o'clock and marched to Fort Ellsworth 2 miles from Alexandria. It is 9 miles from Washington. Ellsworth is a Hospital and convalescent camp. All the sick, wounded, and disabled soldiers of the whole army are sent here.

We had six gum blankets amongst nine of us and we made a very passable tent. We had plenty to eat. The sun shines as hot here now as it did any day last harvest at home but the nights are very cool so that we can sleep well. We stayed here very comfortably until last Sunday morning. We got up quite early and commenced getting breakfast intending to have a good time reading, writing, singing, and thinking about home when the war would be over and all other things.

But alas our earthly hopes! Just then an order came for Burnside's [Ninth Army Corps] men with many others to report to headquarters immediately. But we have become used to such orders and went on quietly with our breakfast. After finishing it we packed up and went to headquarters. About 10 o'clock we started for Long Bridge. There were about 1200 of us [included] for almost every regiment in the U.S. service. After marching, halting, and counter marching for about 6 hours we found ourselves 2 or 3 miles from Long Bridge in the brush where we are at present. And we understand we are to get guns here and then go on to our regiments.

The men who are now with us are principally the worst men of the whole army. Skulkers and stragglers and worked out men and as wicked as men can be. Many of them have said that unless a man can drink, steal, lie, and swear he is not fit for a soldier. If the whole army is composed of this class of men God save our country, for the men never will. War is indeed a calamity. Not because it destroys life and property, this is the smallest loss. But it makes men wicked. I dread to see the day when this army goes home. Religion will be driven from the country.

I am still in good health and spirits.

Yours as ever,
F. Pettit"

CHAPTER TWO

PETTIT JOINS THE ROUNDHEADS

South Mountain and Antietam
Encampment at Antietam Furnace
Camp Israel

"Through the protection of the Almighty I have come off safe."

Fred Pettit joined the Roundheads at Brookeville, Montgomery County, Maryland, on September 10, 1862. The 100th Pennsylvania Roundheads had just entered the Maryland Campaign of 1862 after their participation in Pope's Virginia Campaign and two battles, 2nd Manassas and Chantilly. Pettit was promptly assigned to Company C now under the command of Lt. David Critchlow as its former commander, Captain J. E. Cornelius had just been wounded at Chantilly on September 1.

Written to parents:

> Near Frederick, Maryland,
> Sept. 13th, 1862.

"Dear parents:

I overtook my regiment on the 10th at dark at Brookville, Md. [Brookeville, Montgomery County, Maryland] and found most of the

9

boys well. Evans [John R.], J. Wilson [John P.], Lary [Andrew Leary], and McElwain [John] are here and well. I have marched 2 days with the regiment. I got on well. We are living Well. We expected a fight here yesterday but the rebels left before we came. Some of the Ohio boys had a skirmish with them yesterday. About 30 rebels were killed and 16 union wounded.

We can see them cannonading this morning away on the hills. We can see the flash of the guns.

I find the regiment in much better condition than I expected. The worst men are the poorest fighters. I will write you a full account when we stop. We march from daylight until almost sundown. I am well. Write me a long letter when you get this.

F. Pettit''

The battles of South Mountain and Antietam were fought on September 14 and 17 respectively. There was little time for letter writing, even for avid writer Pettit. It was two days after Antietam before another letter was composed to his parents. The 100th Pennsylvania regiment was camped near Antietam Furnace for several days after the battle on the 17th, and Pettit took the opportunity of telling his family of his stirring experiences after joining the Roundheads on the 10th.

There is some repetition in the following five letters but they have been quoted in full in order to eliminate any omission of details in the story of the battles of South Mountain and Antietam.

The reader is referred to Maps 1 and 2 which illustrate details of both South Mountain and Antietam.

Written to:
Mr. N. Pettit
North Sewickley
Beaver County, Pa.

Maryland,
September 19th, 1862

"Dear Parents:

I have a chance to send you a few lines this morning. We were in another battle [Antietam] day before yesterday. We were sent in advance as skirmishers [for Welsh's Brigade]. Our army had just driven the rebels across a small creek with high hills on each side. We advanced to the top of the first hill where we could see their riflemen firing from behind a stone wall at about 400 yards distant. There were two noble [respectable] batteries about 800 yards from us which piled shot, shell and grape, and railroad iron at us thick and strong.

We first fired at the riflemen, and soon made them run. We then ran forward about 100 yds. to some grain stacks and commenced [firing] on their artillerymen, at about 700 yds. We soon made them leave their guns. The other battery was out of sight so we could not get at it.

I then became separated from my regiment but went forward some distance with other regiments, but not finding our regiment I came back again and found John Wilson[1] wounded in the leg. I then helped him off towards the hospital but did not find it that night as it was almost dark. We found a good place in an orchard, made some coffee, lay down and slept until morning when we went to the hospital.

Wilson's wound is not bad. It was a buckshot wound an the knee cap. He took it out without any trouble. There were 4 wounded and 1 killed.

The firing on Sunday (South Mountain battle) was much hotter but did not last long. On Sunday there were 44 wounded and 8 killed in our regiment.[2] Our company [C] went in with 13 men of whom 2 were killed and 6 wounded.

I am still well and contented. Through the protection of the Almighty I have come off safe. Write soon.

The last battle (Antietam) was fought about 7 miles from that on Sunday.

Give my respects to all. God bless you.

Your son,
F. Pettit

Address:
100 Reg't P.V.
9th Army Corps
Washington, D.C.

Written to: Family

Camp near Sharpsburgh, Md.,
Sept. 20th 1862

"Dear parents, brothers, and sisters:

Having a little spare time this morning I will commence to give you a short account of what our regiment has done since I came to it. I overtook it about 20 miles from Washington at Brookville, Md. It was dark when I found them. They had been resting a day to get provisions.

[1] Samuel P. Bates, *History Of Pennsylvania Volunteers, 1861-1865.* Harrisburg, Penna., 1870, Volume 3, Page 572. This soldier was John P. Wilson, Co. C., 100th Pennsylvania Volunteers. Wilson survived the war. He was promoted to Corporal and then to Sergeant in 1864 and was discharged March 20, 1865.

[2] *Official Records*, Series 1, Volume 19, Part 1, Page 186. Casualties in the 100th Pennsylvania at the Battle of South Mountain were 8 killed and 37 wounded. Pettit's figures are not far from being correct.

The next morning we started for Frederick City, Md. We traveled about 15 miles and encamped a little before dark. Our rations are crackers, coffee, sugar, and beef when the cooks have time to boil it.

The next day we started on our march again and passed through New Market were the rebel pickets had been the night before. This town is 8 miles from Frederick. After passing about 2 miles from the town we halted and the cavalry and artillery were sent forward to reconnoiter. After waiting about 4 hours we again moved forward. About 3 miles from Frederick we again halted. The front skirmishers loaded their guns and advance cautiously. The artillerymen ran two guns to the top of a hill on the right. But the rebels had gone. A shot or two at their rear sent them flying. We marched about a mile further and encamped 2 miles from the city [Frederick].

The next day we could plainly see the cannonading from 8 miles distant on the mountains [South Mountain range]. We lay in camp here until about 6 o'clock in the evening when we took up our line of march again. We passed through Frederick City. It is about as large as New Castle. We then marched on to the mountains [following the National Road] where we saw the cannonading. We could not see any effects of it except a dead horse or two and houses turned into hospitals. After going some distance further we encamped and lay down and slept during the remainder of the night.

The next morning [September 14] we started early toward Middleton [Middletown, Maryland]. It was not long before we heard cannonading in front. About a mile from Middleton we found a large barn and bridge burned. But the stream [Little Catoctin Creek] was shallow and we had no difficulty in crossing. After going a short distance further we could see the batteries at work and hear the whizzing of the shells. The rebels occupied a wooded pass [Turners Gap] in the mountains. The turnpike [National Road] runs through the middle of the pass. On the right of it the rebels had a battery in a ploughed field and others on the left in the woods. When we came in sight of the enemy our division halted and our regiment was sent forward as skirmishers. We advanced along the turnpike in plain view of their batteries on the right until we came within ½ mile of it when we halted and protected ourselves as well as we could under the bank at the side of the road. The enemy sent their shell amongst us thick and fast. They exploded about and all around us.

Shortly an orderly came and told us to fall back. When we commenced to move the shot and shell flew faster than ever. Our loss this time was only one man wounded, but if we had stayed 15 minutes longer we would have been cut to pieces.

After going back a short distance we started up a valley on the left of the turnpike between our batteries and the rebels. After going up this for a short distance we again started up the mountain by another road [Old Sharpsburg Road which passes through Fox's or Reno's Gap]. At the top of the hill our men were trying to plant a battery [Cook's 8th Massachusetts Battery] and on the other side the rebels had a battery and were trying to drive them away. We advanced up the hill steadily under a shower of shot until we came near the top of the hill where the road ran between two high banks. Just here we halted when a number of cavalrymen and artillerists came rushing down upon us crying, "clear the road for the cannon — we are beaten!" And just then the artillery came galloping down with the guns and caissons. And to make things worse the rebels were sending grape shot and shell amongst us in a perfect shower. It was here that Andrew Lary [Leary] was struck on the hip and disabled but he soon got over it and is now as well as ever.

We clambered out of the road as fast as we could, and our officers soon formed us in line of battle on the right of the road. We were ordered to fix bayonets and expected to make a charge but we soon started down the hill again and marched on up the valley about a mile where we halted, about faced, and started back across the hill. While coming up the valley a number of men gave out amongst them Lieutenant Morton[3] and we saw him no more that day. We soon met General Wilcox [Orlando B. Willcox, Brigadier General, commander of the First Division, Ninth Army Corps] and as we were exhausted he ordered us to lay down and rest. We did so, but the grape and cannister flew a few feet over our heads thick and fast, but no one was hurt as we lay close to the ground.

After resting about 3 hours we were formed in line of battle. [Thomas Welsh's brigade was formed with their right on the Old Sharpsburg Road with the 46th New York on the left and the 45th Pennsylvania on the right with the 100th Pennsylvania in close support in second line. On the right of the brigade was the 17th Michigan with their left resting on the Old Sharpsburg Road.] The rebels had advanced upon our cannon and we must drive them back. The 45th Reg. Pa. and 17th Michigan went in before us and drove them behind a stone wall [at the crest]. We then advance to the top of the hill through a shower of musket balls. When we came to the edge of the woods [near present day Reno Monument] we halted and commenced firing. We were about as far from them [rebels] as from our corn crib to the barn. They were in a lane behind a stone fence and we were in the edge of a woods with a clear lot between us.

---

3 1st Lieutenant Philo S. Morton. Morton tendered his resignation from the service on October 4, 1862. Bates, *History of Pennsylvania Volunteers*. Volume 3, Page 572.

I fired 11 shots. Most of the boys fired 15 before the rebels ran. When they ran I went over with J. Wilson and we took 3 rebels from amongst the killed and wounded that were not hurt. The lane was piled full of killed and wounded rebels. We counted 27 dead in one place the next day. 13 men of our company went in and 2 were killed [Privates John C. Miller and Archibald G. Slater][4] and 6 wounded. We encamped for the night near the battlefield.

[P.S.]
September 20th 1862.

I have a chance to send this now. We are all well and near the Potomac River [Antietam Furnace]. We move soon. I send you a rebel envelope I picked up on the battlefield.

F. Pettit"

Pettit's next letter, written one day later, gives an excellent description of uniform, arms, and equipment of the 1862 Union soldier. He is obviously very proud to be a member of the army.

Written to: Family

Camp near Sharpsburg, Md.,
Sept. 21st 1862.

"Dear parents, brothers, and sisters:

I have been so busy marching and fighting since I came to the regiment that I have not had time to write about anything else, but this pleasant afternoon I will write something about other things. As to playing soldier such as lying in camp, drilling etc. I know nothing about it. I never drilled a day in my life. [Interesting commentary. Pettit was committed to combat without any basic training whatsoever.] All the soldiering I have done is marching and fighting. Anybody can do this that is brave and strong enough.

I will commence with my equipments. My uniform is a pair of light blue pants and dark blue dress coat and cap. I have a haversack to carry grub, and a canteen to carry water. Every soldier must have these. Then I have a knapsack to carry clothes, blankets, etc. Besides these I carry a cartridge box with 40 cartridges, a cap box full of caps, and a bayonet in a scabbard on a belt round my waist supported by a strap over my shoulder.

---

[4] Samuel P. Bates, *History of Pennsylvania Volunteers*, Volume 3, Pages 574 and 575.

I use a Springfield rifle the best gun made. The cartridge box hangs on the right hip, the cap box in front, and bayonet on the left side. The haversack and canteen hang under the left arm. The knapsack is strapped upon the back.

My gun I carry on my shoulder. I have a woolen blanket and a gum one. We have shelter ["pup"] tents. They are made of muslin and in two pieces each about 2 yds. square. Each man carries a piece and two go together, button the pieces together, stretch them on our guns, fasten down with pegs and we have a house. Andrew Lary [Leary] and I go together.

We put down a gum and woolen blanket for a bed and another over us. Our knapsacks serve for pillows. When we don't march or fight we write letters, read our bibles, and cook and eat. We get along first rate.

Your son and brother,
F. Pettit

Directions
F. Pettit, 100 Reg., Co. C. P.V.
9th Corps, Washington, D.C."

Pettit now writes a vivid and detailed description of the part played by the 100th Pennsylvania regiment in their advance upon Sharpsburg after crossing the Burnside Bridge during the afternoon of September 17.

Written to:
Mr. N. Pettit
North Sewickley
Beaver County, Pa.

Camp near Sharpsburgh, Md. Sept. 23rd '62

"Dear parents, brothers, and sisters:

You will see by the date of this that I am where I was when I wrote last. We have been in camp here since last Friday evening. In my last letter I gave you an account of our doings up to Sunday Sept. 14th the day of South Mountain battle. That night we lay near the battlefield and notwithstanding the excitement of the day I slept soundly.

The next day I went over the battlefield. Our wounded and dead had been removed during the night. The rebel wounded were being carried off and cared for. Their dead lay in heaps. We counted 27 rebel dead within a few rods of each other.

On Monday evening we marched 2 or 3 miles beyond South Mountain and encamped. About midnight we were roused and marched 6 or 8 miles farther and encamped for the remainder of the night. [This bivouac was on the Locust Spring or Geeting farm, just west of Keedysville, Maryland.] During Tuesday we lay in camp. The rebels kept up a cannonading all day. Some of their balls struck near our camp and we could hear the shells whizzing nearly all day.

Wednesday morning we marched a short distance where we lay as a reserve [vicinity of Porterstown, Maryland] for some time. While we were lying here we witnessed a very severe battle going on toward the right. [This was the early morning assault by the Federal right against the Confederates in the Miller Cornfield and the Dunker Church area.]

In the afternoon our troops took a bridge across the Antietam creek [Burnside Bridge]. We were then thrown across the creek to take the advance as skirmishers. [The 100th Pennsylvania was acting as skirmishers for Welsh's brigade that day as they advanced on the left of the road into Sharpsburg from the Burnside Bridge.] We advanced to the top of the hill above the bridge. Just as we came to the top of the hill the rebels opened upon us with two batteries and their sharpshooters. We commenced on the sharpshooters who were behind a stone wall [on the Otto farm]. We soon made them leave. The batteries still kept sending shell, grape, and cannister, shot, and chunks of railroad iron amongst us. It did not hurt many for we could easily dodge it by lying down behind the brow of the hill. When the rebel sharpshooters ran some us who were separated from our regiment went with other regiments after them.

Our regiment was not ordered from the brow of the hill. J. Wilson and I went to where the rebel sharpshooters had been. The troops in this part of the field had advanced too far and were obliged to fall back to our regiment under a cross fire of musketry and cannon. While coming back I overtook John Wilson and found him wounded in the knee. I helped him to the hospital and did not get to the regiment again until the next morning. Wilson's wound is not dangerous. It was a buckshot in the knee. It struck the knee cap but did not injure the bone. It will soon be well.

Our loss was 4 or 5 wounded and 1 missing. The regiment did not fight any after I left it. The next day, Thursday, we lay as an advance guard near where we fought. In the evening we were relieved and encamped. On Friday the rebels had fallen back and we advanced with great caution to our present place of encampment. We are about 2 miles from Sharpsburg on the back of the Antietam creek below when the battle was fought.

Last Sunday [September 21st] we had preaching in the morning by our chaplain Mr. Brown [Reverend Robert Audley Browne was the chaplain of the regiment from September 1861 until December 1863]. There was preaching in the afternoon but our company went out on picket at 3 o'clock and I did not hear it. We remained on picket until last evening about 5 o'clock.

There are not many in our company now that I know. [Phineas] Bird, Lary, [John] McElwain, and [William] Smiley are all. They are well. McElwain is driving ambulance and does not get into our fights. We have no officers in our company now. They are either killed, wounded, or sick. I am well and living first rate. Be good boys and girls.

F. Pettit."

Written to:
Mr. Evan Pettit

Camp Antietam, September 28th, 1862.

"Dear Brother:

I received your letter of the 22nd and 23rd today and was very glad to hear from you. I have just come from church and eaten dinner. It may seem strange to you for me to get a letter on Sunday, but in the army things are much the same on Sunday, as other days only there is no drilling.

This morning we were ordered out with knapsacks, guns, and equipment to have them inspected. After inspection the drums beat the church call and we assembled for church. After our chaplain had preached a short time and order came from General Wilcox [Orlando B. Willcox] to come to his headquarters immediately for religious services. Our regiment formed immediately and marched to headquarters. The whole division 7 regiments and a Co. of Artillery were assembled. Gen. Wilcox spoke as follows:

'Fellow soldiers and associates; having been brought by Almighty God through the dangers of two battles I thought it proper to assemble you this morning to return Him our thanks.'

The services were conducted by 4 chaplains and consisted of singing, prayer, and short addresses.

We like General Wilcox very much.[5] He was with us in both

---

5 General Orlando B. Willcox was associated with the 100th Pennsylvania throughout much of its four years of service in the Ninth Corps. He was an outstanding combat general and at times commanded the Ninth Corps. Willcox was a graduate of West Point in the Class of 1847. He was brevetted major general in both the volunteers and regulars. He won the Congressional Medal of Honor for "most distinguished gallantry" at First Manassas. He was the division commander of that division of which the 100th Pennsylvania was a part for the last several months of the war.

fights. I have seen Gen. Burnside several times. He was with us in the last battle. I never heard either of them swear.

We have religious services nearly every evening in our regiment. We are still encamped near where we fought the last battle. We have moved about two miles from where we were when I wrote last. We are encamped about 1 mile from the Potomac and 4 miles above Harpers Ferry. [The Ninth Corps encampment at this time was in the valley about 1 mile from Antietam Furnace and was on the road leading from there to present day Dargan.]

Diarrhea is about the only disease in the army. Almost all have it more or less. I have had it several time but have always succeeded in checking it.

John Wilson is back again with us. His knee is almost well. Wilson, Leary, and I occupy one tent. The tents are for two but 3 can sleep in them very well. We get along first rate. Our rations are crackers 10 a day, and a tinful of coffee twice, meat once, beans occasionally. Our rations of sugar are about 3 tablespoonfuls daily. We get candles and soap besides. I think you will find your other questions answered in my other letters.

Bird, Wilson, McElwain, Lary, and I are all well. We get along first rate.

We do not get any apples or peaches now but while we were marching we managed to get plenty of them. When you write again, I want you to me whether you got my carpetsack, and whether anybody went out in the militia from your parts. There were several Lawrence Co. men here last week that belonged to the militia. They were encamped about 16 miles from us.

I hope that John Marshall and his wife may have much happiness and that he may never be alarmed by the booming of cannon and the whizzing of bullets. Write soon a good long letter.

Your brother,
F. Pettit

[P.S.] Remember now thy creator in the days of thy youth. Ecc. 12:1.
Tell me whether there is preaching at Centre and about the Sunday School. Send me 2 or 3 Stars to read. Direct the same as before.''

Written to:
Miss M. A. Pettit

Camp Antietam, September 29th '62.

"Dear Sister,

It is now some time since I received a letter from you and indeed I have received but one since I left home. I will try and give you some account of what I have been doing.

I left home Aug. 26th and arrived in Pittsburgh the same evening via New Castle and Enon Station. There were 9 for our regiment none of whom I knew. We remained in Pittsburgh 2 days and then started for Harrisburgh [sic] which we reached on the 29th having run through the night.

We were marched to Camp Curtin when received our equipments and $29 bounty. We remained here 5 days and judging the place by its inhabitants I can truly say the less of it the better. The food and treatment were 5th the worst I have yet received in the army.

Our equipments consisted of cap, dress coat, pants, 2 pair drawers, shoes, knapsack, haversack, canteen, and blanket.

From there we went to Baltimore where we remained one night and part of a day. We were well treated here. We ate 2 meals at the Union Relief Association's rooms. The food was boiled ham, cheese, soft bread, and coffee.

From here we went to Washington, remained at the Soldiers Retreat until next day when we left of Alexandria by steamer. From here we went to Fort Ellsworth about two miles from Alexandria. The camp at this place consisted of recruits, sick soldiers, stragglers, etc. the most of them are totally demoralized.

We remained here until Sunday Sept. 7th when we left camp near Long Bridge where we were supplied with arms and on Tuesday morning started to find our regiment. We overtook it on the evening of the 10th.

The next day we started for Frederick City, Md. We arrived within sight of it on Friday evening. Several guns were fired, scouts sent out, but the evening had gone.

The next day we saw and heard cannonading far off in the mountains. In the evening we took up our march through Frederick toward Middleton [Middletown] a short distance from which we camped. The next day Sunday 14th early in the morning we heard cannonading at no great distance. We were shortly moving toward it. Shortly after passing through Middleton, we could see the artillery at work. Our regiment was moved to the front and after making a number of maneuvers which we did not well understand we halted until near sundown. This maneuvering was rather trying to new recruits but our loss was only two wounded.

Just before sunset we were formed in line of battle with the 17th Michigan [on the right of the 100th Pennsylvania]. We lay for a short time under the fire of a large body of rebels, the balls flying past us like hail, until the 17th moved to the right when we marched through a small strip of forest and opened upon the rebels across a narrow field. They were behind a fence of stone and rails and we were in the edge of a woods [near the present General Reno monument]. After firing a short time the rebels ran. We were then relieved and commenced carrying off the dead and wounded. Our loss was 8 killed and about 40 wounded. Our company lost 2 killed and 5 wounded. This was large considering we had but 13 men engaged. J.R. Evans was wounded in the leg but not seriously.

That night we lay on the battlefield. The next morning I visited the battlefield. Our dead and wounded had been removed and they [Union troops] were engaged carrying off the rebels. Their loss in killed was much greater than ours. In front of our regiment the dead lay literally in heaps. We counted 27 dead rebels in a space of a few rods. I picked up a blanket and some rebel envelopes.

F. Pettit''

After camping near Antietam Furnace for nearly three weeks after the battle of Antietam, the Ninth Corps was moved to Pleasant Valley, just two miles east of Harpers Ferry. Called Camp Israel for the small stream Israel Creek which flows through a valley known locally as Pleasant Valley, the camp was about one mile from the Potomac River and very near to present day Sandy Hook, Weverton, and Knoxville, Maryland.

Pettit and the Roundhead regiment arrived at Camp Israel on October 7th and remained in this pleasant locale until October 26. While this made for easy soldiering, history shows that actually General George B. McClellan allowed six fine weeks of campaigning weather to be wasted after the battle of Antietam before finally moving the Army of the Potomac in force into Virginia in pursuit of Lee and the Army of Northern Virginia.

Fred Pettit wrote four letters from Camp Israel which provide excellent details of the encampment there.

Written to: Family

Camp In Pleasant Valley, Md., Oct. 9 '62

"Dear parents, brothers, and sisters:

You will see by the date of this that we have changed our camp again. We left our camp at Antietam Iron Works Tuesday 7th and marched across the highest part of the Blue Ridge a few miles north of Harpers Ferry. [The route of this march took the troops over the Blue Ridge (Elk Ridge) on a steep and difficult road through Solomon's Gap into Pleasant Valley. Although the march was a fairly short one, it was a most tiring one.] The Blue Ridge Mountains are not all one ridge but are made up of several ridges.

Our old camp was west of the highest one. Our present camp is between two of the highest ridges in a deep valley [Pleasant Valley] about 1 mile wide. This is called pleasant valley. At the point where the Potomac flows through the western ridge is Harpers Ferry and where it flows through the eastern ridge is Sandy Hook. We are 1 mile from the latter and 2 miles from the former place.

We have plenty of good water close by and there are chestnuts and walnuts in the mountains not far off. But above all our health is good.

There are a great many troops encamped in this vicinity but they are mostly new regiments. I have only received one letter yet.

Afternoon: We received a mail at noon today. I received three letters one from Evan [brother], one from Meg [Sister, Margaret] and another one. I was very glad to hear from home but quite sorry that Evan was wounded in the foot. I suppose he went to the hospital but hope he will soon get well. I think by the time you get this Lieutenant Morton will turn up. I saw George Weller and a number of others this week on their way to the 137th Reg.

Saturday Oct. 11th. A wet day and a cool north wind blowing. Last night was the first wet night for me in the tents, but we kept dry and slept well. Soldiering is not such a bad business after all if a fellow can only content himself. Our rations are 1 pound crackers, about 11, daily. Fresh beef 3 times a day and sometimes port or salt beef, and a tinful of rice or bean soup for dinner, thought I had 3 tinfuls of rice for dinner yesterday. We get about half a tinful of sugar in three days, and a tinful of hot coffee twice a day. I can easily drink a pint of coffee at a meal now.

We have had not frost yet but expect it soon. We have sent for overcoats. We do not know as much of the movements of the army as you do. We know when our regiment moves and when it stops and that is all. In peace times this would be one of the most pleasant places to live I ever saw. The soil is rich, water good and plenty. There is a small stream running through the valley called Israel creek. Our camp is now called Camp Israel. We expect the colonel [Colonel Daniel Leasure, brigade commander of the 100th Pennsylvania who had been wounded at Second Manassas and was recuperating] back every day. Yesterday we marched to the railroad to meet him, but he did not come.

I sent a letter to Mary Ann last week but have received no reply yet. We received a letter from J. R. Evans this week. He is in Washington and getting better. The rest of the boys are all well. When you write again, tell me how Ploughmans meeting succeeded and whether Gill has come back. Have you heard from J. W. Gallagher? How are Grandfathers getting along? Give my respects to them and

J. B. Hazen's folks. When you write again write a long letter. If your letter is not too heavy cut some good pieces out of an old *Star* that I have not read and send it in your letter. We have little to do in camp and would read a great deal if we could get it.

Yours affectionately,
F. Pettit

[P.S.] Therefore all things whatsoever ye would that men should do to you, do ye even so to them. Matt. 7:12."

Written to:
Miss M. [Margaret] Pettit

Camp in Pleasant Valley, Md. October 9th '62

"Dear Sister:

I received your most welcome letter of 28th ultimo [of this month] today and was very glad to hear from you. You said you read the letters I sent home so you know all I have been doing up to last Sunday.

We left our camp at Antietam Iron Works on last Tuesday 7th inst. [instant]. We crossed a high ridge of mountains and are now encamped in Pleasant Valley, Maryland. The valley is about 1 mile wide with high mountains on each side. We are 1 mile from Sand Hook on the Potomac and about 2 miles from Harpers Ferry. I like our camp better than any other we have had. Water of the best quality and convenient. Almost all the water here is so hard that we cannot do much good washing with it, but the water here washes very well. And then the mountains are so close and nearly all woods [so] that we have plenty of shade these warm days.

John Wilson and I are writing letters this afternoon on the side of the Blue Ridge Mountains. There are 3 regiments in our brigade: the 45th Penna. and 36th Massachusetts, a new regiment.[6] We have no drilling to do at all. I have *never* [Emphasis added] drilled any since I came to the regiment. It does not require a well drilled soldier to fight well. Some men who have been with the regiment 13 months have never been in a fight yet. All that is needed is plenty of courage, a good gun, and ammunition for it and I will insure the fight.

I sent Mary Ann a letter some time since but have received no reply yet. I received a letter from home today.

---

[6] These two regiments were to be affiliated in the same brigade with the 100th Pennsylvania for several more months. Both were competent regiments and served with the Ninth Army Corps until the end of the war.

I have not seen any frost yet though there has been some in places. We received a letter from J. H. Evans today; he is at Washington. He says his leg is getting well and he is now able to walk with crutches. You spoke of the paroled prisoners as being very dirty. I presume they were like the most of our soldiers. When soldiers are on the march it is impossible for them to keep clean. They are as often marched by night almost as by day and when they halt to rest or sleep they cannot get a clean place to lie down always but must take it as it comes; and always on the ground in the dust or mud so that their chances for cleanliness are very poor. There is but little excuse for being infected with vermin.

We have religious meetings in our regiment every evening when the weather will permit and two sermons on Sunday. I wrote home for them to send me a few *Stars* to read. I wish you would see if they have sent them; if not, please send them. We have but little religious reading here.

Write soon and tell me all the news and whether you got to Sunday School. Give my respects to G. Grieb and wife.

> Your brother,
> F. Pettit
> Co. C, 100th Reg't P.V.

[P.S.] Don't forget to read your Bible. 'Offer the sacrifice of righteousness and put your trust in the Lord'. Psalm 4:5.''

Written to: Family

> Camp Israel, Md. Oct. 16th, 1862

"Dear parents, brothers, and sisters:

It is with much pleasure that I commence to write you another letter. We have just returned from a most unpleasant tramp. You have no doubt heard before this reaches you of Stuart's raid into Maryland and Penna., but perhaps you have not heard of the part we took in it.

On last Saturday 11th inst. [instant] we had cleaned our guns and accoutrements for Sunday inspection, when just at dark an order came to pack up and be ready to move at a moments notice; but to leave our tents. We marched to the railroad [and] were put on the cars and run to Frederick city distance 22 miles. All this time we were ignorant of what was going on. After leaving the cars we were marched to the principal street, ordered to load our guns and lie with them in our arms. This we did and went to sleep. The pavement stones were so cold I caught a cold and have not got well yet.

On Sunday morning we marched to the outside of the town and had some hot coffee. We lay all day on one road and another. In the evening we camped near the Railroad bridge across the Monocacy river. This night was cold and wet, but John Wilson and I managed to keep dry with our gum blankets. We remained here until about 10 o'clock Monday night when were put on the cars and taken to Point of Rocks. We then marched 3 miles down the Potomac and encamped for the rest of the night.

The next day we were relieved and started for our old camp and arrived at dark, having marched 15 miles in half a day. We found our tents all standing as we left them. We wrapped ourselves up in our blankets and slept soundly. All though we did not meet the rebels in battle yet we no doubt saved U. S. many thousand dollars worth of property. There were immense commissary stores at Frederick and but few troops.

On Saturday night the rebels were 10 or 12 miles west of Frederick but Sunday morning they were 6 miles east having passed around it in the night. Our regiment expect to received their winter clothing shortly of which they stand in much need.

I received a letter today from Mary Ann, dated Oct. 6th. She was well. I also received two papers from home by the same mail which were very welcome. Please send two or three every month.

There is one thing I have never said anything about yet [and] that is the size of our regiment. There are 300 men in our regiment with us now. There is but little going on in this part of the army now.

Give my best respects to all the friends.

> Yours affectionately,
> F. Pettit
> Co. C, 100th Reg't P.V.

[P.S.] Write whether Grandfathers are all well."

Written to: Family

Camp Israel in Pleasant Valley, Md. Oct. 23, '62

"Dear parents, brothers, and sisters,

I received a most welcome letter from you yesterday written the 11th and 14th. I was very glad to hear that you were all well. I have not been well for a week past, but am much better now.

Evan said he had been helping Grandfather to make apple butter. I should like to have been there to eat apples and drink cider, and a piece of soft bread and apple butter would not taste bad. I have not tasted soft bread for more than a month, but we get along very well with crackers.

The weather is getting quite cold but we have our overcoats and manage to keep quite comfortable.

There is nothing of importance going on here now. We do not know whether we will remain in quarters here this winter or whether we shall have more marching, but expect to move soon. I was glad to hear the Ploughman's protracted meeting was so successful. It would be a good thing if could continue his labors in that vicinity for he reaches a class of persons no other men would.

I am sorry that Gill left as he did. It was better no doubt for him to leave if he had done it fairly.

I hope the Centre Sunday School has not been forgotten all this time. Sunday Schools should never be neglected. I find that men remember the Sabbath School better than the Church. I fear there will be a bad division at Hazel Dell soon likely to cause much bad feeling. The best way in such quarrels is to let them alone unless they try to impose upon our rights and privileges.

By the time you get this letter I suppose the fall work will be almost all done, and the boys and girls will be almost ready for school. They must learn all they can this winter. They can have a good warm house for studying in while many poor fellows must stand in the cold to keep the rebels from coming and burning their school houses and taking away all they have that is so comfortable. When the children think of these things this winter some cold day it should make them study very hard. But some day perhaps not this winter some of us will be at home again to teach school and go to school, and I think we will teach and study twice as hard as we used to for we can see more need of it now than we used to.

But I have written enough without anything to write about so I must stop for this time. Give my respects to Grandfathers, James B. Hazens, and the rest of the friends.

When Meg. comes home you must write me a longer letter, all go together. The rest of the boys are all well. We heard from J. Evan a few days ago. He is getting better.

> Yours affectionately,
> F. Pettit
> Co. C, 100th P.V.

[P.S.] Don't forget to send some more *Stars* soon. Don't forget to write a long letter. Take your time like the last one. F.P.''

Written to: Sister

> Camp Israel in Pleasant Valley, Md. Oct. 23, '62

''Dear Sister Mary:

I received your very welcome letter of the 6th inst several days ago, but owing to indisposition I have not answered it until now.

For a week past I have been quite unwell but am much better now. It is so long since I wrote to you that I almost forget where we were at that time, but I think it was Antietam Iron Works. Well, we are not a thousand miles away from them yet.

About the first of this month we crossed the ridge of mountains above Harpers Ferry and encamped in the valley beyond. Our camp is named from the small stream running through the valley called Israel creek. The valley is called Pleasant Valley. Our camp is about 3 miles from Harpers Ferry and 1 mile from the Potomac.

Nothing of importance has occurred since we came here except a short chase to Frederick city to prevent Stuart's cavalry from destroying the government stores at that place. On Sat. 11 inst. [instant] we had cleaned our arms and accoutrements ready for Sunday inspection and expected to spend the day in peace and quiet, but just at dark we were ordered to pack everything except our tents. We then went to the cars go on and were run to Frederick city about which we lay for several days in the cold and wet.

On Tuesday night following we were on picket along the Potomac below Point of Rocks. The next day we came back to camp, having been gone 4 days. During our absence I caught a cold which resulted in a weeks sickness. But I am getting over that and will soon be ready for another trip.

We get along in camp very well. There is but little to do except stand guard about 2 times a week. We have small shelter tents designed for 2 persons each which by a little extra work we make quite comfortable.

You talked of going home to teach this winter. I hope you will as teachers will doubtless be scarce. It would be very pleasant for you to teach near home if possible but you might succeed better in some other part of the county. You can judge of this matter best for yourself. But wherever you teach make it tell. I should certainly like very much to be with you at school [Edinboro] this fall and to be teaching this winter, but that seems impossible under the circumstances. But I hope it will not be many winters until we can all come home and enjoy its comforts.

Our regiment is very poorly officered at present. Our Colonel [Leasure] is wounded. In our company there are no officers. A private has command of the Co. Capt. Cornelius[7] is wounded. Lieutenant Critchlow is sick and Lieutenant Morton has resigned on account of his health and gone home. You said Captain Oliver's Co. was on Bolivar Heights, and that he would be glad to see me. I should certainly be glad to see him but unless I know the No of his regiment it will be impossible for me to find him.

---

[7] Captain James E. Cornelius, wounded at Chantilly 1 September 1862 and resigned his commission 4 March 1863. Samuel P. Bates, *History of Pennsylvania Volunteers*, Harrisburg, 1870, Volume 3, Page 572.

I received a letter from home yesterday and they were all well. We are now very comfortably clothed for the winter having received our overcoats. Give my respects to Professor Thompson's folks and Mr. Hofins and the others I know. You did not tell me where you boarded, I should like to know.

> Your brother,
> F. Pettit
> Co. C. 100th Regt. P.V."

After McClellan wasted six weeks of precious time, he finally ordered the Army of the Potomac to move south against Lee's forces. On October 26, 1862, the Ninth Corps began crossing the Potomac River at Berlin [Brunswick], Maryland on pontoon bridges. Forty days had elapsed since the Battle of Antietam, and the Ninth Corps had enjoyed two pleasant encampments at Antietam Creek and at Camp Israel in Pleasant Valley in lovely autumn weather.

There was now to be much marching and maneuvering as the Army of the Potomac began to concentrate in the Fredericksburg, Virginia area for further offensive movements against the Army of Northern Virginia.

CHAPTER THREE.

THE MARCH TO FREDERICKSBURG
BATTLE OF FREDERICKSBURG
THE FREDERICKSBURG ENCAMPMENT

"it has been in five battles and always did its duty!"
[Reference to 100th Pennsylvania (Roundheads) Infantry]

The 100th Pennsylvania went into camp near Lovettsville, Loudon County, Virginia, a short distance south of the Potomac River after crossing at Brunswick, [Berlin] Maryland. Here, Pettit found a few moments to write his family.

Written to:
Family

Camp in Virginia October 27th, 1862. [Monday]

"Dear parents, brothers, and sisters:

I received a letter from Margaret last Friday and was very glad to hear that you were all well. You will see by the heading of this letter that we have been making another move and this time onto the sacred soil. We had just fixed ourselves comfortably in our old camp when an order came on last Saturday to be ready to move the next morning at daylight with 2 days cooked rations.

Accordingly next morning (Sunday) we were roused at 4 o'clock but alas it was raining. Just before day it quit raining when we got up drank our hot coffee and started down the Potomac. About 3½ miles down we found a pontoon bridge across the river. On this we crossed and marched 1½ miles into Va. where we encamped. It was now about 3 o'clock in the afternoon and it had been raining steadily since 10 o'clock. We built a good fire but it rained so hard we could not dry any, so we pitched our tent, got an armful of dry straw, took off our wet overcoats and socks, wrapped ourselves in our blankets and tried to sleep, but we were so damp and cold we did not sleep well. Toward morning it quit raining but got colder, in the morning it commenced again and quit at 10 and cleared off and we have now, sundown, got our things dry and do not feel much worse.

Henry Altan was in our camp on Saturday but left us at the railroad yesterday. It is uncertain whether I will ever get home again; but I want you all to live so we may meet in heaven. I do not write this because I think I am in more danger now than I have been before but because I want you to be prepared.

[This letter continues two days later]

Wednesday, October 29th, 1862.

We are still in camp. Our camp is 1½ miles from Berlin [Brunswick] a small town on the Potomac. There are a great many troops in this vicinity and they are coming over daily.

Perhaps you would like to know what a pontoon bridge is. Well it is built on boats instead of piers. The boats are like skiffs only larger and are fastened with anchors about 12 or 16 feet apart. Sleepers are laid on those and fastened with ropes and then planks are put on.

Colonel Leasure is here now and commands our division. R. Walker Weller is back in our company and has been appointed 2nd Lieutenant. He was formerly orderly sergeant. Critchlow is now 1st Lieutenant. I wrote to Captain Hamilton [Captain Thomas J. Hamilton, Recruiting Officer, of Company D, 100th Regiment] last week about the bounty. I expect an answer soon. If Father is in New Castle soon he might see the Treasurer. But I think Hamilton will attend to it.

The weather remains clear but the nights are cold and frosty. I cannot tell Mag. [sister] what she had best do; but I think she had better go to work with a milliner until spring.

The boys are in middling good health but if the weather gets wet and cold and we march much it will be hard on us. Give my respects to all the friends. Don't forget me in your prayers.

F. Pettit
Co. C 100th Reg't. P.V.

[P.S.]   I'll die when'er my Savior calls,
                       Like spring, when stormy winter flies;
                       Like house, when sunset's shadow falls,
                       I'll met my Savior in the skies.
                              'American Messenger' "

    The march of the Ninth Corps to Fredericksburg started with the cross-
ing of the Potomac River at Brunswick on October 26 would take a little over
three weeks to reach its final destination. From Lovettsville, the 100th travelled
through Waterford and then south to Fredericksburg. They arrived there on
November 19 and went into camp. The route took the troops over the meander-
ing roads of rural Virginia through Upperville, Marshall, Orleans, Waterloo,
Bealton, and finally Fredericksburg.
    The slow and leisurely pace utilized by the Federal army destroyed any
opportunity the Army of the Potomac would have had for a quick thrust against
the Army of Northern Virginia.
    Pettit continued to write home frequently whenever the opportunity
presented itself. His honest and reputable view of the pillaging and foraging
done by Union soldiers during the march is refreshing for its candor.

Written to:
Family
                       Faquer [Fauquier] Co., Va., November 8th, 1862

"Dear parents, brothers, and sisters:

    The last letter I wrote to you was from Waterford [Virginia. Near
Leesburg]. Since that time we have made so many moves that I can
scarcely keep account of them.
    On last Sunday we left Waterford and marched to Snickersville
near Snickers Gap. On Monday we marched to Ashby Gap about 6 miles
from Snickers Gap where we lay until Wednesday. Our camp at this
place is said to be on the farm of the rebel General Ashby now dead.
On Wednesday we marched to Rectorville and encamped about 1 mile
beyond the town near the railroad which runs to Manassas Junction
from the Cap. [Washington, D.C.]
    The next day we started and marched very fast to Orleans. We
stopped here overnight. The next day, Friday, we marched to our
present camping ground about 3 miles from Orleans. In all we have
marched about 50 miles since we came into Virginia. As to what we
have been doing you can tell better than I.
    A cold wind had been blowing all night and in the morning it
commenced to snow and snowed all day. Last night it was quite cold
and snowy but we got some dry straw for our tent and slept quite
comfortably.

Today Saturday the snow has melted but there is a cold raw wind blowing. The health of the boys is as good as usual and mine is the same.

Our march so far in Virginia has been mostly through the richest farming country I ever saw. But alas for secession; everything is doomed to destruction. By a law of Congress the property of all rebels is confiscated that is they have no right to any property.

The soldiers carry this out to the fullest extent. Every hog, chicken, duck, turkey, and bee-hive is sure to be taken. There is no order against it, the officers *encourage it* and the law allows it but still it looks hard. Yesterday I saw a hard sight yet it was in accordance with the law. A secessionist owning about 40 acres of land and a mill lived near Orleans. The soldiers took all his turkeys, chickens, ducks, geese, and a great many bee-hives. The teamster took his corn and left him with scarcely anything. This occurs every day.

I almost forgot to say that I saw the reserves [Pennsylvania Reserves regiments] George Price came to us and I talked with him awhile. The boys are all well that are with them. They have not heard from Gallagher.

I have been in Virginia 2 weeks and have not got any letter from home yet. By the time you get this Mary will be at home and I will expect you to write as often as I write. Give my respects to all the friends. Pray for me for I find it requires much watching to live right in the army.

> F. Pettit
> Co. C. 100 Reg't. P.V.''

Written to:
Family

> Carters Run, Faquer Co., Va. Nov. 13,
> 1862.

[Carter Run is near the Rappahannock River, approximately five miles west of Warrenton, Virginia].

"Dear parents, brothers, and sisters:

Once more I write you from this out of the way place. Why we are here we do not know or why we stay here, but we have been here for the last six days.

We can hear cannonading almost every day and hear reports of the rebels being almost all around us but we have seen none yet. One thing is curious I have not received a letter from home since I came to Va. now almost 3 weeks. I suppose you have written but they have mis-carried. I received a copy of the *Star* this week from home and also a package of 15 papers sent I think by Elder Plowmen for which you will please return him my thanks.

The changes which are taking place in commanders I fear will cause much dissatisfaction in the army. The report now is that McClellan is removed from office [and] I fear for the result. I never saw men have so much confidence in a man as the soldiers have in McClellan.

This part of Virginia is not so rich and well improved as that we have passed through in coming from the Potomac. There are but few able bodied men left. The suffering of the women and children this winter in this part of Virginia must be very great. The soldiers have taken everything, and the inhabitants will have neither property nor money. An order came this morning against this wholesale robbery, but it is too late everything is taken almost and the men will not stop now even if the penalty is death.

By the time you get this letter I suppose you will know who the schoolteachers are about home and tell me who they are. What do the people think about the war at home? Things look very gloomy here.

The weather has been quite pleasant for a few days past. The health of the army is better now than it was early in the fall. Our clothing is excellent. The only thing need is gloves or mittens.

It is very cold to hold a gun in frosty weather with the bare hands. If you have a chance I wish you would send me a pair of woolen gloves or mittens, but do not go to much expense or trouble. Perhaps someone will be coming to see the regiment and you can send them, but don't go to much trouble as I may get a pair some other way. The boys from our neighborhood are all well.

How are grandfathers getting along? Give my respects to them and all the rest of the friends. Let us all try to serve our Maker and live as the Bible tells us to live.

> Your affectionate son and brother,
> Frederick Pettit
> Co. C 100 Reg't P.V.''

The Roundheads [100th Pennsylvania Regiment] reached Fredericksburg during the early afternoon of November 19, 1862. They soon established a semi-permanent camp approximately 1½ miles east of Fredericksburg on the north side of the Rappahannock River near the road to Belle Plain, and near Burnside's army headquarters, the Phillips House. Shortly after arrival, Pettit had time to write a lengthy letter home.

Written to:
Family
                  Camp near Fredericksburg, Va., November 23rd, 1862.

''Dear parents, brothers, and sisters:

Once more I sit down to write to you, but I cannot say it is to answer your last letter for I have almost forgotten it. I think the last letter you wrote me was dated October 18th. The last letter I wrote you was from Carters Run [preceding letter]. Since that time we have moved round a number of times.

We left Carters Run Nov. 15th and marched to Sulphur Springs distance about 6 miles. While we were on the road we heard cannonading in our front and on arriving at the Springs we learned that the rebels had driven in our pickets and commenced shelling a wagon train that was passing at the time. When we arrived they had all gone except a few cavalry and our artillery were throwing a few shell__ at a wagon train still in sight.

Our regiment was ordered forward to prevent the enemy from crossing the river while our train was passing. Sulphur Springs was once a noted summer resort for the rich and fashionable. The water of the springs has quite a sulphurous taste and is said to be quite wholesome. The buildings were once quite extensive but are now in ruins. The bath house and one or two boarding houses are the principal ones left. There is no person living in the village now. Our regiment passed through this place last August on their way to Manassas.

The next day Sunday 16th we left the springs about 11 o'clock and marched until dark and encamped 3 miles from Bealton station on the railroad. We marched about 12 miles this day. Rather hard marching for Sunday.

When will this war be over and we be allowed to spend our Sabbaths in peace and quiet [?] But I almost forgot to say that we had a sermon before leaving the springs by the chaplain.

Monday Nov. 17th left camp about noon and marched 6 miles in the direction of Fredericksburg without a halt. I was very tired tonight but slept very soundly. Tuesday 18th we were roused by reveille at half past three this morning with orders to march at 5 o'clock. Our regiment had the advance today and we marched and rested as we pleased. At 11 o'clock we had marched about 10 miles. We turned off the road into a field at the same place where the regiment stopped for dinner August 13th, 1862. It was raining a little and we expected a wet afternoon's march but Col. Leasure said we must put up our tents as we would stay until morning. This news was quite welcome you may be sure, and we were not long in pitching our tents.

November 19th started shortly after daylight for Fredericksburg. On our way we passed large bodies of troops from whom we learned that the enemy occupied Fredericksburg in force while our troops were on the opposite side of the river. We passed within sight of the city and encamped about 2 miles from it on the North side of the river.

It rained some today but it is not so cold. We passed the camp of the 145th Reg. P.V. Captain Oliver of Edinboro is in this Regiment but we were marching so fast I could not stop to see him. The 100th started from this place Fredericksburg last August 13th and have been marching almost ever since.

Thursday Nov. 20th. Our regiment was detailed to repair the wagon road from Bellplain landing [Belle Plain and Acquia Landing were the new supply bases for the Army of the Potomac] to our camp. We reported to General Wilcox about noon and were ordered to move our camp about 3 miles towards the landing and repair the road. We packed our knapsacks and were ready to march in a few minutes but did not start again for some time. Just as we took down our tents it commenced to rain and rained heavily until the next day. We arrived at our place of destination about dark thoroughly soaked with rain. We however put up our tents got some dry hay and made ourselves as comfortable as possible in our wet clothes.

Friday Nov. 21st. The regiment went out to work on the road today but as I was on guard last night I was left in camp today. Nothing occurred worthy of note today except that I got my clothes dry toward night and began to feel comfortable again. Our camp is 4 miles from Bellplain landing on the Potomac and about 5 miles from Fredericksburg. The soil is light and sandy and much of it looks as though it had been worn out. Much of it is now covered with pine and cedar brush. The inhabitants are mostly poor ignorant whites.

Here are a few market prices here. Corn meal $12 per barrel. Flour from $30 to $40 per barrel. Salt from $6 per bushel to $1.00 per pound. Course boots $16 per pair. Butter 75 to 100. Sugar 75 cts per lb. Coffee there is none.

Saturday Nov. 22nd. I went out today with the regiment to work on the roads. The mud is getting quite deep in places. We cut brush and poles and put in the road and cover them with dirt. We do not work very hard. Commencing at 9 o'clock, quitting at 11, commence at 1, and quit at 4.

Sunday 23rd. Today I commenced to write expecting to have the whole day but just as I commenced we were ordered to pack up and start toward our old camp. After stopping to fill several mud holes and eat our dinners, we arrived at the old camp near sundown and put up our tents again. Tonight we had religious services again in our regiment.

Monday 24th I am just finishing this morning. Last night was quite frosty [and] the ground froze quite hard but we slept quite comfortably in our little tent.

Remember J. Wilson and I tent together. The rebels can be seen any day by going to the bank of the river and our men and they have some hard talk with each other but they never fire at each other.

I have thus given you an account of my rambling and marching so far. Through it all the Lord has preserved my life and health. I and the boys are well. Give my respects to the friends and write soon.

Your son and brother,
Frederick Pettit

[P.S.] I received a letter from Captain Hamilton [Recruiting Officer] about the bounty. He said no recruits for old regiments had got any yet from the county and if they did he would let me know. Some of the boys got woolen gloves by mail. If you have no other chance send them that way for I cannot get them here. Roll them tight, past a paper round them and direct as a letter and they will come safe.

F.P."

Fortunate indeed, was the 100th Pennsylvania, as their regiment was not heavily involved in the bloody battle of Fredericksburg on December 13. The regiment, part of Burns' Division, was not committed to the combat of December 13th, and remained near the center of the Federal line in a support role, but was designated as one of the leading assault regiments in the attack planned for December 14th. They undoubtedly would have suffered severely in a frontal attack on the Maryes Heights position. Propitiously, the attack was never made and the regiment survived the disastrous battle unharmed.

Pettit wrote a detailed account of the Roundheads' role in the battle.

Written to:
Parents

Camp opposite Fredericksburg, Va. Dec. 16th, 1862.

"Dear parents:

Through the mercy of God I am still alive and well. There has been a terrible battle on the other side of the river but we were not in it. We crossed the river in front of the city on Friday morning the 12th and lay in and near the city until last night when we crossed back again. On Saturday we were on the reserve and did not get into the fight.

In the 9th Reserves [Pennsylvania Reserves, Meade's Division, who attacked the Confederate right in the area of Hamilton's Crossing] I am sorry to say that George Prices was killed. He was shot dead on the field. In the 134th [Pennsylvania] James Shoemaker was killed. I saw one of his comrades today who saw him fall. The battle was terrible, but you will get the news in the papers. None of our regiment was hurt.

Since I wrote last we have been paid. I received $31.60 I sent $20.00 home by Lieu. Critchlow. You can get it at his house. I received a pair of gloves some time ago and they were very useful.

The weather has been quite cold but has moderated. We did not suffer much with the cold. I received a letter last night from Mary by J. Wilson. I have received but 2 since Oct. 18th. Perhaps you had better mail them at some other office as I got the one sent from New Brighton.

We have no ink just now so I wrote with the pencil but I think you can read it. I will write soon again.

Your son,
F. Pettit."

Written to:
Parents

Camp opposite Fredericksburgh [sic], Va. Dec. 21st 1862

"Dear parents, brothers, and sisters:

I have received 3 letters from you within a week, one from Mary dated Dec. 7th, one from Mag. [Sister Margaret], one from Amelia Dec. 10th. It will be very tedious to answer these separately so I will write one long letter and answer them all.

First thing I must write is that I am well and doing my best to keep comfortable. Perhaps you would like to know what I have been doing all this cold weather. I have not been idle I can assure you. First I must tell you about getting those mittens. I received them on Sunday Dec. 7th, the day Mary and Mag. wrote their letters and I suppose you remember how cold it was. Just as I received them we got orders to go on picket that night. I can tell you I thought those mittens came about the right time before Monday morning. My post was along the river opposite Fredericksburgh. The rebel pickets were on the other side of the river but were very peaceable as they did not disturb us. We came off picket on Monday.

Nothing more of importance transpired until Thursday Dec. 11th when an attempt was made to lay pontoon bridges across the river. We were ordered out ready to march early in the morning and lay all day near our camp. The pontoons were finished in the afternoon but we did not cross until the next morning when we were marched over and drawn up in line on the wharf where we remained all day.

In the afternoon the rebels threw a few shells at us but none of our regiment were hurt. That night we lay in the streets of Fredericksburgh. The next morning early we marched a short distance below the city and placed behind a bank to support a battery, but it was not used during the day and we did not get into action. [See Map #3]

On Sunday we lay in and near the city expecting every moment to go into action. In the afternoon we had a short sermon by our chaplain in the streets of Fredericksburgh. Sunday night and Monday we lay near where we were on Saturday. Monday evening General Burns' [Brigadier General William Wallace Burns, Division Commander] aide came and took our regiment from the brigade and we were almost sure we were going into a fight. As we marched past Col. Leasure he said 'Roundheads, do your duty'. We and the 2nd Michigan were marched into a ravine a short distance from the picket lines and in a short time were ordered to rest on our arms. We made down our bed expecting to sleep until morning, but just as I got to sleep we were ordered to pack up quietly and fall in. Scarcely a word was spoken above a whisper and we were soon on our way to the river. When we arrived at the wharf we found all our division there and crossing the bridge very quietly. We were soon across and back to our old camp where we slept until the next day. This is all we saw of the retreat. The next morning all the army was safely across.

Since we came back nothing of importance has transpired. We were on picket again night before last. We were not on post but it was so cold we had a very uncomfortable time and were glad to get back to camp again last evening.

We have built up a pen of poles about a foot high, banked up the ground round, put the little tent over for a roof, shut up one end with a gum blanket, built a fire before the other end, and so we have a middling comfortable house for two. At night we shut up both ends with old grain sacks and sleep quite comfortably.

We now get plenty to eat having rice, beans or potatoes almost every day for dinner. Our regiment is now pretty well clothed and if we could be certain of remaining any length of time in one place we would soon have comfortable quarters; I wish those who write and talk so much about no winter quarters for the army of the Potomac could be here and spend one of these cold days and nights with us. I think it would make them break for winter quarters.

I do not know what the people at home think of the war but I know what the soldiers think of it. They think that fighting will never stop it and the sooner it is over now the better.

I saw Dan Thamer and M. C. Rose the other day. They were well. George Price was shot dead on Saturday. The ball passed through his head. George Smith was wounded in the side and back very dangerously. Edward Matheny was shot through both legs. His wounds are not dangerous. James Shoemaker was shot dead the same day. The dead were left on the field, the wounded were all brought off. [The soldiers referred to, all known to Pettit, were members of Company H, 9th Pennsylvania Reserve Regiment, which was recruited in Beaver County, Pennsylvania. This regiment was heavily involved in General George Meade's attack on the Confederate right at Hamilton's Crossing during the battle of Fredericksburg, December 13th.]

You said the weather had been very cold at home. It has been the same here. I should like to be at home to help eat the puddings and sausages, but we get fresh beef about once a week which tastes excellent.

I hope Mary will succeed well with her school. Tell Albert and Alice they must learn as fast as they can and be good children at school. Tell Amelia I was glad to hear from her and hope she will write again. She and Evan must study hard at that Geography for it is very useful. Cyrus and Amelia must study hard at the written Arithmetic for they have a start now and ought to go right along. The rest of the children must study hard too, and I want you all to be good children and remember the golden rule. 'Do unto others as you would have others do unto you'. Let all the children write to me for I like to read their letters. I hope your letters will come a little more promptly.

Are there any singings, spellings, or meetings about home this winter? Are grandfathers well and how are they getting along? I sent $20 to Critchlow's at New Brighton which I suppose you got. If you have got it let me know.

The next letter you send, send me 25 or 30 postage stamps as I cannot get them here. We have preaching today (Sunday) at 11 o'clock and although it was very cold and in the open air yet there were quite a number present. Tomorrow we go on picket again. Thus we put in our time.

By the time you get this it will be Christmas and New Years and you will all be having a good time. I hope this war will soon be over and we may all return to our homes. Give my respects to all the friends. The boys from our neighborhood are all well.

Do not forget to read your Bibles and remember me when you pray.

Your affectionate son and brother,
F. Pettit
Co C 100th P.V."

Written to:
Mrs. Barbara Pettit [Mother]
North Sewickly, Beaver Co., Pa.

Camp opposite Fredericksburg, Va., Dec. 27th '62.

"Dear Mother:

I this day received a letter from you and Evan dated November 24th and also one from Mag. and Evan dated Nov. 1st. Although these letters are old yet they were quite welcome because they contained news from home. It is just such letters as these that I like to get. Letters that talk to me as the writers would if I were there to talk to them. The best letters I have gotten from home are those written by Evan, Amelia, and you. Mag's do pretty well but Mary's are too learned and abstract. Perhaps you do not understand that so you can get her to explain it to you.

You complain that the girls are not contented at home: They think it too old fashioned, and not enough quality like. I am very sorry for this, for it is a very wrong spirit. If they could see things as I now see them I think they would act and think quite different.

This part of Virginia was inhabited by much the same class of persons in regard to wealth as those about New Brighton and New Castle. No doubt their children were dissatisfied with their old fashioned parents and homes, and complained because they did not live in style like the fashionables of Fredericksburgh. But look! How changed is their condition now. The most of them have left their homes and are now wandering through the South in a naked starving condition; while those that remain are but little better. Everything of value has been taken from them not even their personal clothing and household furniture being left. I have seen young women here who were once comfortable, dressed in clothing made of old grain sacks and blankets. These sights do not make the feeling soldier very contented when he knows that his own sisters may be in the same condition in a few years if the war continues. And then to hear that they are discontented with their present comfortable house makes me fear that God may yet bring them to see the road of need.

I have nothing now to write. I am still in good health. The weather is quite warm for the season. Christmas passed very quietly. I procured a pint of beans and boiled them with a piece of pork for my Christmas dinner. They were excellent.

You said Mr. McCoy was sick. Did he get well? His son Charles was to see me this week but I was on picket and did not see him. They are near here and I may see him yet.

I have received no letters from home later than Dec. 10th. The boys here are all well. I am glad to hear that you still pray for us. Write another long letter soon.

Give my respects to grandfathers folks. Tell Evan and Amelia to write again and I will write them a letter soon. Tell May not to get affronted her turn will come yet.

Your affectionate son,
Frederick Pettit
Co. C. 100th P.V.

P.S. We have a very comfortable little hut with a chimney at once and straw in the bottom to sleep on. Be careful how you direct your letters. I will give you the address again. Be sure to write it as I do.

Fred Pettit
Co. C 100th Reg. P.V.
9th Army Corps
Washington, D.C.

[P.P.S.] It is now 4 months since I left home. My 2 pairs of socks are about done and I have sent for 2 new pair. I can get them from the government cheaper than you can send them.

F.P.''

Written to:
Miss M. A. Pettit, North Sewickly, Beaver Co., Pa.

Camp opposite Fredericksburgh, Va., Dec. 30th, 1862.

"Dear Sister Mary:

I received your very welcome letter of the 22nd inst. today and was very glad to hear much cheering news from you and your school. I am particularly glad that you are beginning to like your profession as you will now have ample opportunity to practice it. The interests of our public schools must be principally entrusted for a number of years to the female teachers of our land. You spoke of Thursday morning Dec. 19th as being very cold. It was indeed so here.

Our regiment had been thrown out as a reserve picket the day before and that night and Thursday morning we lay in an open field on a hill along the bank of the Rappahannoc [Sic]. It was so cold we could not sleep and so windy the fire did but little good and altogether we had such a night as soldiers only can stand, but we made full time sleeping the next night in our comfortable little tents.

I presume your "Knitting Party" at father Abram's was nice and wish I could have been there. Did they all knit? Do you and Erskine stand in the relation of reciprocals yet? I hope Ann G's change may be for the better. Mr. Morton's end was sad indeed. Oh, when will our people take warning by such miserable end. I hope Mr. Morrison's bragging about your school will not stop you from striving to improve it still.

Since we returned from the other side of the river [Battle of Fredericksburg] nothing of importance has taken place. An account of our proceedings over there I have sent home which I suppose you have seen. You wished to know how I spent Christmas. Doing nothing. Emphatically nothing. It was as quiet a Christmas as I ever spent in my life. For my dinner I had a mess of beans and pork boiled, which were equal to anything I have eaten lately. We now have good rations and plenty of them.

We have fixed our little tent quite comfortable having a fireplace at one end. We do not drill now and have but little to do. The weather has been delightful the past few days, but this evening it rained some and I presume we will have another cold time. If it were not for the want of the accustomed society I could be as contented here as any place. When there is a firm reliance on divine Providence it does not require all the luxuries to which we have been accustomed to make us contented.

You said there had been no preaching at Centre for some time. This is indeed a bad state of affairs but not to be bettered now. I believe the best thing to do in this case is to withdraw and unite with some other Church where we can feel at home without compromising any doctrine. This is the course I think I should pursue if I were now at home, but act as the Spirit of God directs. Whatever you do, do it to the honor and glory of God, and still continue to trust and serve Him. I never felt until lately the full force of these words: God moves in a mysterious way, His wonders to perform. The realization that they are true inspires me with more confidence in the Creator.

Give my respects to all the friends. I am still in good health.

> Your affectionate brother,
> Fred Pettit
> Co. C. 100th Reg. P.V.

P.S. Be careful to write the address in full on your letter. Co. C 100th Reg. Pa. Vol. -9th Army Corps, Washington, D.C.

Give the other letter to Evan.

Dec. 31st

It rained some last night and today is cold and windy.

F.P."

Written to:
Evan Pettit

Camp opposite Fredericksburgh, Va., Dec. 31st '62

"Dear brother Evan:

I have received several letters from you and I thought I would answer them today. The oldest one I have now is dated Oct. 11th and you said you had been at grandfathers making cider and that there had been a meeting at Hazel Dell. At that time I was in Pleasant Valley, Maryland. The next letter is dated Nov. 3rd. At that time I was traveling in Virginia. Though this letter is old I did not get it until last week.

You said it snowed very hard a week before. That was the time we crossed the Potomac Oct. 26. It did not snow here but the rain was very cold. That week it got quite warm and we stayed three days in a small town called Waterford. The people were nearly all Union and we could buy plenty of bread, pies, butter, and apples from them. I got a pass one day and went to town and bought 2 loaves of fresh bread, half pound of butter, and some apples all for half a dollar. We lived well while the butter and bread lasted as I had none for 2 months before and have had none since.

The last letter is dated Nov. 23rd. It came last week with the other one. You said it was a cold snowy day when you wrote. The wind was quite cold here but it did not snow.

I think the wheat turned out middling well.

I suppose you would like to know what we are doing here and what you could see if you were here. We do not have much to do. In the morning we are awaked at daylight by the drums beating reveille. The orderly sergeant then calls the roll the men all standing in two ranks in the street between the tents. We then wash and fold our blankets. By this time breakfast is commonly ready. It consists of coffee, boiled meat, and crackers. After breakfast 4 or 5 men are detailed to clean up about our tents. 1 man for guard around the camp and 1 to go to the woods and cut wood to be hauled for our company fire. The rest of us have not much to do. Some washing their clothes, write letters, fix their tents, get wood for their fires, read books and papers etc.

Once or twice each week we have review or inspection or both. At the inspection an officer comes around and takes each gun and examines it to see if it is clean and bright, and if it inspection of knapsacks we open them and he examines their contents. At a review an officer rides along our lines and looks at us and then we march past him.

About once in two weeks we go on picket. Pickets are the outside guards next the enemy and must not let anybody pass them. When we stand along the river as here, it is not very troublesome. There are generally 4 men on a post and they must stay 24 hours. This is about all we have to do now.

We have meeting every night in our regiment. It is something like a prayer meeting. Mr. Brown [Browne] our chaplain leads.

Today is quite cold and windy but our little tent is quite comfortable.

I suppose you are going to school this cold weather. Learn all you can. The next time you write tell me how you are getting along, what you are studying, what kind of a teacher you have, and who is [in] your written arithmetic class.

Tell Cyrus to write me a letter too when you do. I want to hear from him. Ask Albert what he wants to tell me and you write it in your letter. Tell him I often think of him and Alice and would like to see them at school.

Dear brother be a good boy and read your Bible.

> Your affectionate brother,
> Frederick Pettit
> Co. C. 100th Reg. P.V."

January 1, 1863. The new year found the 100th Pennsylvania still encamped in their same Fredericksburg location, near the Phillips house, about one mile from the town. Morale was low in the Army of the Potomac at this time. Particularly depressing were the memories of the tragic "over the river" offensive which had resulted in the disastrous battle of Fredericksburg.

The weather continued cold and life in camp was monotonous. No progress was being made against the enemy, and it seemed to many that the entire future of the war was questionable. On the 17th, six men from the 100th Pennsylvania deserted in a single day according to one of the future regimental historians, Private Silas Stevenson.

On January 20th, Burnside attempted another move against the Confederates which has been labeled the "Mud March". During the operation, a flanking movement against Lee's left flank, the weather turned extremely bad, and the entire project had to be cancelled. The 100th Pennsylvania was spared as their brigade was one of the last scheduled to move during the affair. Fortunately, the waiting regiment received no orders to move out.

The Roundheads remained in the Fredericksburg camp for the balance of January and the first 10 days of February, when they received the welcome news that they were departing from the area and were to be detached from the Army of the Potomac.

Pettit wrote several letters during this period of 40 days and they present an excellent picture of life in the regiment during their last few weeks at Fredericksburg. The first 1863 letter continues in the same vein.

Written to:
Family

Camp opposite Fredericksburgh, Va., Jan'y 5th '63

"Dear parents, brothers, and sisters:

I received a letter from Mary yesterday dated Dec. 29th as she wanted me to write all I know about the battle of Fredericksburgh I thought I would write a letter to all of you. I was glad to hear that you were all well and had a good time on Christmas. Tell grandmother I would like to be there to get my Christmas presents but if she waits until next year I think I will be there.

I was sorry to hear of the death of Rev. Kirk. He will certainly be missed but has no doubt gone up higher. Mary's letter was very good, and plenty of it. I like to read such letters and hope she will write more of them.

Nothing of importance has transpired since I wrote last. New Year's day passed very quietly and pleasantly. The weather has been uncommonly fine during the past month. There has been so little rain that the roads are getting dusty.

I wrote a letter to John Serverus last week and if you will send me Hannah Pettit's address I may write to her.

You wished me to write all I know of the battle of Fredericksburgh which I will proceed to do. We arrived opposite Fredericksburgh Nov. 19th on our way to Richmond. We were then at least 20 miles nearer Richmond than the main part of the rebel army. General Burnside had ordered the pontoon bridges to be at Fredericksburgh the very day we

arrived Nov. 19th but they did not arrive until Nov. 26th. By this time
the whole rebel army was there to oppose our crossing and we had not
three days rations ahead nor did we have until Dec. 1. Gen. Burnside
was unwilling to move until he had at least 12 days rations on hand.

On Dec. 9th everything was arranged and the whole army massed
near the river ready for an attack the next day. At 5 o'clock the next
morning the engineers commenced putting down the pontoon bridges, 2
opposite the town and 2 about 1 mile below. Those below the town were
put down without much trouble, the rebel sharpshooters being driven
away without much difficulty; but opposite the town it was different.
The engineers proceeded very quietly until they had lain the bridge about
⅔ of the way across, when the sharpshooters opened upon them and
compelled them to leave. Our artillery then opened upon the town.

At 10 o'clock another attempt was made to finish the bridges
but with no better success. The batteries now poured in an incessant
fire of grape, cannister, and shell riddling the houses along the river
where the sharpshooters were concealed and setting fire to several in
the back part of the town.

In the afternoon skirmishers were sent over in boats who drove
the rebels back and the bridges were then completed. On our left at the
lower bridges Franklins men crossed during the day and advanced some
distance without much fighting. On the right opposite the city but few
troops crossed until the next day Dec. 11th when Sumners Grand Division crossed. There was but little fighting this day, the fog being so
heavy during the forenoon that little could be seen on either side.

During the night preparations were made for an attack on the
enemies [sic] works the next day. The rebel artillery was planted on
a range of hills from 1 to 2 miles from the river while their infantry
were in rifle pits in front and below their artillery.

The ground sloped gradually from here to the river so that our
infantry must advance against the fire of both infantry and artillery
and our artillery could not fire for fear of killing our own men.

Hooker's men crossed on Saturday, part going with Franklin
on the left and part with Sumner on the right. The fighting must
necessarily be done by infantry.

The fight was commenced by Franklin about 10 o'clock on the
left and by 11 it was a continuous road of musketry and artillery on
both right and left. Remember the right was in front of the town and
the left about 2 miles further down the river.

On the left the enemy were driven by the Pa. Reserves out of their
rifle pits and across the railroad, but still their rifle pits continued and
their batteries were effective as ever. About 3 o'clock the rebels made
a desperate charge upon our forces and drove them back with great
slaughter to the place they occupied in the morning. Here a stand was
made and at dark the fighting ceased on the left. It had been very severe.
For six hours there was a continued road of musketry and cannon.

On the right the fighting commenced about 11 o'clock by our forces charging upon their rifle pits and batteries. A part of these were at first carried, but the cross fires from batteries and riflepits not before seen soon drove the assailants back. Again and again they charged, one brigade after another, as often were driven back. The fighting continued on the right until late at night, several charges having been made after dark.

Our forces at night occupied the same ground as in the morning. On Sunday and Monday there was no fighting the rebels not daring to venture outside of their entrenchments to attack us, and our forces being satisfied that it was useless to attack them again.

It must be remembered that the whole army was lying under range of the enemies cannon and that there was danger of the river rising and destroying the bridges, this leaving the army in a very dangerous situation. In view of all these things our general determined to recross the river. This they did Monday night Dec. 14th.

The truth is we were fairly beaten in our attempt to take the enemies works. The enemy did not drive us and we were unable to drive them. We did not fail for want of troops for twice as many could have done no more. We did not fail through any mismanagement of our general for everything was planned and executed well. We did not fail for want of bravery in our troops for the rebels say we fought with uncommon bravery.

The reason was simply this, the works were too strong to be taken by storm. The loss was about 1200 killed and 8000 wounded. That of the rebels was not so large as ours. All the wounded that could be obtained were brought over the river. The dead and wounded were stripped by the rebels of everything except their underclothing.

By means of a flag of truce our men buried all their dead and the wounded were exchanged or paroled.

This is what is known amongst us here as the battle of Fredericksburgh. The enemy have since greatly strengthened their works making it next to impossible to cross now. The pickets are very friendly but are not allowed to talk to each other.

F. Pettit"

Pettit's letter of December 21st gave many of the details of the Roundheads' regimental operations in the battle. His January 5th letter gives a fairly accurate summation of the primary combat operations on December 13 of the entire army. It is a remarkable letter considering its overall accurate account of the battle. Further, it must be remembered that it was written just three weeks after the contest with only limited detailed and factual information available to the writer.

Written to:
Miss Margaret Pettit

Camp opposite Fredericksburg, Va., Jan'y 7, 1863

"Dear Sister,

I have received quite a number of letters from you, but have written few in answer. Your letters were the only ones I received from home for some time [and] when I write home I like to write to all so I did not write to you in particular. The last one is dated Dec. 12th. I received 2 papers from you with Mary's letter. Tell Mary I received a letter from her yesterday dated November 30th. The reason your letters do not come to me is you do not put on the full address. I will give you the full address at the end of this.

Mary wrote to me that you talked of going to school and again I hear you are preparing to work at your trade. A good education is very desirable but perhaps in your case it would be as well to continue at your trade. Be contented to commence on a small scale, learn to do your work well and rapidly, and you will soon rise in your business. I know it is inconvenient to commence work at home but persevere and perhaps next spring you may have a chance to better yourself.

There is but little going on of interest here. All is quiet. The weather is cool but pleasant. Mother wished to know if any of the boys received Christmas presents. None except it be some small article of clothing of which I need none now.

We are all well. Write soon a long letter. Remember thy Creator now in the days of thy youth.

Give my respects to the friends.

Your affectionate brother,
Fred Pettit

Address

Co. C. 100th Reg. P.V.
9th Army Corps
Washington, D.C."

Written to:
Evan Pettit

Camp opposite Fredericksburg, Va. Jan. 13th 1863

"Dear brother Evan,

I received your very neat letter of Jan'y. 4th and 5th on Sunday evening. I am glad to see that you are improving in letter writing. Your letter was certainly written very neatly and I hope you will continue to improve.

I would have answered your letter yesterday but we went on picket at 9 o'clock and did not come back until 11 o'clock today.

Picketing is about the only duty we do now. Our Division of 12 regiments furnishes pickets about 1½ miles along the river. The men are so divided that we go on once in 9 days and perhaps I cannot describe it better than by telling you what we did yesterday and today.

In the morning we were ordered to be ready for picket at 9 o'clock. We do not take our knapsacks and tents, but roll our woolen blankets in gum ones and tying the ends together throw them over the shoulder. We also take our canteens and haversacks with all the grub we can get for we eat a great quantity on picket. Our guns and cartridge boxes complete the rig. Thus equipped we assemble at the top of the drum and march to the river 2 miles. About one half the men go on post and the rest stay in some convenient place near by ready if they should be needed. They are called the reserve picket. The posts are about one fourth of a mile apart and about 30 men are put on a post. In the day time a small squad stay where they can see along the river but at night guards are placed close to the river and must keep a sharp watch. When not on guard we can sleep if it is not too cold.

The weather is not so cold here as it is at home. The nights are frosty but the days are not generally very cold. My health is still good. The rest of the boys are well. I almost forgot to say that I received 21 stamps in your letter. They came when needed as I had but one left. You wished to know whether I wanted a pair of boots or shoes. Shoes I can get here of the government. Boots would be very convenient and useful in muddy weather for marching. But the trouble is to get them. It is almost useless to send them by express as expressed goods scarcely ever reach us. The only certain way is to send them with some person who is coming to see us. If any one is coming from our neighborhood you might send them. But do not trouble yourself much as I can get along without them. If sent they must be large heavy soled No. 10. Boots are plenty here at from 6 to $8 per pair.

January 14th

[letter continued]

This morning is foggy and chilly. We have orders to drill 1 hour before and after noon.

Are there any singings about home this winter? Who belongs to the regulars and who to the volunteers at Hazel Dell this winter? Has Joseph Rowser come back? What is the price of pork, beef, and butter. How many head of cattle, sheep, and hogs has father this winter. How many cows are giving milk. How many beeves did you butcher? Has Dick Ramsey come home yet?

These are perhaps enough questions for one letter. Tell me all you can about the school. The verses you sent me were very good, especially the last one which is this:

'Be ready — many fall around,
Our loved ones disappear;
We know not when our call may come.
Nor should we wait in fear
If ready, we can calmly rest
Living or dying, we are blest.'

Your affectionate brother,
F. Pettit"

Written to:
Margaret Pettit

Camp opposite Fredericksburgh, Va.   January 28th, 1863.

"Dear sister Margaret:

Your letter of the 23rd was received today and with it came one from mother. I was glad to hear that the most of you were well and hope Evan is too by this time. I am still in good health.

We just came off picket at noon today having been on 24 hours. It rained yesterday, commenced to snow last night and is still snowing. From this you may judge how we fared last night. Our only protection against the storm was a gum blanket thrown over the shoulders. I have spent 2 nights on picket lately which were enough to stir any man's patriotism. The night of the 21st we were on picket. The wind blew a perfect hurricane and it rained all the time. I do not write to complain for I expected as much before I enlisted, but to let you know what the Army of the Potomac endures.

On the 20th a grand movement of the army was commenced. [Burnside's famous 'Mud March'] Hooker's and Franklin's divisions and Sigel's corps moved on that day to Banks Ford 8 miles above Fredericksburgh. We (Sumner's division) had orders to move the next morning but that night a heavy rain and wind storm commenced which lasted 2 days and nights. By this time the roads were impassable. Wagons, cannon, and pontoons were all fast in the mud and the rebels tauntingly told our pickets Burnside had stuck in the mud. The army has now moved back to its old place.

General Burnside has been removed and Gen. Hooker appointed in his place. Report says he has resigned. I should not wonder considering the treatment Burnside has received. We think Burnside did all he could do and cannot understand why he was relieved of the command. Burnside appeared much like Washington to the troops that knew him best.

Col. Leasure and son left for home yesterday on a furlough. We do not know when this war will end but now we think if we live we will be in the army next winter yet.

This is a very stormy afternoon but we are getting our clothing partly dried and expect to make full time sleeping tonight, for we did not sleep much last night. It is not much trouble for me to remain awake 2 days and a night now. When I was at home I thought it terrible. But this is not the only thing I have learned. I sleep as comfortably on the ground in our little tent with 2 blankets over me as I ever slept at home.

Let mother read this as I have nothing new to write to her. I received a letter from John and Susannah Severus dated Jan. 12. They were all well.

Write soon and tell me all the news and how you are getting along with your trade. Be contented with your lot. Despise not the day of small things. Make it your aim to serve God and be of use in the world. Give my respects to all the friends.

Your brother,
F. Pettit.''

Written to:
Family

Camp opposite Fredericksburg, Va. Feb. 3rd '63.

"Dear parents, brothers, and sisters:

As I am at a loss for employment this cold day I will commence writing you a letter. Now don't think because it is to all of you that no one need answer it, but all answer it. Let each one write a little at least no difference how poorly. The last letter I received from you was written by mother and Margaret Jan. 23rd. There were several things in it I forgot to mention in Mag's letter, and first I must say I did receive a Christmas present in a letter from you. All I can say of it is that it was small but sweet. I was glad to hear in mother's that Albert had commenced to read small words. I think he will soon be able to write me that letter. You must be taking uncommon interest in the school this winter. I think you were very fortunate in getting a good teacher. How are Wirtenberg, Hope Dale, and the other schools getting along?

Perhaps you would like to hear something more about the army. Let me first tell you something about the situation of our camp and what troops are near us. There are 3 regiments in our brigade viz: the 36 Massachusetts, 45th Pa, and 100th Pa. We first encamped in a large field where troops had been encamped last summer. About a week afterward we moved to the woods leaving the field to drill in. The place our brigade encamped on was an old field covered with small pines. We were ordered to put up our tents as best we could without cutting any brush; consequently our camp is very irregularly laid out. Commonly a camp is laid out in regular streets.

Our camp is on a high sandy ridge opposite Fredericksburgh and about 2 miles east of it. The front of our brigade that is the lines of the different regiments runs north and south. On the south is the Fredericksburg road and the 46th N.Y., a German regiment lies on the opposite side. [The 46th New York Infantry was in the same brigade with the 100th Pennsylvania for many months earlier in the war and participated with them in the battles of 2nd Manassas, Chantilly, South Mountain, and Antietam.] On the East are the 29th Mass., and 50th P.V. On the west is the large field in which we drill. North of our camp are the commissary and sutler tents. I may here say Virginia is one field as there are no fences and the timber is disappearing rapidly.

I must say a word about the regiments of our brigade. The 36th Mass. is a new regiment. It joined us at Antietam after the battle. It is composed of respectable Yankee mechanics and farmers and has a good reputation though never in battle. The 45th P.V. has been in service over a year. It has been in 2 battles, South Mountain and Antietam. It is composed of very civil respectable men from eastern Pa.

The 100th needs little description. You know it well. It was formerly composed of eleven companies. One [Company I] has been broken up and put in the others. One Co. [A] is from Washington County, one from Westmoreland [M], and the others from Beaver [D], Lawrence, Mercer [G], Butler [C] Co's. It has been in 5 battles and always did its duty.

The 134th P.V. [A nine months regiment from northwest Pennsylvania] bears a hard name here. They are discouraged, dirty, and careless compared with our regiment. Our regiment is now comparatively healthy, and in good spirits.

The soldiers are well pleased with their new commander Gen. Hooker. They see that it is useless to be in haste to attack the enemy, and are willing to wait for a good opportunity. Extensive preparations are being made for a spring campaign by putting the whole army in good condition.

They are building ovens here to bake bread, and various other improvements are being made. The party at home that find fault with the government and try to hinder its operations find but little sympathy among the soldiers. The soldiers are for the government and the prosecution of the war. If enough of us ever get home there will be quite a change in the politics of the country. I was surprised to find all the soldiers opposed to the part that carried the last election in Pa. We intend to right these wrongs after the war is over.

February 5th, 1863.

[letter continued]

I did not send any letter immediately hoping to receive one from you first; but none has come yet and I will delay no longer. The weather during the past few days has been the coldest this winter. Today (Thursday) it is snowing and is quite cold.

Our hardest work is getting wood. We carry most of it half a mile. Though when not too stormy it is good exercise.

I still remain well and hearty. Wilson, Lary, and Bird are well.

Lieutenant Critchlow told me there are 2 pounds of butter on the way for me. He said he received the key of the box Sunday night. He did not say who sent it but I think I can guess. It will be a great luxury for me when I get it.

None of has received any word of our books except what Mag. wrote, but we suppose you intend to send them. We can buy many things at the sutlers here but they are very dear. Butter 50 and 60 cts per lb. Sugar 20 to 30 cts and scarce, ham 25 to 30 cts. Dried Beef 20 cts lb. Air tight peaches and tomatoes in quart cans from 75 cts to $1.00. As a soldiers pay is but $13.00 per month you can calculate now many of the luxuries he can afford to buy. Bread sells at 25 cts per lb., and crackers and cakes about the same. We can get plenty of newspapers here but they cost 10 cts apiece.

I cannot think of anything more that would interest you. Write soon a long letter. Tell Cyrus and Amelia to write and Ruth and Harriet too.

> Frederick Pettit,
> Co. C. 100th Reg't
> Pa. Vol."

The foregoing letter is the last one written from the "Camp opposite Fredericksburgh". With little notice, the Ninth Corps was ordered to Fortress Monroe and Newport News, Virginia, in early February. This move detached them from the Army of the Potomac. Because the Lincoln administration considered Burnside as the permanent commander of the Ninth Corps, it is probable that the move to Newport News was made in anticipation of their joining Burnside in his new assignment in the Department of the Ohio with headquarters at Cincinnati.[1]

The men of the Ninth Corps were pleased to leave the mud, misery, and monotony of their Fredericksburg encampment on February 10 and be "on the march" once again.

---

[1] William G. Gavin, *Campaigning With The Roundheads, History of the 100th Pennsylvania Veteran Volunteer Infantry*, Morningside House, Dayton, Ohio, 1989. Details of the decision to detach the Ninth Army Corps from the Army of the Potomac in February 1862 will be found in Chapter Nine of this work.

CHAPTER FOUR

CAMPING AT NEWPORT NEWS VIRGINIA FEBRUARY - MARCH 1863

The Journey to Kentucky

"We are in excellent health and spirits."

After the dismantling of their old camp opposite Fredericksburg on February 10, the 100th Regiment moved a short distance to the Falmouth railroad station where trains took them to the nearby Federal base at Acquia Landing. Delaying only briefly, the vessels were then boarded and the convoy was underway down the Potomac by the 11th.

On the 13th, the brigade landed and marched about eight miles to the banks of the James River just above the town of Newport News. The troops were gratified with their new location and considered it to be one of the choicest camp sites that they had yet occupied. The soil here was dry and sandy, a most welcome change from the muddy topography of the Fredericksburg area.

By February 15, Private Fred Pettit was settled and started writing his family once again.

Written to:
Family

Newport News, Va. February 15th, 1863

"Dear parents, brothers, and sisters:

We are safe at last at this far famed place and are encamped near the place the regiment occupied last summer. [The 100th Regiment

53

was in the area the previous summer after coming north from South Carolina on their way to participate in Pope's Virginia Campaign as well as the battles of Manassas and Chantilly.]

We broke camp on the Rappahannock Tuesday the 10th. The forenoon have been very warm and pleasant and our company had been at a game of ball. About noon the order came to pack up, and never did troops do it with more good will. At 2 o'clock we marched to the railroad station, got on the cars towards evening and arrived at Acquia Creek shortly after dark. After considerable delay we got aboard the steamer Sylvan Shore and lay in the river until next morning. Our vessel was small carrying only 300 men with no bunks for sleeping. Wilson and I made our bed on the hurricane deck and slept very well only it was a little cool when the boat was running.

At daylight Wednesday morning we started down the Potomac bound for Fortress Monroe distance 180 miles. Nothing of importance occurred on the way down the Potomac. The day was cool and windy and on arriving at the mouth of the river the signals indicated that the bay was too rough for our boat so we lay to in St. Mary's harbor until the next morning. We had now run 80 miles in about 6 hours.

The next morning we hoisted anchor and started for Fortress Monroe. There was a strong tide and wind against us so that we ran very slowly and did not arrive in sight of the Fortress until sundown. It was dark when we arrived there, so we ran past and anchored in Hampton Roads until morning. The night was cold and very windy and we were glad when morning came. In the morning we steamed to the Fortress and had a good view of it and the Rip Raps. The last is simply a large heap of rock in the harbour. It is indeed a solitary look place. The Fortress looks quite formidable with its bristling cannon.

After reporting here we were ordered to go to Newport News distance 8 miles. We were not long in reaching our destination and soon landed. We marched a short distance from the wharf and stacked arms until a camping ground should be selected.

In the meantime we could look around us. All was life and animation. A few days ago there were but 10 men here; now there are thousands. Sutlers were plenty and things were so cheap compared with what we were accustomed to that the sales were enormous.

About 3 o'clock the Brigade started to camp but our company was left to unload our baggage and we did not get to camp until dark. The next morning we were up early and off to the woods for poles to put up our tents. By night we had quite comfortable quarters built.

Our camp is on the James river about 1 mile above Newport News landing. The land along the river has been cleared about ½ mi. wide and is dry and sandy. Our camp is on the ridge. Back of it the ground is low and swampy and covered with timber. This is the best location we have ever had for a camp.

We are in excellent health and spirits. Our trip here was very long and tedious considering the distant. We do not know how long we will stay here nor where we will go when we move. We received two mails yesterday the first since leaving the Rappahannock, but there were no letters from you. The last letter from home was mailed the day the Box was started. We expect to get our express goods in a short time. Some regiments have received theirs already.

Colonel Leasure arrived here this morning from home. We will doubtless have a pleasant time here if they let us stay long enough to enjoy it.

This is Sunday and is warm and pleasant with a little rain. We expect to have a sermon by our chaplain.

Write soon. Give my respects to all inquiring friends.

> Yours with affection,
> Frederick Pettit,
> Co. C. 100th Reg't. P.V.

[letter continued]

February 15th, 1863.

P.S. Direct your letter as usual until further orders. I send you two clippings [not found] from a paper. The one conveys a true idea of a soldier's life. The other conveys a true idea of the present and what will doubtless be the future condition of the soldiers of our country.

F. Pettit"

Written to:
Family

Newport News, Va. February 22nd, 1863.

"Dear parents, brothers, and sisters:

Last Wednesday I received a letter from Margaret dated the 9th and one yesterday from Mary, Evan, and Amelia. I was very glad to get these letters as they are the first I received from home since we came to this place. As there are so many of them I will answer them all by writing a long letter to all of you.

I think some people about Hazel Dell do not like to hear anything about the army from the soldiers or they would not have used Mr. Roberts as they did. Your teacher of course did what the law says he should do by not giving the house, but if the soldiers ever get home they will not dare do such a thing again.

Does anybody write essays in opposition to Mrs. Johnston? The soldiers belong to the blood letters. They do not want the war to stop until the rebels lay down their arms and promise to behave themselves. We would like to be at home to go to spelling, etc. but have patience will be along some day. Are you sure Mr. Marshall of whom you wrote was John Marshall of the regiment? We had not heard of his going blind. Mary said she was sorry we were going farther south, it seemed so far way. We are not at all sorry.

We hope to be more successful here than we have been in Virginia. I do not know that I can write anything more interesting than an account of what we have been doing the past week.

Monday was warm and pleasant and we intended to fix our tent, but we learned that we were to get new tents of a different kind so we did not fix any.

I was down to the landing in the morning. Things sell about one half cheaper here than opposite Fredericksburgh. Monday night it rained. Tuesday it rained all day. We had not built a chimney in our tent and we now felt the need of one. We wrapped up in our overcoats and to pass away the time we commence working at a puzzle sent to John. Towards evening we got it. It was this 1-Plant 19 trees in 9 straight rows and 5 trees in each row. We did it. Can any of you do it?

Monday Night Feb'y 23. It became so cold I could not write any more yesterday and I have been busy today. I will now continue last weeks diary.[1] Wednesday it rained again most of the day. We got the new tents today. They are made in the shape of the letter A and are called A tents.

Thursday: cold and windy. I was on guard today. My post was before Col. Leasure's quarters. By the way his quarters are close to the bank of the river and just opposite them lie 5 gunboats blockading the James River. While I was on guard an officer and 4 marines from one of the boats came to visit Col. Leasure. The marines look quite neat and clean compared with the soldiers. But they have not such hard fare on board the boats as we have on land and can of course look better.

Friday clear and pleasant and a busy day in camp. The new tents are to be put up. There will be 4 or 5 in a tent. They are to be built up 2½ feet from the ground with logs, two tents together with a double chimney between them. Perhaps I will send you a drawing of our camp. By night we had ours built and slept in it. There are 4 in our tent. Robert Weimer, [Robert Wimer, Died May 30, 1863, Camp Nelson, Kentucky,] Robert C. Dunwoody, [Died August 19, 1864 of wounds received July 30, 1864 at the Battle of the Crater], Wilson [John], and I.

[1] From this comment it is obvious Pettit kept a detailed diary and often consulted it for dates and events when he compiled his letters home. One diary only has survived and is in the archives with Pettit's letters at U.S. Army Military History Institute, Carlisle Barracks, Pennsylvania. The diary covers the period from September 1863 to January 1864.

Saturday quite springlike. We put a floor of pine puncheons in our tent and daubed it today and got some brick to build a chimney.

Sunday 22nd. The weather took a sudden change last night. The wind became very cold and it snowed all night. This morning it turned to rain. About noon it quit raining and commenced to get cold very fast. I commenced to write in the afternoon but it got so cold I was obliged to quit. Last night was quite cold and it did not thaw any in the shade today.

This morning we were busy cleaning our guns. This afternoon we have been carrying wood and fixing at our tent and tonight I am writing to you.

I saw John McElwain this morning. He arrived here night before last. He is as well as usual. Lieutenant Critchlow gave me some butter this morning. He said his wife sent it to me, and he said he supposed it was made at our house. It was very good.

Do you not think it was very kind of her to send it to me? I do. Critchlow is, or soon will be, captain of our company. [Lieutenant David Critchlow as promoted to Captain of Company C on March 4, 1863][2] Captain Cornelius will never be fit for duty again and it is reported he has been discharged. [Captain James E. Cornelius, wounded in action at Chantilly, resigned from the service March 4, 1863][3]

We are getting along finely here although it has been quite wet. They boys are all as well as usual. Nothing displeases us more than the conduct of our pretended friends at home rightly called copperheads. We would like to be there to talk to them and you may be sure that fellows who are not afraid to face shot, shell, and bullets will not be afraid to talk to them if they are 'copperheads'. They will need to keep very quiet when we get home for we will not have much patience with them.

I hope the war will soon be over that we may get home and save the government from passing into the hands of its enemies. We will doubtless give the enemy some hard knocks next summer.

Tattoo is beating and I must close.

Give my respects to all inquiring friends. We have not received our box yet but expect it soon as Cap. Cornelius started 3 boxes from Washington the 18th.

May our Heavenly Father protect you all.

> Yours affectionately,
> F. Pettit
> Co. C. 100th P.V.''

---

2 Samuel P. Bates, *History of Pennsylvania Volunteers*, Harrisburg, 1870, Volume 3, Page 572.

3 Ibid, Page 572.

Written to:
Miss M. A. Pettit

                              Newport News, Va., Feb. 28th 1863.

"Dear Sister:

I received your very kind letter of the 22nd inst. today. I was sorry to hear that you had been unwell but was glad to hear that you were better. You said it was very stormy the day you wrote. It was the same here. The wind blew a perfect gale, but most of the snow disappeared before noon. The week has been quite pleasant until this afternoon when it commenced raining and promises to rain all night.

Last Wednesday we had a grand review and inspection by our corps commander General Smith [General William F. Smith]. The troops made a good appearance generally though some regiments showed a lack of discipline. Since that time we have drilled 4 hours daily.

Today we were mustered for pay. According to the army regulations the troops must be mustered for pay at the end of every two months. An officer closely inspects the arms, accoutrements, knapsacks, and quarters, and every man must be accounted for in the muster rolls.

We now have excellent quarters as far as the rain and cold are concerned I am almost as comfortable as though I was at home tonight sitting by the grate.

We do not expect to stay here very long though for we have been ordered to be supplied with shelter tents immediately. This would indicate that we are soon to be on the march again but when or where we cannot tell. The probability is that we will go to either North or South Carolina. Wherever we go you need not fear but we will do our duty.

I am sorry to inform you that we have given up all hopes of receiving the box you sent us by express. This will no doubt be a great disappointment to you as to us, but it cannot be remedied. We know the risks we ran before we sent for it and agreed to bear the loss of it if it did not come. You need not therefore lose anything by the operation. A great many boxes are lost that are sent to the army, at least one third. Send an estimate of the cost of articles in it for me and I will send you the money as soon as we are paid again.

We do not need the boots near so much here as we did on the Rappahannock. Do not send anything more until we order it.

I shall not answer your question in relation to J. & R. as I do not like to reveal the secrets of my friends.

Erskine E. Allison formerly sent me a copy of the American Messenger and childs paper. He now sends me 20 copies of the Messenger monthly for distribution in the regiment. The March number was received today. The men are glad to get it. Erskine and I correspond occasionally.

I received two numbers of the Star yesterday. They were welcome visitors.

I find it as easy to serve God here as at home. Disappointment, danger, and temptation seem to drive me nearer the cross. God is indeed the only refuge of the soldier. I have no doubt but I shall be a better Christian if I get home for having served in the army. It is infusing me with more courage and perseverance. But it is growing late and I must close for tonight.

Your brother,
Fred Pettit
Co. C 100th Reg. P.V.

[letter continues]
March 1st, 1863 Sunday Afternoon.

This is quite a pleasant Sabbath day. The rain ceased this morning. We had regimental inspection this morning at 8 o'clock. Our regiment has improved very much in appearance since last Wednesday. The soldiers are in much better spirits now than they were months ago. They now feel confident of crushing the rebellion though it may take time to do it.

There is nothing I miss so much as the Sabbaths of home. I often think or try to imagine what you are doing at home on the Sabbath. I think I shall praise it more than I used to when I get home.

That is certainly a terrible misfortune which has befallen Miss Fisher. Her mother is having much trouble in her old age. I hope her trust is in God. I must close. Write soon again.

Who does Jordon Nye's feeding this winter? What is Alvah doing? I should like to be at home to go to school this summer.

Give my regards to all the friends.

Your brother,
Fred Pettit
Co. C. 100th Reg. P.V."

Written to:
Family
Newport News, Va., Thursday March 12, 1863.

"Dear parents, brothers, and sisters:

I generally wait until your letter comes before commencing to write, but forget a great many things I intended to write. This is the reason I commenced so early this week. The last time I wrote I said the weather was quite warm. That night it changed and the next morning was windy and cold with a heavy rain commencing about 9 o'clock and continuing until about the same time yesterday. The weather is now clear, cool, and windy.

About 3 o'clock yesterday we were called into line and as Col. Leasure was out with his staff officers we supposed that there would be a Brigade drill, but in a short time Gen. Wilcox [Willcox] came along and ordered the Colonel to march his brigade to another drill ground. We marched to the 1st Brigade and found it and the 2nd Brigade out in line. We formed in the rear and soon learned that a new flag was to be presented to the 8th Michigan regiment.[4] The flag was presented and speeches made by citizens of Michigan, but we could not hear them. After this we marched in review and then to our quarters, got our suppers and so ended the day.

By the time you get this I suppose your school will have closed and as it will now do no harm I will tell you what I know and think about your school and teacher. I will first tell you what I know. I know that your teacher was a very poor scholar when he commenced to teach. When I hear he kept so many long rods I knew he could not manage that school and keep good order. I know he is an old fashioned teacher. I know that some of the people said they wished the teacher they had last winter was back again. I know that he could not solve a very easy question in mental arithmetic about a man shooting pigeons and I know that someone sent it to a teacher in Rochester to solve and he solved it correctly and the answer was 28. And finally I know your teacher goes down to the mill with Miss Hannah sometimes.

Now I will tell you what I think about your school. I think Mr. Johnston at last found the kind of teacher he wanted last winter. I think Hazel Dell school has not improved any this winter. I think Mr. R. G. McGregor is getting up the exhibition and your teacher is only helping him. I think R. G. M. will write most of the pieces for the paper you intend to give. Do you not think these things are true?

The boys are all in good health. We are improving very fast in drill. The quarters of our regiment are said to be the best of any regiment in the 9th Corps.

Friday Evening March 13th. This has been quite a cold windy day and tonight it is freezing hard. We drilled as usual. Col. Leasure's wife arrived here today. Chaplain Browne's has been here but left for home yesterday. Soldiers can now get furloughs to go home on business

---

[4] The 8th Michigan Infantry served in the Ninth Army Corps with the 100th Pennsylvania throughout the war. It took part in Sherman's South Carolina expedition in 1861 and had an outstanding part in the assault on Battery Lamar at Secessionville in June of 1861. There was a close association between the 8th Michigan and the 100th Pennsylvania in all of the Ninth Corps operations of 1862-1865 and prior to the establishment of that Corps in South Carolina.

from 10 to 15 days. The soldier applying must state the business for which he wishes to go, and none need apply but those who have been good soldiers and keep their arms and accoutrements in good order. Several have applied from our company. Hazel Dell is getting a bad name here by Sergeant Robert's letter in the New Castle *Courant* stating that the democrats would not let him have the school house to lecture in. But the explanation of his conduct set it all right.

Monday March 16th. I did not receive a letter from you as usual last week. The weather since Friday evening has been quite cold and disagreeable. It does not freeze hard, but the wind blows very damp and cold from the ocean.

Last Saturday the regiment was called together to adopt resolutions expressing the sentiments of the regiment on the war, and the conduct of the people at home. The resolutions were unanimously adopted. They will appear shortly in the papers at home.

Are you taking any political paper now? I have heard some reports of Bob McGregor's speech at Hazel Dell. If they are correct he should be hung without further delay. When I came through Pittsburg I found he was a low debased scoundrel and I would advise you and all the girls in the neighborhood to have nothing to do with so vile a man. He is a hyocrite in more ways than one. I am willing he should read all that I have written about him. I hear that they threaten to hang him if he makes such a speech at Hope Dale as he did at Hazel Dell. I tell you the democrats of the north (copperheads) have gone as far as they can go without bloodshed at home. Before they rule us in the army we will carry the war to their own doors. The army must and shall govern the country.

You may think that I write things about men at home that I should not write. But I tell you it is nothing more than I and all the soldiers feel. We have endured untold sufferings and risked our lives for our homes and country's rights, while these copperheads have been enjoying all the peace and comforts of home. They have done nothing but find fault with us so far and now they wish to rule us after doing so much for our country. It is that so exasperates us. We will never submit to it. We will carry war and bloodshed over the entire north rather than submit to rule of these traitors. This is the opinion of nine tenths of the army. And it is the opinion they will never give up. They believe a Negro has rights as a dog had rights and they think his rights should be respected. They think the Negroes should be made to fight for their freedom.

Frederick Pettit
Co. C 100 P.V.

[letter continued]

Newport News, Va.   March 16th, 1863
Monday Afternoon.

Two days mail has arrived but it has brought no letter for me.
I will therefore detain this no longer. Perhaps yours was detained or
you had no time to write. When school is out you will have more time
to write. All of you write and tell me all about the exhibition. Mary,
tell me what you think of it. Will you have one? Tell me about Hets
[?] whether those big girls have improved any since last year. I see in
the late *Star* which you sent me that Gill was to preach at the late Q
meeting at Croton. Have you heard or seen any of them yet about
Centre? I think Gill acted rather traitorous to the people at Centre.

Today we see in the papers that Colonel Thomas Welsh[5] of the
45th Pa. Vol. of our brigade has been made Brigadier General. This
is rather cruel. Colonel Leasure has been in the service longer than he,
has been in harder service, and is a much smarter man. It is said that
he has been promoted for gallant conduct at South Mountain. We were
in his brigade at that time. His own regiment say that he lost them,
and that he hid behind a tree. This was certainly very brave and valiant.

Colonel Leasure says he will not serve under him nor will his
regiment.

I am well with the exception of a slight cold. The rest of the
boys are well. What is the general opinion concerning the war now?
I often think of the time when we shall come home. We are well contented to remain as long as it is necessary, but I long for the time when
I can engage in some pursuit that will better suit my inclinations.

Give my respects to all the friends especially the Grandfathers.

Your son and brother,
Frederick Pettit
Co. C., 100th P.V."

The five weeks spent in the Newport News encampment were one of the
most pleasant sojourns the 100th Pennsylvania regiment ever enjoyed. Communication from the north, usually by boat, was convenient and there were
many visitors. Many officers' wives took the opportunity to visit their husbands

---

[5] Thomas Welsh of Columbia, Pennsylvania, was born May 5, 1824. He was a Mexican War veteran. He served
as a company commander in the 11th Pennsylvania (90 day regiment) at the outbreak of the Civil War and later organized
the 45th Pennsylvania in October of 1861 and became Colonel of that regiment. He was brigade commander during
the battles of South Mountain and Antietam when the brigade included the 100th Pennsylvania and the 45th Pennsylvania.
He was promoted to Brigadier General in March 1863. He served as a division commander in the Ninth Corps during
the Vicksburg and Jackson campaigns but contracted some sort of malarial fever which caused his death in Cincinnati
on August 14, 1863.
    Judging from several contemporary accounts from the 100th Pennsylvania records, he was never popular with
the rank and file of the 100th Pennsylvania.
    Ezra J. Warner, *Generals In Blue,* Louisiana State University Press, 1964, Pages 550-551.
    William G. Gavin, *Campaigning With The Roundheads,* Morningside Press, Dayton, Ohio.

which gave the camp a very "home-like" appearance. The mail service was excellent and both parcels and letters were received in abundance. Food was good and plentiful as well.

There was constant speculation concerning the next move of the regiment, and all the men of the regiment knew they would not remain much longer at Newport News. With spring approaching, active campaigning was once again a certainty. Many of the men convinced themselves that they would return to South Carolina once again under General Burnside. The men were enthusiastic about the possibility of another extended stay in a pleasant place such as Beaufort.

However, on Thursday, March 18, orders were given to prepare to move on short notice. The drums beat reveille at 4 o'clock the next morning and the regiment was on the way to nearby Hampton to board steamers for a trip up the Chesapeake Bay. Shortly after embarking, the men learned that they were headed for Baltimore where they would entrain for the "west", probably either Kentucky or Tennessee.[6]

Pettit's company along with several other companies of the 100th Pennsylvania embarked on the steamer *John Brooks*. This gave Pettit a chance to write home once again.

Written to:
Family

On board steamer John Brooks, Chesapeake Bay,
March 22, 1863.

"Dear parents, brothers, and sisters:

By this time you will see we are on the move again. Last Tuesday [March 17] we had orders to cook rations and be ready to move at a moments notice. This was on account of the skirmish at Suffolk the day before. These orders were countermanded before morning.

Late Wednesday night orders came to cook 5 days rations and be ready to move at 6 the next morning. I knew nothing of it until awakened by the drums at 4 the next morning. At 6 we started for Hampton 6 miles distant where we arrived in due time accompanied by 2 batteries of artillery.

Ex-president Tyler's residence is here. It is a brick building and looks very neat. Hampton is 2 miles from Fort Monroe. It was once a place of some importance but it was burnt by the rebels at the commencement of the war. It now contains a few whites and a great many negroes.

---

6 William G. Gavin, *Campaigning With The Roundheads*, Morningside Press, Dayton, Ohio, 1989, Chapter Nine.

When we arrived here Thursday forenoon it commenced to snow. We were told we would remain here until we went aboard a boat. The most of us took lodging in a three story brick building that was being repaired. After considerable talk with the owner and Provost Marshall we obtained permission to remain in it. We remained here until last evening when we marched to Ft. Monroe and went aboard the bay steamer John Brooks.

But all this time you will be wondering where we are going. When we started we were going south, then again to Suffolk. But such is not the case. We are going to Baltimore as we are to take the cars [and] we expect to go west, perhaps to Kentucky or Tennessee, nothing would please us better.

We started from Ft. Monroe this morning. As we have 2 schooners in tow it will take 24 hours to make the trip.

I received 2 letters from home last week, one from Mag. and one from Mary and mother. If I had known that A. Metz was in the 134 Regiment I might have seen him as I visited that regiment in Virginia.

I should be very glad to go to work with Gottlieb Grieb this spring. Tell him I would be very glad if he could keep the place for me until the war is over.

We will probably arrive in Baltimore tomorrow when I will mail this. If we go west we will pass through Pittsburgh, Wheeling, or both.

F. Pettit
Co. C 100th P.V.

[P.S.] Baltimore, Mar. 23. We arrived here at daylight. We are well as usual. We have not landed yet but will in a few minutes. Direct your letters as usual. Goodbye for the present.

F. Pettit"

Pettit's next letter details the journey from Baltimore to Cincinnati. Since General Ambrose Burnside had been appointed the commander of the Department of the Ohio, the Ninth Corps had been ordered to join this Department at his request. Thus began a new phase in the varied and interesting history of the 100th Pennsylvania Regiment.

Written to:
Family

On board Boat Jennie Rogers--Ohio River,
March 27th, 1863.

"Dear parents, brothers, and sisters:

The last letter I wrote you informed you of my safe arrival in Baltimore. Since that I have ridden 400 miles by railroad from Baltimore to Parkersburgh. On landing in Baltimore we marched to the common and stacked arms to await further orders. In the evening we get in the cars to sleep. The next day we remained until about noon when we started on our journey. We had not passenger cars to ride in. They were only freight cars with rough board seats. There were 33 men in each car. It was hard sleeping at night.

The first day and night we ran to Harpers Ferry. The next morning Wednesday 25th we got hot coffee and a loaf of bread at Harpers Ferry and went on our way rejoicing. In the forenoon we passed through Martinsburgh, Va. At noon we arrived at Cumberland, Md. Here we got hot coffee and some boiled meat. At dark we arrived at Piedmont a small mountain town. As it was dark and I was asleep I saw no more of the country until we came to Grafton in Western Virginia.

Awaking at daylight and looking out of the car I found we were still amongst the mountains and that it was snowing. Here we got some more coffee, bread, and meat. At this place (Grafton) the railroad branches, one branch going to Wheeling and the other to Parkersburgh. The distant to Parkersburg is 102 miles. The country from here is the hilliest I ever saw. Still the soil must be fertile, for the farmers have good houses, and good schoolhouses. On the 102 miles of road from Grafton to Parkersburgh there are 23 tunnels varying in length from 40 rds to 1½ miles.

We arrived at the Ohio about sundown. There were quite a number of gentlemen from Lawrence Co. waiting to see us at Parkersburgh. I saw none that I knew. They did not have much time to talk for we immediately went aboard the boats and by 8 o'clock we were on our way down the Ohio. We stopped at Pomeroy to coal but started again at daylight. The Ohio is in very good running order. We passed Portsmouth a few minutes ago or about 2 o'clock P.M. We expect to be in Cincinnati early in the morning.

Now if you want to trace my track in this move get the largest map of the United States you can find. Now on your map find the Chesapeake Bay. Look near the lower end of the bay and you will find Ft. Monroe. Here I first started on a boat and went up the bay, passed the mouth of the Potomac River, and stopped at Baltimore near the upper end of the Bay. Here I got on the cars. Now find Harpers Ferry in the edge of Virginia on the Potomac river. Here we got coffee Wednesday morning Mar. 25th. Next find Cumberland on the same river in the edge of Md. Here we ate dinner. Next find Grafton in Western Virginia. At this place we got coffee Thursday morning. We here took the railroad to Parkersburgh. Here we got on the steamboat and are now sailing down the Ohio for Cincinnati. The whole distance is between 900 and 1000 miles.

Sunday March 28th.

We are now in or at Cincinnati. We arrived at 2 o'clock last evening. We ran 350 miles in 24 hours. We are still on the boat. We expect to go to some town in Kentucky. The weather this morning is warm but it is raining. I write this letter in the hold of the boat by candle light. After this direct your letters as before except for Washington, D.C. write Cincinnati, Ohio.

F. Pettit
Co. C 100th P.V.

[P.S.]We are just leaving for Kentucky."

The Ninth Army Corps had been ordered to join General Ambrose E. Burnside who now commanded the Department of the Ohio in Cincinnati. Reinforcements were required to bolster his Department and to insure peace and tranquility in Kentucky. There were projected plans to advance into east Tennessee and drive the Confederates from this territory. After several months of delay, these plans were eventually carried out in late 1863.

The 100th Regiment spent the next two months in Kentucky. In general, it was a very relaxing tour of duty, with performance limited to short and occasional marches. Pettit had considerable free time on his hands and he wrote several letters while on duty. These are included in the next chapter.

CHAPTER FIVE

CAMPAIGNING IN KENTUCKY
APRIL — MAY 1863

"The citizens are about two thirds Union and the friendliest people I ever saw." Kentucky, April 1863.

During the early afternoon of March 28, the regiment entrained at Covington, Kentucky, for the trip to Lexington, Kentucky, their next destination and camping site.

Shortly after arrival in Lexington the next day, Sunday March 29, the troops were occupied with provost duty in the town and in the construction of a fortified position. Colonel Daniel Leasure, commander of the brigade which consisted of the 45th Pennsylvania and the 36th Massachusetts, was designated as Post Commander at Lexington. The encampment, although in a scenic setting in a beautiful grove of black walnut trees, was an unhealthy one because of the dampness of the spring weather. Cold, chills and intermittent fevers were rampant according to the historians of the 36th Massachusetts Infantry.[1] Much of this illness was precipitated during the cold and windy two day rail trip from Baltimore to Parkersburgh.

After being in camp at Lexington for nearly one week, Pettit found time to write the first of his Kentucky letters on Friday, April 3.

---

[1] Committee of the Regiment, *History of the Thirty-Sixth Regiment, Massachusetts Volunteers, 1862-1865.* Boston, 1884, Pages 39 and 40.

Written to:
Parents

Lexington, Kentucky April 1st 1863.

"Dear parents,

We arrived at this place last Sunday morning. We left Covington, opposite Cincinnati, on Saturday about 2 P. M. The railroad as far as we ran by daylight was along the Licking River. This is the richest farming country I ever saw. Lexington is a place of considerable size. I have not been in the city yet. The railroad runs by one side only. I must continue my account of our journey.

We found ourselves in the cars at this place last Sunday morning at daylight. After remaining in and about the cars for some time we were ordered to get out, and about noon were marched about ¼ of a mile from the station and encamped in the most beautiful walnut grove you ever saw. The grain and grass looks quite green here. This is certainly the finest country I ever saw.

Close by our camp is the cemetery where Henry Clay is buried. There is a beautiful monument in it erected to his memory. He lived about 2 miles from here.

Colonel Leasure now commands this post. The citizens are about ⅔ Union and the most friendly people I ever saw. But I will write particulars soon. We are about 100 miles from Cincinnati by railroad. We traveled just 1000 miles. [Since leaving Newport News.]

We have just been paid off. I will send some money home soon. Direct your letters:

> Fred Pettit
> Co. C 100th P.V.
> 9th Army Corps
> Cincinnati, Ohio."

Written to:
Family

Lexington, Kentucky   April 3rd, 1863

"Dear parents, brothers, and sisters:

We have been here almost a week and it is true I was writing you some more detailed account of our whereabouts. But we have received no mail for 2 weeks. The last we received was at Hampton, Va. The last letter I received from you was dated March 15th. In my last letter I informed you of our safe arrival at this place.

I will now try to give you some account of Lexington and its surroundings. Lexington is about 100 miles southwest of Cincinnati by railroad. The surface of the surrounding country is rolling and un-dulating but there are no high hills. It is situated in one of the richest farming districts of Kentucky. The farmers and farms are the richest I ever saw. The famous Kentucky horses and cattle are here fully developed. The horses are the most beautiful I ever saw, the cattle are equal to any I have seen. The citizens are very friendly and courteous. They have a warm side for Pennsylvania but do not like the Michiganders, New Yorkers, and Yankees.

Our camp is situated north west of the town. It is in a beautiful black walnut grove. The cemetery is a few rods west of our camp. It is indeed a beautiful place. Henry Clay's monument stands near the centre. It is built of Kentucky marble. It is 132 ft. in height. A statue of Clay stands on the top of it.

General Morgan [Confederate General John H. Morgan] is a native of this town.

There is but little of interest transpiring. The weather is not cold here as it is at home, but the citizens say it is uncommonly cold for the season. The days are cold and windy with some snow flying. The nights are frosty.

The 45th P.V. of our brigade are about 12 miles from here guarding the railroad. The other night 25 rebels rode up to a railroad bridge where 12 of the 45th men were on guard. They remained quiet until the rebels rode up to the bridge when they fired a volley and then charged upon them. They captured 7 of the rebels and put the rest to flight.

We are better pleased with our present position than any other we have had. We all caught bad colds on our journey but are getting better. We were paid last Monday for 4 months to the first of March last.

Eatables are very plenty and the boys are spending money very fast.

Give my respects to all inquiring friends. Write soon again and tell me all the news. Direct your letters:

> Fred Pettit
> Co. C., 100th Reg. P.V.
> 9th Army Corps
> Cincinnati, Ohio

[letter continues]

April 4th, 1863. Dear Father: Enclosed you will find ten dollars ($10.00) a part of my pay. I will send you rest in small amounts by letter. Most of the boys are sending by mail.

> Your son
> Fred Pettit"

The 100th travelled about the state of Kentucky extensively over the next several weeks and camped in several different locations. MAP #4 illustrates the moves of the Roundheads during this period. Pettit's next letter is written from Camp Dick Robinson, a short distance south of Lexington.

Written to:
Family

Camp Dick Robinson, Ky., April 10th, 1863

"Dear parents, brothers, and sisters,

Our pleasant stay in Lexington was of short duration. We had a very pleasant time while we were there and had a good rest after our long journey.

Last Tuesday the 7th we worked on the fort being built at Lexington. That night we received orders to be ready to march the next morning. We started about 10 o'clock the next day and marched to Nicholasville 14 miles arriving before dark. The day was quite warm though the night was frosty. The road was good but very dusty. As we had marched but little since last November it made us feel very weary and sore.

The next day Thursday we started about 8 o'clock for Camp Dick Robinson 14 miles further. Traveling was much the same as yesterday but fortunately for us we succeeded in getting our knapsacks hauled. This relieved us greatly. About noon we crossed the Kentucky River 8 miles from Nicholasville. We arrived marching at this place before sundown. Considering our condition for marching this is the hardest marching we ever did. There are but few of us this morning but have blistered feet and sore limbs. But I think we will not march today, at least there are no orders to march yet and if we get to rest a few days we will be all right again.

I do not know where we are going but think it is to Cumberland Gap, Tennessee or wherever the rebels make a stand.

The country over which we have traveled is the richest farming country I ever saw. There is a great quantity of stock raised here. Cattle, hogs, mules, and horses are abundant. I also noticed considerable hemp standing in shock in the fields.

Camp Dick Robinson is a large wood pasture used as a camp ground. I have [not] seen nor heard of any fortifications around it.

We are all in usual health. We have received no mail yet from Washington. A few letters have come that were sent to Cincinnati but none for me. Direct your letters to:

F. Pettit
Co. C., 100th P.V.
9th Army Corps
Cincinnati, Ohio.

[P.S.] I will send no money until I hear whether my letters arrive safely. Give my respects to all inquiring friends.

> Yours truly,
> Frederick Pettit
> Co. C 100th P.V."

Written to:
Sister, Miss M. A. Pettit

Camp Dick Robinson, Ky.   April 12th 1863

"Dear Sister:

Our long detained mail reached us yesterday. It brought me two letters from you, one from Evan, and one from S. Hofius Mercer Co., and one from Miss H. J. Pettit, Ohio. These letters were all very welcome but especially those from home.

Mr. Hofius taught 3 months in Erie Co., was at home when he wrote, and had engaged to drive team 3 months from April 1st. He seemed a little suspicious of the coming draft.

Miss Hannah said the folks were all well. Her letter was very evasive on the war question. I fear she is slightly tainted with copperheadism. She says none of the Pettits of our relations have joined the army from the west. I am glad to hear that you beat the copperheads at home in the Hazel Dell affair. I did not think there was so much firmness in the loyal men at home. Hurrah for the pluck of your teacher and the Johnstons. Who would have thought of it? I am glad your teacher was of the right stripe. He is a man after my own mind. I am sorry I was misinformed concerning him. I tell you the spirit and firmness of the loyal Hazel Dellians will be an everlasting honor to them.

I heard of the scheme of the copperheads to have it all their own way and supposed everything would be submitted to them. But I am glad to hear it was not so. I tell you these enemies at home are an ignorant, cowardly set, led by a set of unprincipled villains. Let them resist the draft if they dare.

If the 100th ever returns to Western Pennsylvania they will have something else to resist.

I think the title of the paper read at Hazel Dell very appropriate and the motto still better but will not send for it until we are sure of remaining at one place long enough to get it.

We are still in camp but expect to move soon. I suppose by the time you receive this you will have left for school or have determined on some other employment for the summer. You can best judge what is best.

The weather since we came here has been quite warm and pleasant. We expect to do much marching this summer. General Burnside now commands this department and we will be occupied in keeping the rebels out of Kentucky.

The people in this part of the state are mostly loyal and have suffered very much on account of their loyalty. They hail us with delight as the defenders of their homes. Still there are some who are inveterate enemies and will do all in their power to injure us. On the other hand there are a few men in every regiment who disregard all law and plunder the property of friend and foe alike. These are a great nuisance in the army.

We are all well. Remember me in your prayers. Give my respects to all inquiring friends.

> Your brother,
> F. Pettit
> Co. C 100th P.V."

Written to:
Brother, Evan.

Camp Dick Robinson, Kentucky, April 12, 1863

"Dear brother Evan,

I received your letter of March 26th yesterday. I was glad to hear that your exhibition succeeded so well, and that I was wrong in my statements about your school and teacher. I heard these things and wished to know whether they were true. I am glad they are not.

I suppose by this time you are busy getting the oats sowed, the manure hauled out, the early potatoes planted, and the corn ground ready.

As we were marching the other day saw some farmers planting potatoes. They will soon plant corn here. I suppose the Sunday Schools will soon commence at home. Tell me all about them when they commence. I was sorry to hear the grandmothers was so unwell. I hope she will get better as the weather gets warm.

Where are you planting corn this year? How far did you get in Arithmetic last winter? How far did Cyrus get?

Write soon.

> Your brother,
> Fred Pettit
> Co. C. 100th P.V."

Written to:
Father, Nathaniel Pettit

Camp Dick Robinson, Kentucky, April 18th 1863

"Dear father:

It is a long time since I wrote you a letter and perhaps a short one from here will be interesting to you. First I must tell you where we are. Our camp is called Dick Robinson. It is about one hundred and twenty-six miles almost south of Cincinnati. There is a railroad as far as Nicholasville 14 miles from here. One branch runs to Louisville and the other to Covington opposite Cincinnati. We are six miles south of the Kentucky river and about 50 north of the Cumberland.

There has been a camp here almost ever since the war commenced. It has been occupied sometimes by our forces and sometimes by the rebels. There is a great quantity of cannon balls of different sizes scattered over the ground. These were left by Bragg [Confederate General Braxton Bragg] last fall when he retreated. The rebels left here two weeks before we came. That was the last raid into the state.

They took many good horses with them out of the state. It appears there were about 5000 troops [Federal] at Danville 7 miles beyond this place, but their commanding officer became frightened not knowing the force of the enemy and retired across the Kentucky river pursued by 1200 of the enemy. The citizens think this was very cowardly. The only reply we can make is that it was not Burnside's men who did it.

We get great praise here for cleanliness and good behavior. The western troops are generally very careless in their habits.

This is the finest country I ever saw. It is moderately hilly, the soil is very fertile and the climate is mild and healthful. The farmers are now engaged in planting their corn. It is the principal crop. Most of the labor is done by slaves.

A short time since I sent you ten dollars in a letter. This I suppose you have received before this time. In this letter I will send you 20 dollars more which is all I will send at this time. Try by all means to have the money ready to pay that land debt as soon as it becomes due. I will send you all I can to help pay it. Do not delay a single month after it is due. After the war closes money matters will be in the worst condition they ever were in this country. It will be well then to have debts all square.

We are in good health.

Your affectionate son,
Frederick Pettit
Co. C 100th P.V.
9th Army Corps
Camp Dick Robinson, Ky."

Written to:
Sister, Miss Mary A. Pettit

Camp Dick Robinson, Ky.   April 20th, 1863

"Dear Sister,

I received your welcome letter of the 8th inst. last week but as I wrote to father I did not answer it then. The weather still continues quite warm and pleasant. Yesterday was Sunday but as it rained most of the day we did not have any religious services until sundown when it having cleared off Chaplain Browne addressed us a short time. He is an earnest live preacher. Our evening exercises still continue.

Last week one day Andrew Lary [Leary] and I got a pass and started out to see the country and get our dinners. We went about three miles east of camp and found ourselves at a farmhouse on a hill. The occupants were a man and wife aged about 80 yrs. We found them quite sociable. The man's name was Stone. He had resided in the state from infancy. His father came from Virginia at an early day. Although owning 10 or 12 slaves he is a strong Union man. His motto was "United we stand — divided we fall". He hoped we would kill the rebel leaders. He was very confident the slaves could not support themselves if free. He with all the rest of the citizens thought it very strange we should look so neat and clean. He said they never saw soldiers walking about with blacked boots and clean clothes. They were surprised to learn we had ever seen rough service. It would do you good to see our regiment.

Thursday, April 23rd. I went on picket Tuesday and did not get back until yesterday and therefore did not write any. My picket post was in Bryantsville a small village about 1 mile from camp.

Time passes very pleasantly. We are stationed here to prevent the rebels from invading the state. The 36th Mass. started yesterday after a body of about 400 rebels. They have not returned yet.

Last Monday evening all the troops of this post were reviewed by Brigadier [General Thomas Welsh] commander of the post. Our regiment is said to be improving in appearance very rapidly.

By the papers which we get daily from Cincinnati, I see the butternuts [rebels] are causing some trouble in Indiana. I hope they do not become so bold in Pennsylvania. If they do you must arm yourselves and resist them. If necessary you cannot put my money to a better use than to buy fire arms with it. If the copperheads commence to arm themselves I will make you a present of 15 dollars to buy one of Colt's army revolvers and father may use the remainder of my money to get a couple of good rifles. Don't be afraid to use them if necessary. These men who resist the government at home but who are too cowardly to join the rebels and fight against it do not deserve any respect at all. Death should be their doom.

We are not all disheartened. The present prospect is encouraging yet the war may last 2 or 3 years yet and I believe it will. [Extremely prophetic.] I should not be surprised if there was fighting over the entire north this summer. Everything at present indicates it.

We are all well. We expect to be engaged in chasing guerrillas this summer. We may have a skirmish any day.

I have received no letter from home this week yet but may. As I expect to go on guard again tomorrow I thought I would finish my letter today.

If you have gone to school at Edinboro tell me all about its present condition. Give my respects to all inquiring friends.

Your brother,
Fred Pettit
Co. C., 100th P.V.

P.S. [This P.S. is directed to Pettit's parents] If Mary has gone to school you can do as you see fit about sending this to her. Don't neglect to write. Evan's letters are very welcome. I wish the others would write too. I won't criticize them much.

Fred Pettit''

Written to:
Sister, Miss Mary A. Pettit

Camp Dick Robinson, Ky., April 26th 1863

"Dear Sister:

I received your letter of the 16th and 18th inst. last Friday, and was very glad to hear from home once more.

We are still in our first camp and shall probably remain here during the summer, and then again we may move at any time. There are scouting parties out almost every day after spies from the rebel army.

Our Brigade is praised highly here for its fine appearance, and our regiment is considered the best in the brigade. Some of the most distinguished men of this state have visited our camp and they pronounce our regiment the best they ever saw. Burnside's troops have gained him a high reputation in this state.

Nothing of importance has transpired since my last [letter]. I was sorry to hear that Grandmother has become so feeble. I did not expect to hear that she was failing so rapidly. I think you have acted nobly in volunteering to take care of her in her declining years. It may appear a great sacrifice to stop in your studies and no doubt it is; but duty's path will never lead us astray.

I was surprised to hear that Uncle Josiah was in our neighborhood. We have prayer meeting almost every evening when the weather will permit, which I generally attend. Our chaplain always leads and none take part in the exercises except those with whom he is acquainted. The meetings are not what could be desired but still they are much better than none and I supposed the best in the army.

Tuesday, April 28th. All is quiet but we have orders to be ready to move at a moment's notice. This is on account of rebel raids. Last Sunday we had orders to fill our canteens and be in readiness to move but we did not move. That night an order from General Burnside was read ordering us to keep 15 days rations on hand and for each man to be supplied with an extra pair of shoes. This looks like a march. It may not be for several weeks yet. I think it will be to Cumberland Gap, Tenn. The troops that were there last summer almost starved, became almost naked and entirely shoeless before they obtained supplies. Burnside is providing for these things.

Furloughs are now being granted again and perhaps you will see some of our boys at home shortly. For my part I do not want one until the war is over.

We hear some fearful tales of starvation in the south both from the citizens who have friends there and from the papers.

Write as usual. If we moved the letters may not go regularly but there will be more when they come. Give my respects to all inquiring friends.

Your brother,
Fred Pettit
Co. C 100th P.V."

Written to:
Brother, Evan

Stanford, Ky., May 1st 1863

"Dear brother, Evan,

I received your letter written April 22nd and 23rd last night after dark. We left Camp Dick Robinson yesterday and marched to this place. Stanford is 16 miles from Camp Dick Robinson. We have now fairly commenced soldiering for this summer. Day before yesterday we packed our overcoats to send them to Cincinnati, Ohio, but just before we started yesterday they said they could not be hauled back and we were obliged to take them again. Half of them were not carried from camp. Many tore theirs to rags, and for 2 or 3 miles the road was lined with overcoats. I carried mine a mile or two and tossed it away. My knapsack felt much lighter after it was out and I had no difficulty keeping up. Overcoats are of no use here now. The weather is quite warm.

This is the first of May and as beautiful a day as I ever saw. We expected to march again today but we have received orders to lay over today. We are cooking rations and I expect we will move again tomorrow. I do not know where we will go, but I suppose it will be toward the enemy. There is not much news that I can write.

We passed through two small towns yesterday Lancaster and Stanford. They are almost one size. Stanford is perhaps the largest. Lancaster is the county seat of Garrard County.

We are camped about 1 mile from Stanford. The country is a little more hilly here than about Camp Dick [Robinson]. The farming is done mostly by slaves and is very poorly done. The soil is very rich and grain will grow without much cultivation. I suppose you will be planting corn by the time you get this. I sent father $20.00 in a letter some time ago. I suppose you have it by this time.

Write soon again and tell me what you are doing and where you are going to Sunday School this summer.

Your brother,
Fred Pettit
Co. C 100 P.V."

Written to:

There is no salutation to the following letter and presumably it was sent to parents, brothers, and sisters. The content of the letter indicates it may have been taken from a daily diary which we have indicated that Pettit was keeping.

"May 1st 1863. I commenced writing this at Hughstonville [Hustonville]. I had mailed Evan's letter [above letter] but a short time when orders came to pack up and report to Gen. Welsh for provost guard duty. This was about 12 o'clock and the regiment was ordered to march at one. Upon reporting to the General we were ordered to go to town and drive out all soldiers and officers belonging to our division. We started out about 50 men and officers arrested several rowdies and sent them to jail, reported to the General again and were ordered to march in the rear and drive up stragglers. You must understand this was only our company.

Shortly after we started we chartered an ox wagon to haul our knapsacks 5 miles at 5 cts each. In this way we got along finely until our able driver said he must leave the road. Then came the tug with our knapsacks for about a mile when we succeeded in getting another wagon to haul our knapsacks the remainder of the journey. About sundown we arrived at Hughstonville 10 miles from Stanford where we [had] started. We camped close by the village. Hughstonville is a small village of 200 or 300 inhabitants.

May 2nd. A beautiful day but very warm. We remained in camp until 1 o'clock and rested ourselves. At one we started in a southerly direction. Yesterday we traveled almost west. The officers hired citizens to haul our knapsacks this afternoon for which we paid 10 cts. each.

After ascending a high hill south of the village we traveled several miles on the top of a high ridge and had a fine view of the surrounding country with its fine farms and pleasant looking farm houses. This is indeed a beautiful country. The soil is very fertile. The farms look beautiful. The climate is all that could be desired, but alas! There is something pervading the very air, it seems, that kills energy, enterprise, sociability, and all that makes a people enlightened and happy. That poison is slavery.

But to return to our journey. After leaving the ridge we descended into a narrow deep valley, the hills rising high and abrupt on each side. We continued our way some distance through this valley and arrived at a small cluster of houses called Middleburgh [Middleburg]. It is about one fourth the size of Wurtemberg. We camped close by. The pike ends here and we are now on the head waters of the Green River. We marched 10 miles today.

Sunday, May 3rd. This being Sabbath we did not march but have spent the day in peace and quiet. Our new General certainly deserves respect for observing the Sabbath, a thing so uncommon in the army. Oh that we could once more spend our Sabbaths as we used to only better. Chaplain Browne preached us a short sermon this afternoon. How refreshing and how much like the happy days of yore to listen to the precious words of divine truth as they fall from the lips of the faithful servant of Jesus. And how it reminds us of the many pleasant Sabbaths we have spent in other society, to spend one here in peace after a week of toilsome marching. Ah those home influences. They will save many of our brave soldiers from a fate worse than death on the battlefield.

But I must close for this evening. The weather is quite warm and pleasant. We have had several showers of rain today and a heavy thunder-shower is just coming on. Our tent shields us nicely from the wet.

> Fred Pettit
> Co. C 100 P.V."

Written to:

No salutation again on this letter. Presumably sent to Pettit's family.

> Camp near Middleburgh, Ky.   May 6th, 1863.

"My last was mailed on the 5th and gave account of us up to that date. I was on picket today. There are pickets on all the roads leading from camp to prevent stragglers without passes from leaving camp. I was on reserve and was quartered in a church ½ mile from camp. Nothing of interest occurred. The day was damp and cloudy.

May 7th. When I came off picket this morning I received a letter from Mary. I was very glad to hear that you were all well. There has been great excitement in camp all week concerning Hooker's movements. [This was the celebrated Chancellorsville Campaign which resulted in Hooker's defeat and the withdrawal of the Army of the Potomac to the north of the Rappahannock River.] Our reports are up to Sunday. If he continues successful it will go far towards putting down the rebellion. Further results are anxiously looked for.

May 8th. Nothing of importance transpired in camp. This evening report reached us that Hooker has been driven across the Rappahannock. Great discouragement and indignation. The troops are very indignant against the Germans of the 11th Corps for running.

May 9th. Nothing of interest transpired in our brigade except the arrival of the furloughs. There were three granted in our company. G.W. Fisher and Oliver Tebay of Portersville and S. A. White of Perry Twp. Lawrence Co. Pa. But few papers were received today. Hooker's retreat confirmed.

Sunday May 10th. A beautiful Sabbath day and one of the few Sabbaths which we have the privilege of spending in peace and quiet. How many congregations are this day engaged in worshiping Him who created heavens and the earth? But how few of those who are battling for our country enjoy those privileges! War is indeed a great calamity. It not only destroys life and property but it also destroys the morals of those engaged. How remarkable are the providences of God.

Our leaving the Army of the Potomac, short stay at Newport News, and eventual transfer to Kentucky appeared but a move occasioned by the chances of war. But who that reflects can fail to see the hand of the Almighty in all this.

During the past week what fierce strife and slaughter has swept that army. But we have been kept safe. Far away amongst hills and wildernesses of Kentucky we are shielded safe from the storm of war which is howling all around.

In the afternoon Chaplain Browne preached us a sermon from Hosea 6:1. 'Come and let us return unto the Lord; for he hath torn and he will heal us; he hath smitten and he will bind us up'. He [Browne] made no reference to the army or politics in his sermon. Afterward he was requested to make some remarks to show its application to our present condition as an army and nation. He promised to do so in the evening.

About 5 o'clock in the evening a dispatch was received stating that Hooker recrossed the Rappahannock and Stoneman and Dix had captured Richmond. The other regiments of our brigade received it with loud demonstrations of joy. Our regiment was silent. They assembled at the tap of the drum for the usual evening service. And while the other regiments were noisily proclaiming their joy for the victory, our regiment was quietly returning thanksgiving and praise to Him whom they believe has granted victory. After service the colonel ordered three cheers. Most of the crowd cheered. I could not. Such news has proved false too often to be credited by me without better confirmation, yet I hope it is true.

After this the regiments were formed, each man having a candle in the end of his gun. The night was quite dark. The regiments went through a number of maneuvers presenting a grand and imposing sight. After this Colonel Leasure made a short speech and we quietly dispersed to our quarters.

May 11th. A beautiful day. 9 A.M. No news. Nothing going on. All quiet.

F. Pettit
Co. C. 100th P.V."

Written to:
Brother, Evan.

Middleburg, Ky. May 17th 1863.

"Dear brother Evan:

I received your very welcome letter of the 7th last Thursday. You said you had received a letter from me dated March 20th. That was a mistake. I wrote no letter at that time. It should have been April 20th.

The first of last week the 45th P.V. left here with General Welsh. Col. Leasure then took command of the post and we moved our camp to Middleburg where we now are.

Last Wednesday I was on picket. Thursday afternoon a story was circulated that Morgan's pickets were within 3 miles of camp and that he was about to make a dash and gobble us up. The Colonel said he would give him a warm mouthful if he came. About 100 men including our company were sent out the Summerset [Somerset] Road with orders to hold it against any force. We remained there very quietly until the next evening when we were relieved. In the meantime we learned that neither Morgan nor any of his men were on this side of the river. I think Morgan will have to fight a little harder to drive the 9th Corps than he did to drive some other troops through Kentucky.

Yesterday I was on guard and came off about 2 hours ago. Tonight I expect to go on picket again.

You think the copperheads are too cowardly to fight, I do not. I used to hear that the rebels were cowards but they have never shown it yet at least not when I saw them fight. The copperheads in Indiana have killed several soldiers already and I expect to hear that some dark night they will kill some crippled soldier about Hazel Dell and scare the Union folks almost to death. Then you will have to get a gun and fight or turn traitor. I hope such times may never come but I fear they will and that soon.

The weather is quite warm. I saw the other day the farmers were plowing their corn. I am well as usual. Write soon.

Your brother,
Fred Pettit
Co. C. 100 P.V."

Written to:
Pettit's Mother

Middleburg, Ky.,   May 17th 1863

"Dear Mother,

I received your letter with Evan's and was glad to hear from both of you. I have but little to write more than I have already written.

We are kept pretty busy on guard now. All our hopes of the war ending soon have died away. The spring campaign has not resulted in our favor. Think the summer will wear away without gaining anything but hard fighting. Two things I consider certain. We will some day be victorious and the slaves will be free. The war may end within a year or two, but I expect it to last 5 or 6 years yet. Let it last 1 year or 10 *I intend to be a soldier as long as I am able.* [Emphasis added]

I was sorry to hear that grandmother was so low. The true way to live is to be ready for life or death. Then whether we die in youth or after living to a ripe old age, all will be well.

Your affectionate son,
Fred Pettit
Co. C. 100th P.V."

Written to:
Sister, Miss M. A. Pettit

Middleburg, Ky.   May 20th 1863

"Dear Sister:

Having no military duty to perform this morning I have retired to a pleasant shade in order to reply to your welcome letter of the 7th and 8th inst. which was received last night. I received a letter of the same date from home last Thursday. Yours had been delayed.

I was sorry to hear that you are afflicted with a toothache. About the only prescription the doctors give them [the troops] is a dose of salts or quinine. These are given for almost everything.

You think my fears concerning the copperheads are groundless. I hope they are. But rest assured they will fight. I used to hear the rebels were cowards. But they have never proved such when we have met them. Suppose a copperhead shot some union soldiers home on furlough. Do you think enough home guards could be found to arrest him? I think not. It is time to quit reasoning with the home traitors. Let them either support the government or swing! The poem you sent me suggests the best plan.

I see J. C. Stevenson [James C. Stevenson, Company E, who later became one of the historians of the regiment and who was the Secretary of the Society of the Roundheads, the regimental veterans' association

after the war][2] almost every day. He belongs to Co. E. of our regiment.
I did receive two New Castle papers early in the spring but thought I
had acknowledged them. Mr. Boot's story is quite applicable, only in
this case I think Lucy will hit John a lick to keep him quiet before she
kills the bear. Last night I received a *Star* from home and this morning
a letter from Maggy [sister Margaret] dated the 15th.

We have had numerous reports of the rebels raiding to within
a few miles of our camp but we have seen none of the long haired gen-
try yet. This part of Kentucky is very hilly, almost mountainous. There
is but little of the land cleared. The people are on a par with the country-
rough and uncultured. The most licentious crimes are customs here. The
society is the most heathenish and debased I ever wish to see. Its effect
upon the soldiers is anything but good.

But I must close. Give my respects to grandfathers.

> Your brother,
> Fred Pettit
> Co. C. 100th P.V.

P.S. As our Division is now much scattered it will be necessary for you
to add a little more to the directions of your letters. I will write it in full.

> Fred Pettit
> Co. C. 100th P.V.
> 3rd Brigade, 1st Division
> 9th Army Corps
> Cincinnati, Ohio.''

Written to:
Sister, Miss M. A. Pettit

> Middleburg, Ky.,   May 22nd 1863

"Dear Sister:

Day before yesterday I received your letter written up to the 15th.
It was very welcome as it brought one week's later news from home
and it has been several weeks since I received a letter from you. From
your letter you has as much work as you could wish in the bonnet line.
Now is the time for you by diligence and attention to establish yourself
in business.

There is yet no movements going on in this part of the army.
We came to this place May 2nd and here we are yet. The weather is
quite warm and we are getting so lazy we can scarcely lie in the shade.
It is hard for us to live and eat with nothing to do. But I think our

---

[2] William G. Gavin, *Campaigning With The Roundheads*, Morningside Press, Dayton, Ohio, 1989. There are several references to Stevenson in the regimental history of the 100th Pennsylvania. He continued extremely active in veterans' affairs after the war. Stevenson survived four years of service and was a Sergeant at the end of the war.

rest will not last much longer. I should not wonder if within the next two months we should do some of the hardest marching and severest fighting since the war commenced.

The copperheads of the north are going to cause much trouble and bloodshed. I have received letters stating they are too cowardly to fight. Union men will believe this until they do fight and then be unprepared to meet them. The copperheads are already arming themselves in some sections. The union men at home must prepare to meet these men. The army cannot assist them. They have a foe in front to fight and can-not turn and fight in the rear. If the union men of the north wake up, arm themselves, and put down the rebels at home all will be well. But if they do not they may expect to lose their property and be driven as wanderers from their homes. They must not wait for the copperheads to commence. They must commence themselves and keep the traitors down.

There is nothing going on here worthy of notice. We are all well. You can inform those interested that J. C. Stevenson has so far distinguished himself as to be appointed eighth corporal. Write again at your leisure.

> Your brother,
> Fred Pettit
> Co. C. 100th P.V.

P.S. Our Division is now somewhat scattered and it will be necessary for you to add a little to the directions on the letters. Direct in this way:

> Fred Pettit
> Co. C. 100th P.V.
> 3rd Brigade, 1st Division
> 9th Army Corps
> Cincinnati, Ohio.''

There are no salutations on the next four entries, and they were extracted from Pettit's diary and included in his letter of May 27th directed to his parents, brothers, and sisters.

After three weeks in the quiet but pleasant and comfortable Green River encampment at Middleburg, Casey County, Kentucky, the 100th Pennsylvania was ordered to Columbia, Kentucky, where portions of the Ninth Army Corps were concentrating to prevent any Confederate incursions into Kentucky from the Cumberland River valley. Details of the march to Columbia follow:

Written to:
Family

> Camp near Liberty, Ky.,   May 24th, 1863.

"At last the tedium of camp life has been broken. Yesterday (Saturday) we were ordered to pack up and be ready to move. We started at 2 o'clock and marched 2½ miles below Liberty on the Green River. We marched about 10 miles. The day was very warm and the roads dusty. The country becomes wilder and rougher as we advance.

Sunday 24th. The order to march was countermanded this morning and we were allowed to spend the day in rest and quiet. Our chaplain has gone home on a furlough and we had no sermon today. But we could read our bibles and think of the goodness of God and how you were assembling to worship Him in churches, schoolhouses, and groves. How I wish I could be with you at Hazel Dell this evening! But still if we love God we will be happy any place. Thus it is with me. Dear parents, brothers, and sisters, love Him and you will be happy too.

Camp in the woods near Neatsville Ky.   May 25th

We started at 5 o'clock this morning and arrived at this place at 3 this afternoon. We followed Green River about 2 miles then marched up a long steep hill, then along a level road through woods, down another steep hill to Green River again which we followed and near which we are now encamped. Neatsville is just across the river about 1 mile from camp. We marched 15 miles today and expect to move again tomorrow. The country through which we passed today is hilly and thickly wooded, with few improvements. I think our present destination is Columbia 14 miles from here. If so we will arrive there tomorrow. Our object in going there I do not know. Perhaps to go to Tennessee. The day has been very warm.

Columbia, Ky.,   May 26th, 1863.

"We were roused this morning at 2½ o'clock and marched at 4 o'clock. We arrived at this place before 10, having marched 13 miles. This we considered very good marching. The road and country were very much the same as yesterday — first a long hill and then a long level road mostly through the woods. Today has been very warm but our march was over before the heat became oppressive. Our camp is in the woods about 1 mile east of Columbia. I have not seen the town yet and cannot speak in regard to it.

Camp near Columbia, Ky.,   May 27th 1863.

"We did not march today as I expected. We were ordered to lay our camp out in order, and clean it up. This would indicate we are to remain here a few at least. Since leaving Lexington we have marched 100 miles. I think we will not remain here very long. Our force at this place is becoming quite formidable and I think we will move against the enemy shortly. Perhaps into Tennessee."

Corporal Frederick Pettit, Company C, 100th Pennsylvania Veteran Volunteer Infantry Regiment. Taken September 1862 at Camp Curtin, Harrisburg, Pennsylvania, shortly after joining the service.

Colonel Daniel Leasure, Organizer of the 100th Pennsylvania "Roundhead" Regiment.
U.S. Army Military History Institute Collection, hereafter referred to as "USAMHI"

Brigadier General Orlando B. Willcox. Competent 9th Corps Division Commander. Willcox was a much respected commander.

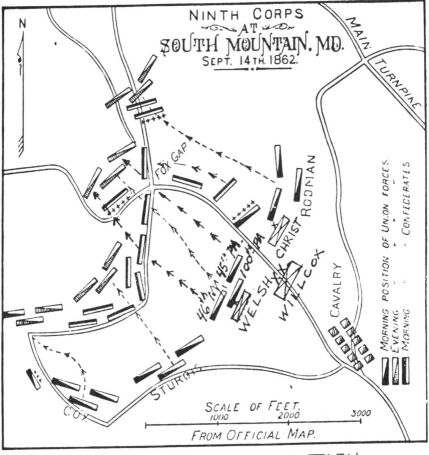

NINTH CORPS
AT
SOUTH MOUNTAIN, MD.
SEPT. 14TH. 1862.

N

MAIN. TURNPIKE

FOX GAP

CHRIST RODMAN

46 IN N.Y 45 TH PA 100 TH PA

WELSH WILLCOX

CAVALRY

MORNING POSITION OF UNION FORCES.
EVENING ·
MORNING · CONFEDERATES

STURGIS

COX

SCALE OF FEET.
1000   2000   3000

FROM OFFICIAL MAP.

SOUTH MOUNTAIN

Map #1 — Battle of South Mountain

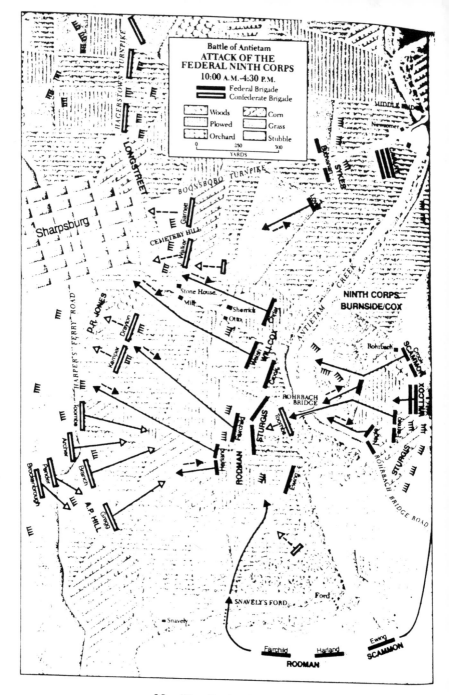

Map #2 — Battle of Antietam

Private Andrew Leary of Company C, 100th Pennsylvania. Leary was a close friend of Pettit's and is often mentioned in his letters and referred to as "Lary".

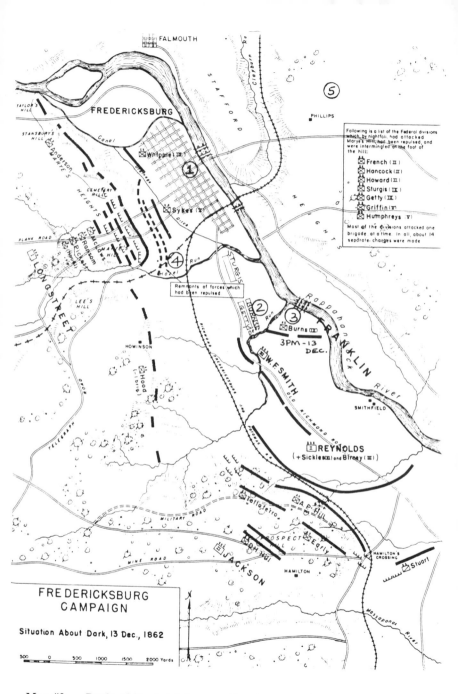

FALMOUTH

STAFFORD

FREDERICKSBURG

TAYLOR'S HILL

STANSBURY'S HILL

Anderson

MARYE'S

HEIGHTS

CEMETERY HILL

PLANK ROAD

McLaws

Ransom

Pickett

LONGSTREET

LEE'S HILL

Hood (-1brig.)

HOWINSON

TELEGRAPH

Canal

Whipple III

Sykes (V)

Sykes

Hazel

Run

STURGIS

Sykes

Remnants of forces which had been repulsed

Deep Run

Burns III

3 PM-13 DEC.

W.F.SMITH

REYNOLDS
(+Sickles III) and Birney (III))

Hazel Run

Massaponax Creek

Richmond Road

Hamilton's Crossing

PHILLIPS

Following is a list of the Federal divisions which, by nightfall, had attacked Marye's Hill; had been repulsed, and were intermingled at the foot of the hill:

French (II)
Hancock (II)
Howard (II)
Sturgis (IX)
Getty (IX)
Griffin (V)
Humphreys (V)

Most of the divisions attacked one brigade at a time. In all, about 14 separate charges were made

HEIGHTS

Rappahannock River

FRANKLIN

SMITHFIELD

Taliaferro

A.P. HILL

Early

D.H. Hill

JACKSON

HAMILTON

HAMILTON'S CROSSING

Stuart

Massaponax River

MILITARY ROAD

MINE ROAD

PROSPECT

FREDERICKSBURG CAMPAIGN

Situation About Dark, 13 Dec., 1862

500   0   500   1000   1500   2000 Yards

Map #3 — Battle of Fredericksburg — Showing successive positions of the 100th Pennsylvania Dec. 12-14, 1862.

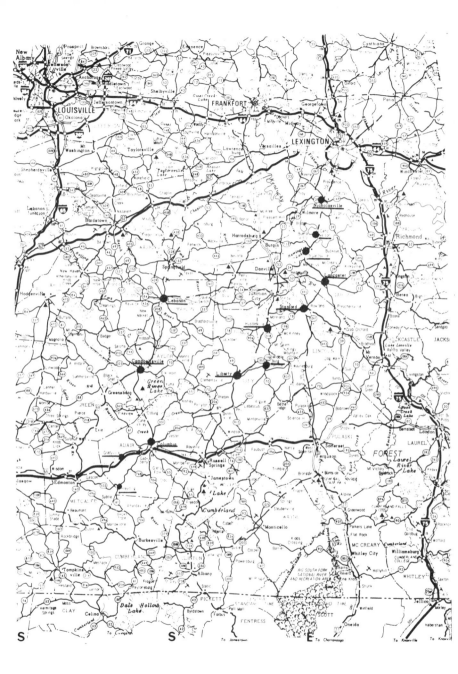

Map #4 — Kentucky Campaign

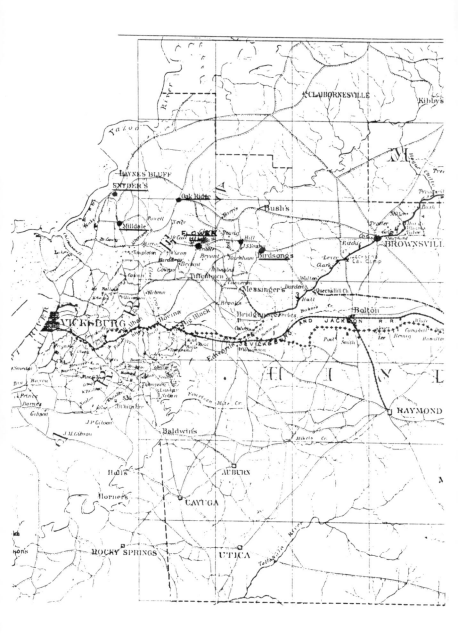

Map #5 — Vicksburg — Showing Positions of 100th Pennsylvania June and July 1863.

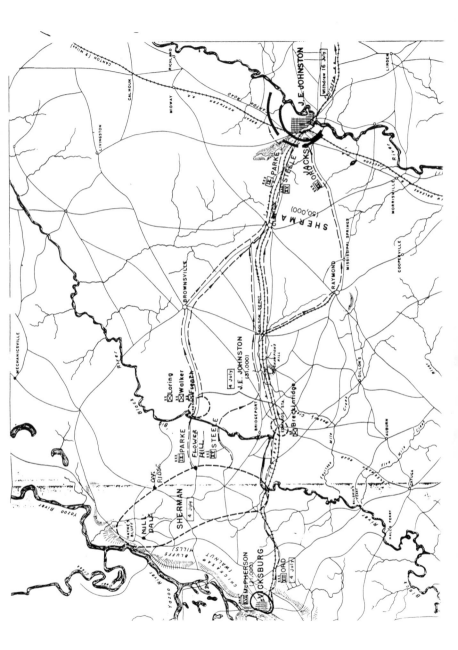

Map #6 — The Vicksburg-Jackson Campaign, July 1863

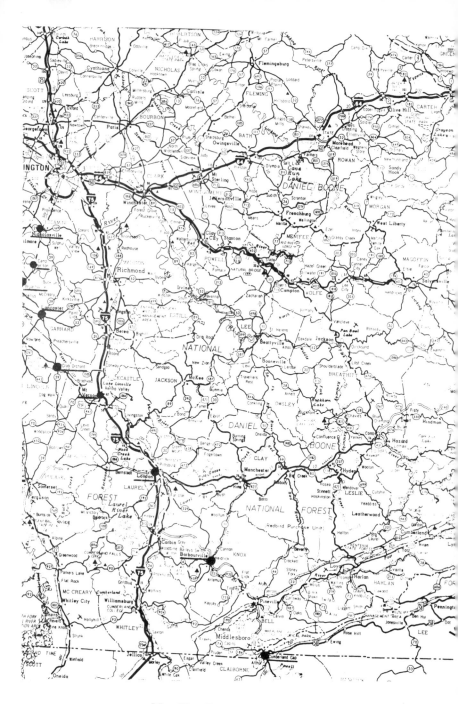

Map #7 — Route to East Tennessee

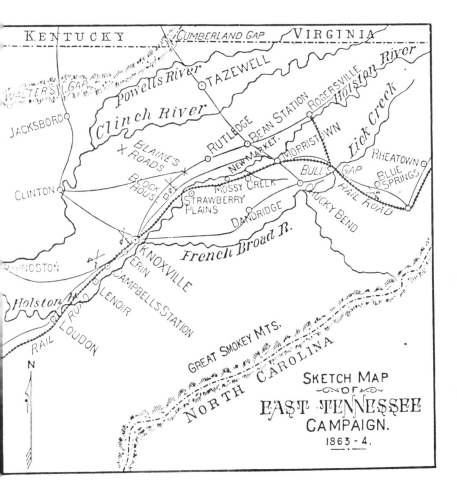

Map #8 — East Tennessee

Private Samuel Cleeland of Company C, 100th Pennsylvania. Cleeland was mortally wounded on May 12th at Spotsylvania.
USAMHI Collection

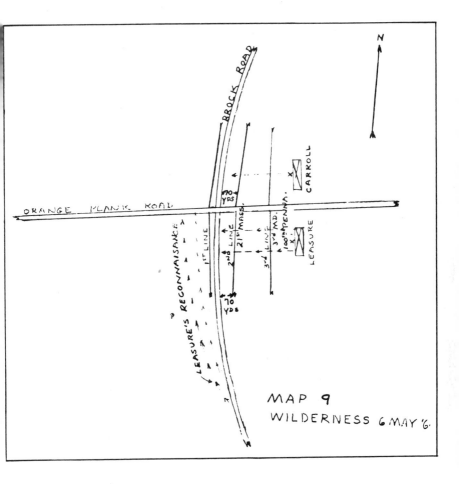

MAP 9
WILDERNESS 6 MAY '6.

Map #9 — Battle of the Wilderness

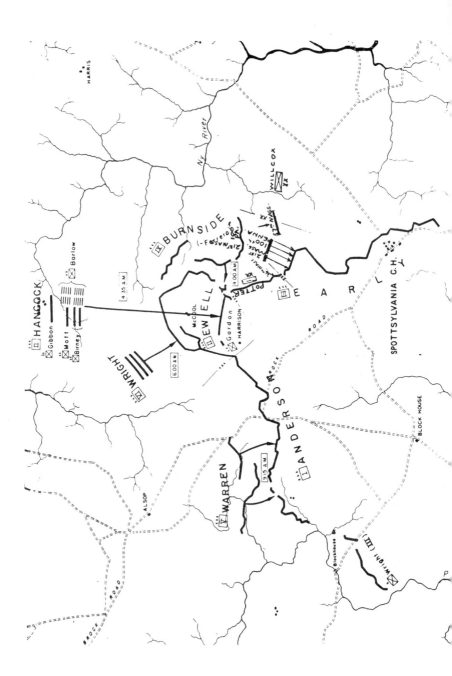

Map #10 — Battle of Spotsylvania, May 12, 1864

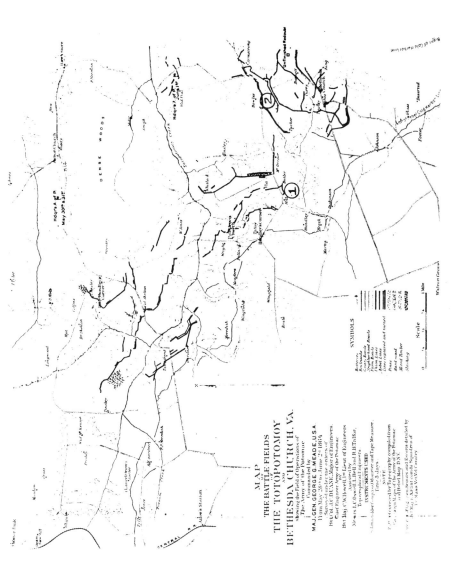

MAP
OF
THE BATTLE FIELDS
OF
THE TOTOPOTOMOY
AND
BETHESDA CHURCH, VA.
showing the Field of Operations of
The Army of the Potomac
Commanded by
MAJ. GEN. GEORGE G. MEADE, U.S.A.
From May 26th to June 2d 1864

Surveyed under the orders of
Bvt.Col. J.C DUANE, Major of Engineers,
Chief Engineer Army of the Potomac,
Assisted by
Bvt. Maj. C.W.Howell, 1st Lieut. of Engineers.
Messrs. Lt.Oswell, L.Bell and R.B.Talfor,
Topographical Engineers.

INSTRUMENTS USED
Lions to Albert Compass, Odometer and Tape Measure.
Time 3 days.

NOTE
Part surveyed the Topography compiled from
Geo. map Maps of the Army of the Potomac
and Rebel Map D.N.C.

Map #11 — Cold Harbor. Positions of 100th Pennsylvania on June 1-2, 1864

CAPTAIN J. E. CORNELIUS, Company Commander of Company C, 100th Pennsylvania. Wounded at Chantilly. Resigned March 4, 1863.
USAMHI Collection

2ND LIEUTENANT J. E. CORNELIUS, Company C, 100th Pennsylvania. Mortally wounded at Cold Harbor, (Bethesda Church) June 2, 1864.
USAMHI Collection

1ST SERGEANT (Later Captain) GEORGE W. FISHER, Company C, 100th Pennsylvania. Fisher is one of the few men who served the complete 47 months of the regiment's service. He commanded Company C during the last months of the war. *USAMHI Collection*

2ND LIEUTENANT WILLIAM SMILEY, Company C, 100th Pennsylvania. Smiley enlisted in August 1861 and was promoted through the ranks. He survived the war and was a veteran of 47 months service. *USAMHI Collection*

SERGEANT MATHEW STEWART (later First Lieutenant) of Company C. Stewart was another soldier who was promoted through the ranks and served in the 100th for the entire period of 47 months service. *USAMHI Collection*

1ST SERGEANT J. W. CRAIG of Company C. Craig served as Company C's 1st Sergeant during the last months of the war. *USAMHI Collection*

**CORPORAL WILLIAM W. McQUISTON,
Company C. Mustered out July 24, 1865,
with the regiment.** *USAMHI Collection*

**PRIVATE CALVIN STEWART,
Company C. Died March 1, 1865, at
Washington, D.C.**
USAMHI Collection

PRIVATE THOMAS BANES, Company C. Banes transferred to the Veterans Reserve Corps, June 1865.
USAMHI Collection

PRIVATE FREDERICK BAUDER, Company C. Bauder was a veteran and enlisted in the regiment in September of 1861. He transferred to the Veterans Reserve Corps in 1865.
USAMHI Collection

PRIVATE JACOB FULLER,
Company C, 100th Pennsylvania.
USAMHI Collection

PRIVATE H. GILL,
Company C, 100th Pennsylvania. Gill's
name does not appear on the company
roster. *USAMHI Collection*

PRIVATE ROBERT McKISSICK, Company C. McKissick was killed in action July 30, 1864, at the Battle of the Crater. He enlisted in the regiment in February 1864 when the regiment was recruiting in Pennsylvania while on veteran furlough. *USAMHI Collection*

PRIVATE JOSEPH MOORE, Company C. There was also a Private John Moore in Company C. This photo could be either soldier as it is labeled "J. Moore." Both men survived the war.
USAMHI Collection

PRIVATE LAFAYETTE SHAFER, Company C. Shafer enlisted February 1864 and was mustered out with the regiment in 1865.   *USAMHI Collection*

SERGEANT HENRY RIBB, Company C. Ribb enlisted August 31, 1861 when the regiment was organized. He survived the entire 47 months of service and was mustered out July 24, 1865.
USAMHI Collection

CORPORAL JAMES W. WHITE.
White was another 47 months veteran. He enlisted August 31, 1865, and was mustered out July 1865 with the regiment.
USAMHI Collection

PRIVATE THOMAS WIER,
Company C. Wier was another February 1864 recruit to the regiment. He survived and was mustered out July 1865.
USAMHI Collection

Written to:
Family

Camp near Columbia Ky.,   May 27th 1863.

"Dear parents, brothers, and sisters:

Although I have received no letter from any of you since I wrote last yet I will send this one now to let you know where we are, how we are, and what we are doing. My diary of the last few days will tell you where we are. Our camp is well located being convenient to both shade and water, both of which are very necessary in warm weather.

I am well and have stood the marches well. Write soon.

Fred Pettit
Co. C. 100th P.V.
3rd Brigade, 1st Division
9th Army Corps
Cincinnati, Ohio."

Written to:
Family

Columbia, Ky.,   June 3rd, 1863.

"Dear parents, brothers, and sisters,

A few hours after I mailed my last letter (May 27th) we were ordered to be ready to move at 7 o'clock p.m. It was to be an expedition against the rebels in the southern part of the state and consisted of 2 regiments of infantry, 250 cavalry, and 2 pieces of artillery.[3]

We marched about 10 miles, stopped at 1 o'clock a.m. and rested until morning. At daylight the cavalry moved forward and the infantry and artillery moved into the woods and remained until the next morning, when we marched 8 miles farther. The cavalry went on another scout and returned about midnight with two prisoners. They were near the Cumberland river and could discover no force of the enemy on this side.

The next evening Saturday 30th we started back to camp. After marching down 5 miles a heavy thunder shower commenced. The rain came down in torrents, the road became very muddy, but we marched on very rapidly. Shortly after dark we stopped, made coffee and ate supper. We then marched to camp arriving about midnight. We marched 16 miles.

The next day Sunday we spent washing, resting, and sleeping. Monday morning we went on picket. The rebels are expected hourly but none have come yet.

---

[3] On May 27, Leisure's brigade, including the 100th Pennsylvania was ordered on a scout to the south and west of Columbia, Kentucky, to feel for the enemy and disperse Morgan's forces and drive them south of the Cumberland River. This three day operation did not locate any substantial Confederate force and returned to Columbia on the 30th. Colonel Daniel Leisure, letter, "Columbia, Kentucky, May 30th, (Sunday), 1863". McDowell Collection, Historical Collections and Labor Archives, Pennsylvania State University, University Park, Pennsylvania.

Yesterday Tuesday we moved our camp about 2 miles. Almost every night we are roused to go on a scout or lie on our arms awaiting the rebels. None have come yet and we do not fear them much.

We now have orders to be ready to move shortly and as other troops are to relieve us we will undoubtedly go to Tennessee. I think Gen. Burnside will command us. We may expect long marches and heavy fighting. But with commanders like Burnside and Willcox we can do anything.

I have received no letters since the 15th of May. We are all well. Write soon. Direct your letters:

> Fred Pettit
> Co. C. 100th P.V.
> 3rd Brigade, 1st Division
> 9th Army Corps
> Cincinnati, Ohio.''

This was the last letter Pettit wrote from Kentucky in June, 1863. General Burnside had been assembling an army consisting of the Ninth Army Corps and the Twenty-Third Corps for an immediate move into east Tennessee. Burnside left Cincinnati on June 2d to take personal command of the force. The First Division of the Ninth Corps at this time was dispersed at Columbia, Somerset, and Jamestown, Kentucky, from which points they could easily invade Tennessee.

However, on June 3, Burnside was directed by General H. W. Halleck, general in chief of the armies, headquartered in Washington, to "immediately dispatch 8,000 men to General Grant at Vicksburg." Confederate General Joseph Johnston had been advancing toward Vicksburg from the east and it was feared that he might break the siege there unless additional troops were sent to block him. Burnside selected the veterans of the Ninth Corps for this assignment and two divisions were dispatched to Grant under command of General John G. Parke.[4]

Colonel Daniel Leasure, brigade commander, received orders on the night of June 3d to march northward to Lebanon, Kentucky, 40 miles away, and proceed by rail to Louisville where orders for the next destination would be received.

Pettit's next letter, dated June 10, 1863, was written from Memphis, Tennessee, on a troop transport headed down the Mississippi for Vicksburg. General Halleck's orders had been executed promptly and in 10 days Leasure's brigade and the 100th Pennsylvania were at Young's Point, Louisiana, in front of the besieged city.

---

[4] *Official Records*, Series 1, Volume 24, Part 3, Pages 383 and 403. Also see William G. Gavin, *Campaigning With The Roundheads*, Morningside Press, Dayton, Ohio, 1989. Chapter Nine of this work gives additional details of the Ninth Corps' assignment for duty at Vicksburg.

CHAPTER SIX

THE VICKSBURG AND JACKSON CAMPAIGNS JUNE AND JULY 1863

"...and several dropped dead from fatigue."

The Ninth Corps under General Parke arrived opposite Vicksburg on Saturday, June 13, 1863. Pettit gives some brief details of the journey from Columbia, Kentucky, in his letters June 10 and 16, written from Memphis and Young's Point, Louisiana. [SEE MAP 5].

Written to:
Family

Memphis, Tennessee, June 10th 1863.

"Dear parents, brothers, and sisters:

The date of this letter will no doubt surprise you. We left Columbia, Ky., the day after I wrote my last letter and made a forced march of 40 miles in one day and a half arriving at Lebanon at noon 5th. The same night we took the cars for Louisville where we arrived the next day — crossed the Ohio river and took the cars for Cairo, Ill.

We arrived at this city of mud Monday morning the 8th inst. We here went aboard the boat *Alice Dean* bound for Memphis. We left Cairo Tuesday the 9th and have just arrived here (Memphis) now noon Wednesday June 10th.

87

I think our destination is Vicksburgh. Troops are going there daily. Our whole corps is on the way. We expect to have something to do soon.

I have been well during the journey so far. We are paid off just before leaving Kentucky. I will write particulars as soon as possible. Write as usual.

> Fred Pettit
> Co. C. 100th P.V.
> 3rd brigade 1st division
> 9th Army Corps
> Memphis, Tenn."

[SEE MAP #5]

Written to:
Family

Youngs Point, Louisiana,   June 16th, 1863.

"Dear parents, brothers, and sisters:

I received a letter from Evan when we were at Memphis dated May 29th. This is the last one I received from home. The last one I sent you was from Memphis. We lay there two days. We arrived here last Saturday the 13th.

We are 4 or 5 miles from the city on the opposite side of the river at the head of the famous canal. We can see the city and fortifications very distinctly. The mortar boats lie in the river about 2½ miles below us. You can see the shells bursting over the city and fortifications constantly. The rebels fire but little in this direction. We can hear Grant pounding away in the rear.

We landed here Sunday. Yesterday, Monday the 15th we were ordered to Warrenton below Vicksburg.

[letter continued]

Chickasaw Bluffs, Miss.   June 17th 1863

My letter was suddenly interrupted yesterday by the order to pack up. I will commence where I stopped yesterday. We went to Warrenton below Vicksburg or nearly opposite there and remained until evening and marched back again.[1] The distance across the bend from Youngs

---

[1] Parke's Ninth Corps was intended to move into the Vicksburg siege lines south of the city. At the last minute, General Grant countermanded this move and ordered the Ninth Corps to Hayne's Bluff north of the city. Grant had received information of an enemy force of 12,000 men concentrating at Yazoo City. The Confederate threat from the direction of Yazoo City was the deciding factor in ordering the Ninth Corps up the Yazoo. Otherwise, Pettit's regiment would have found themselves in the front siege line and would have been first hand observers of the dramatic events leading to the surrender on July 4. See *Official Records*, Series 1, Volume 24, Part 3, Pages 409 and 410. Also William G. Gavin, *Campaigning With The Roundheads*, Chapter 10.

Point to Warrenton Landing is about 4 miles. Yesterday we went on the boats again and came up the Yazoo 15 or 16 miles and landed at Chickasaw Bluffs. Hanes Bluff [Hayne's] is one of the Chickasaw bluffs but is 3 or 4 miles above where we landed. This morning we marched out about 3 miles. The country about here is very hilly, but very fertile.

As soon as we had our tent up I broke for the blackberries. I found them very plentiful and soon had my cap full as well as something else full. When I came in John boiled a tin full of them for dinner. We found them excellent. It is quite warm here, much warmer than Pa. The siege of Vicksburgh still goes on, the lines are said to be 10 yds. apart in places.

Evan said father wanted to know something about that bounty. I thought I settled that last winter. Last winter the legislature of Pa. passed an act declaring the bounty tax unconstitutional, and any tax assessed to pay bounties cannot be collected by law. If father has paid a bounty tax he has been defrauded by the person to whom he paid it.

I am well as usual. Write soon. Direct your letters as usual to:

> Fred Pettit
> Co. C. 100th P.V.
> 3rd brig. 1st division
> 9th Army Corps
> Cincinnati, Ohio.''

Written to:
Family

Snyders Bluffs, Miss.   June 26th 1863

"Dear parents, brothers, and sisters:

I have nothing of importance to write to you today. I have received no letter since I left Memphis. The last one from you was written almost a month ago. I do not know whether you get my letters or not but I shall continue to write once a week.

The troops here are busy throwing up fortifications to prevent Johnston from attacking Grant in the rear. We are getting this place strongly fortified. Johnston will need a large force to get through. Our regiment worked on the fortifications one day.

The weather is very warm. We have made shades over our tents with brush and spend most of our time lounging in them.

The siege of Vicksburgh still goes on. We are gaining upon them little by little, but it may require a long time to reduce it yet. We have rumors of Lee's invading Penna. This will wake the north to the fact that a war is going on. They will perhaps now enter into the struggle with earnest and drive the rebels back.

[letter continued]

July 1st 1863

I intended to finish my letter last Sunday (June 28) but on that day we had to work on the fortifications. On Monday we marched out 6 miles toward the Black River where we are now encamped. We are about 8 miles from Blackwater bridge and about 14 miles from Vicksburgh. Marching is almost impossible here it is so hot and dusty. You can have no idea of the hot days we have here. The hottest days in Pa. are cool compared with this.

There is some sickness in the regiment. The water is very unhealthy. Vicksburgh still holds out. Nobody can get either in or out of it. If we can keep it so it must surrender sometime. It may hold out 6 months yet.

The latest news from the north is that Harrisburg has been captured and the rebels are within 20 miles of Pittsburgh. Hooker is at Washington with his army. I suppose the people of Pa. will soon see some of the glories of war.

We have heard that the ladies of Chambersburg presented the rebels with bread, meat, pies, cakes, clothing, flowers, etc. From the speeches made on the return of the 134th P. V. [9 months regiment] there are no more troops in the service as good as them. The 134th P.V.[2] was called the poorest regiment from the state. They were certainly the dirtiest Pa. Vols. I have yet seen.

I suppose you must be very busy as I get no letters. The last was written in May. Perhaps they do not come.

Fred Pettit"

Written to:
Family

Flower Hill, Miss.,   July 4th 1863.

"Dear parents, brothers, and sisters,

Another fourth has come and with it the same warm, genial sun of other years but how different do things appear to me. How far from my old home have I wandered during the past year. This morning commenced with its usual monotony. Nothing to disturb the stillness except the morning drum and the distant boom of cannon at Vicksburgh. These gradually died away and all is still and quiet again.

---

[2] The 134th Pennsylvania Infantry regiment was organized in July of 1862 for nine months service until May 1863. It was composed of companies from Beaver, Lawrence, and Butler counties which is the same general area from which the 100th regiment originated. There was some feeling of rivalry between the 100th and the 134th as the members of the 100th considered themselves a veteran regiment and felt some resentment for 9 months' volunteers. Samuel P. Bates, *History of Pennsylvania Volunteers*, Harrisburg, 1870, Volume 3.

But why this nervous excitement visible in every countenance? The long looked for news has come at last. Vicksburgh has surrendered at last. After sustaining a siege of 46 days it has at length fallen into our hands. This gives us control of the Mississippi excepting Port Hudson (perhaps) and is one of the greatest blows yet struck at the rebellion.

[There is no signature or closing address on this letter. It is included in the letter of July 24th following the editor's explanation.]

Private Pettit had little time for letter writing during the next three weeks. The 100th Regiment was on the march for Jackson, Mississippi, and was occupied in the siege of Jackson, the destruction of the railroad to the north, and then the endurance of a terrible return march to Hill Dale in scorching July weather with only limited water supplies. The sickness in the regiment was devastating. It took many weeks for the troops to recuperate from their Mississippi Campaign. [SEE MAP #6]

[letter continued]

Mill Dale, Miss.   July 24th, 1863.

We have just returned from one of the hardest campaigns this regiment ever went through. Above you have part of a letter I commenced to write on the 4th. That letter was stopped by the order to pack up and move.

We marched about 6 miles toward the Big Black that evening and lay in that vicinity during Sunday and Monday. Tuesday evening we crossed the Big Black and marched some distance. Our regiment was on picket that night. Shortly after dark a heavy thunder shower set in and continued almost all night. We did not take our knapsacks with us, only our gum blankets.

The next day the 8th we joined the brigade about noon, and started at 4 o'clock p.m. and marched until almost midnight. The next day 9th we started early and marched until late in the afternoon and were stopped by cannonading in front. We were now 6 or 7 miles from Jackson.

The next day we continued our march keeping to the north and were brought to a halt by the rebels in line of battle. We halted half an hour for dinner and then moved on half a mile into a large cornfield when we formed line of battle with skirmishers in front. The skirmishers advanced to a thick woods at the foot of a low ridge on which we could see rebel cavalry. At the edge of the woods the skirmishers commenced firing which showed they had found the enemy.

The whole division now advanced in line of battle through the corn. The enemies force was only a few pickets and was easily driven away and we continued onward through the woods to the railroad. This woods was a brush thicket. You know the thicket near T. Nyes house. This was just as thick. We marched through this brush about 3 miles. Our object was to swing around to the Pearl River which runs in the rear of Jackson. We came in sight of the river in the evening about 2 miles above the city. We remained here until morning and then formed line in a field to the right of the woods. The rebel skirmishers were in front of us on a low ridge and their balls came zipping around us plenty close.

Col. Leasure ordered his brigade to go to the foot of the hill double quick. After getting to the foot of the hill we were safe from the bullets as they flew high over our heads. The skirmishers then advanced to the top of the hill and drove the rebels back. The brigade then advanced to the brow of the hill and sheltered themselves by lying down. Here the bullets flew over us thick with an occasional cannon shot, but no one was hurt.

Shortly afterward our brigade was moved further to the right into the woods. This was on Saturday. We remained here until Sunday morning when we were relieved. The skirmishing was kept up all the time. Some of the skirmishers were killed and wounded. We lay behind the brow of the ridge and the balls flew over us.[3]

After we were relieved on Sunday we were sent on picket in the rear. We stopped at a planters house and threw out pickets on the roads. We now drew but half rations of crackers, sugar, and coffee and were ordered to take everything we could get to eat. Where we stopped there were plenty of chickens, hogs, 3 or 4 barrels of molasses, and a large house filled mostly with costly furniture. All these things were taken whether needed or not. Roasting ears and green peaches were plenty and we lived well notwithstanding the half rations. You must understand the rebels had left their houses and run away.

On Monday night 13th we were again taken back to the front where we lay before, the rebels firing over our heads and our skirmishers in front of us firing at them. Wednesday the 15th we were taken back on picket again. That night the rebels evacuated Jackson and none were to be found. They had taken everything and burned the principal stores. The next day 16th the regiment was ordered up the river along the railroad. I had a very large boil on my leg and was not able to march with the regiment and was left at the hospital. The regiment returned Sunday evening 19th and my leg having got better, I joined them. They had been out 12 miles destroying the railroad. [New Orleans, Jackson, and Great Northern Railroad which ran north from Jackson.]

---

[3] For additional details on the siege of Jackson, Mississippi, reference is made to: Edwin C. Bearss, *The Siege of Jackson*, Gateway Press, Baltimore, Maryland, 1981. Published for the Jackson (Mississippi) Civil War Roundtable. Additional details of the operations of the 100th Pennsylvania are found in William G. Gavin's *Campaigning With The Roundheads*, Chapter 10. Morningside Press, Dayton, Ohio, 1989.

The next day we started at 4 o'clock on our trip back [to Mill Dale]. We marched about 18 miles that day. It was very hot. At least one third of the men fell behind. Many fainted from the heat and several died from the same cause. The next day we started at daybreak and marched about 15 miles stopping near the Big Black. This day at least one third of the corps were behind when we stopped and several *dropped dead* [emphasis added] from fatigue. The next day 22nd we crossed the Big Black but only marched 3 or 4 miles.[4] Part of the wagons were emptied and sent back to gather up the men who had given out along the road.

Yesterday we started at daylight and arrived at this place at noon. This is where we first camped when we landed at Snyders Bluffs. We found our knapsacks here and have a big time washing as we had no change of clothing with us.

We have marched about 130 miles since July 1st. The weather is the hottest I ever felt. We had very poor water [Editor's note: Or none at all] most of the time.[5]

                              F. Pettit"

Written to:
Family

                         Mill Dale, [Milldale] Miss.   July 24th 1863.

"Dear parents, brothers, and sisters,

It is almost a month since I wrote to you. I have not had my knapsack since the 4th and but little time to write if I could. You will find an account (above letter) with this [letter] of what we have been doing. During that time I have received many letters from you, one from Father, Evan, and Maggie 2, and Mary several. The last was from Maggie July 10th. It would take a long time to answer them separately so you must be content with this. My health has been good since the 4th. On our trip to Jackson we got plenty of peaches, roasting ears, chickens, melons, and hard marching.

You wanted to know what we get to eat. In camp we get crackers, bacon, fresh beef, sugar, coffee, beans, and rice. On the march we take

---

[4] [Editor's opinion] There appears to have been no logical reason for marching the troops at this pace on the return march. Jackson had been evacuated with General Johnston's army moving quickly east and Vicksburg had surrendered. Considering the scorching heat, shortage of water, and the exhausted condition of the men, the forced march back to Mill Dale was completely unnecessary. It not only caused many fatalities, but also the hardship was unnecessary on the men. It is a severe indictment on the Federal commanders involved and demonstrated their complete disregard for the welfare of the men. Finally, by the 22nd, the commanders realized the severity of the consequences and allowed the pace of the march to be reduced. For additional details on the hardships and consequences for the 100th Regiment in the Jackson campaign, see chapter 10, *Campaigning With The Roundheads.*

[5] Vivid first hand accounts of the hardships encountered during the 100th Pennsylvania's march to and from Jackson are found in Chapter 10 of William G. Gavin's *Campaigning With The Roundheads.* The time spent in Mississippi created severe health problems with a large number of the regiment and it was weeks before many regained their health in Kentucky.

everything we can get. The talk is now that we are going back to Ky. It is very hot and sickly here. The western troops stand it better than we do. The principal disease is fever [typhoid] and ague. Dysentery is prevalent but not worse than common. Capt. Critchlow [Company Commander, Company C] has had the ague but is better. The rest of us are well. I have just eaten my dinner and had all the roasting ears I could eat.

I think the next time I write it will be farther north. Continue to write as usual.

Maggie and Mary wish me to send them my photograph. We do not have the luxury of such an institution away down south here!

F. Pettit
Co. C. 100th P.V.''

Written to:
Father, Nathaniel Pettit,
North Sewickly,
Beaver County, Pa

Mill Dale, Miss.   July 30, 1863.

''Dear Father,

I received a letter written by you June 1st on the 4th of July. We were then in pursuit of Johnston's force which was retreating on Jackson. We followed him as far as that place, but before Sherman was ready to attack him he was gone.[6] We then came back to this place. The march to Jackson and back was very hard on the troops. Water was very scarce and very poor. The weather was very warm. There are a great many men sick with Dysentery, Fever [both malaria and typhoid], and Ague.

We expect to start north again in a few days. I think we shall go to Kentucky. We all wish to go back.

In your letter you wished me to send you the necessary papers for drawing my bounty. I wrote to you some time ago stating that it was impossible to get the bounty and I believed it at the time. Shortly before receiving your letter I learned that some had already procured the bounty and I began to think of securing mine. But we then started on the Jackson campaign and I did not get the certificate until today.

---

[6] General William Tecumseh Sherman was commander of the ''expedition'' which General Grant ordered east in a thrust against Jackson immediately after the surrender of Vicksburg on July 4, 1863. This ''Expeditionary Army'' consisted of the Ninth Corps (Major General John G. Parke), the Sixteenth Corps (Brig. General W. Sooy Smith), the Thirteenth Army Corps (Major General E. O. C. Ord), and the Fifteenth Army Corps (Major General Frederick Steele). Further details of the campaign are in Edward C. Bearss's *The Siege of Jackson,* Baltimore, 1981.

I will send it and an order for the money in this letter. I have written two orders, one on the commissioners, and one on the treasurer. If you go to the commissioners you will need the one direct to them only and they will give you one on the treasurer. If you go to the treasurer, and not to the commissioners, you will use the order addressed to him. You may either draw the money or take a bond for it as is most convenient. Whatever money I send you use just as you see fit.

I think we will be on our way north in a few days. A. Lary, John P. Wilson, P. Bird, and J. McElwain are well. A. Lary and I now mess together. I messed with John P. Wilson until about a month ago when he left the company to serve in the provost guard at Col. Leasure's [brigade] headquarters. Col. Leasure commands our brigade. Captain Critchlow has been sick but is better.

I should be very glad if you would write again. After you get this direct all letters to Cincinnati, Ohio, as we are ordered to report there.

I am well as usual. While on the last march my health was very good.

> Your affectionate son,
> Frederick Pettit
> Co. C. 100th P.V."

It was a day of great excitement and rejoicing on August 1 when the regiment was ordered to move from the Milldale camp to nearby Snyder's Bluff where they boarded steamers for the long awaited trip north. Spirits were high and although the destination was unknown, they were heading north and away from Mississippi.

After six days on the steamers, the long trip (600 miles) ended at Cairo, Illinois. When the troops arrived in Cairo, many of the men were so weak that they were scarcely able to march through the streets of the town. Even at the town's market house, where the citizens had provided an abundant meal, many fell besides the tables and were carried away to the hospitals.[7]

Pettit took time in Cairo to write home his weekly letter.

Written to:
Family

> Cairo, Ill., Aug. 7th, 1863

"Dear parents, brothers, and sisters:

We landed at this place today. I am well and have been during the trip.

---

7 Augustus Woodbury, *Burnside and History of the Ninth Army Corps*, Providence, 1867, Page 288.

We left Snyders Bluffs August 1st. Nothing of importance took place on the way up. The guerrillas did not disturb us. We stopped a few minutes at Helena. At Memphis we remained almost 24 hours. Being on detail half a day in the city I have a good opportunity of seeing it. It appears to have been quite a business place at one time. Its trade is fast improving. It contains a number of extensive stores.

This morning as we were passing Columbus, about 20 miles from here, we were brought to in a hurry by a cannon shot. After reporting we were allowed to pass.

The distance from Vicksburgh here is 632 miles. We were six days in making the trip. I am heartily tired of steamboating for the present.

Our company was quartered on the hurricane deck — a hot place by day and a middling place at night. But we got along very well. The boys are all well.

We are the first regiment of our corps that has arrived [in Cairo]. We do not know where we will go. Perhaps on up the river by boat to Louisville or Cincinnati and perhaps by railroad. We are awaiting orders.

I have received no letter from home since I wrote last. Write and direct your letters to Cincinnati, Ohio.

We saw a list of drafted men in Lawrence Co. before we started up. I have seen no list of Beaver Co. yet. The soldiers are glad to hear that the draft is being carried out. Fill up the old regiments and the rebellion must be crushed. Write soon.

What do the young people think and say about the war now? I will write again soon.

> Yours,
> Frederick Pettit
> Co. C. 100th P.V."

The Vicksburg Campaign was now history. The forty odd days spent in Mississippi had been arduous ones for the 100th Pennsylvania and tolls in sickness and disease were severe. Although combat casualties had been negligible, the regiment was greatly weakened by the time they arrived in Cairo.

Pettit's regiment had been active participants in one of the most successful campaigns of the entire war. The fall of Vicksburg opened up the Mississippi River and sealed the doom of the Confederacy. The regiment could add the names of Vicksburg and Jackson to their regimental colors.

For the 100th Pennsylvania, it had been a campaign of seven weeks which included the siege of Vicksburg and the fall of Jackson. Although the men did not know it at Cairo, they were destined to rejoin Burnside in the Department of the Ohio with their immediate assignment once again to be in the pleasant state of Kentucky.

CHAPTER SEVEN

BACK IN KENTUCKY
AUGUST - SEPTEMBER 1863

"...Our stay in Miss. proved very disastrous to the health of our corps."

The 100th Pennsylvania regiment entrained August 7 for Cincinnati the same day that they arrived in Cairo. By August 11, the troops were located at Camp Nelson, Kentucky, just six miles from Nicholasville, Kentucky.

Written to:
Sister, Miss Mary A. Pettit

Camp Nelson, Ky., August 13th, 1863.

"Dear Sister,

It has been some time since I wrote you a letter. The last one I wrote home would inform you of my arrival in Cairo. We left it the same evening on the cars for Cincinnati. We changed cars at noon Saturday the 8th at Sandoval, Ill. We arrived in Cincinnati Sunday evening. We marched to the market house and partook of a substantial supper of bread, boiled ham, and coffee. As we were eating General Burnside passed through the hall and was loudly cheered. The General looks well.

After supper we crossed the river and quartered for the night in Covington Barracks. The next day Monday we left in the cars about dark for Camp Nelson. We arrived at Lexington early the next morning and at Nicholasville about 8 o'clock Tuesday morning. The railroad terminates at Nicholasville. From there to Camp Nelson is 6 miles. It is 120 miles almost south of Cincinnati and 8 miles north of Camp Dick Robinson and 2 miles from the Kentucky River.

The situation is a very good one. There are several excellent springs of water within the camp limits. As far as we have traveled the harvest is mostly gathered. Fruit and vegetables of all kinds are very plentiful here, and we are living well. Since we came here we have been very busy fixing up our tents, washing our clothes, cleaning our guns, etc. I just finished mine today. The regiment is improving in appearance very rapidly.

General Burnside's quarters are close by our camp. He came out here with us. He is organizing an extensive expedition for some point in rebeldom. Perhaps Eastern Tennessee. [Pettit's guess was a prophetic one!]

In one of your letters you wanted to know how many corporals there are in a company. I will give you kind of an outline of the organization of a company and a regiment. A company consists of 101 men viz: 1 captain, 2 lieutenants, 5 sergeants, 8 corporals, and 85 privates. A regiment consists of 10 companies and a drum corps of 6 or 8 drums, 3 or 4 fifes, and sometimes one or two buglers. Its officers are a colonel, lieutenant-colonel, major, chaplain, adjutant, who ranks as a 1st lieutenant, quarter master, sergeant major, quartermaster sergeant, and commissary sergeant. Regiments are organized into brigades, brigades into divisions, and divisions into corps. The 9th and 23rd corps are in Ky.

The position in which you are now placed is no doubt a very embarrassing one. Duty says remain and trust an all wise Creator. While self interest says any course that appears to benefit myself. You can choose whichever appears right. What now appears dark and mysterious may shortly appear plain.

I have received no letters from home for some time but hope to soon. Direct to Cincinnati, Ohio. I am well and have been all summer. Write soon.

> Your brother,
> Frederick Pettit"

Written to:
Father

Camp Nelson, Ky.   August 15th, 1863

"Dear father:

I received two letters from you yesterday. One of July 1st and the other the 19th. You wondered why I did not receive your letters sooner. We move about so much our mails do not find us for a month sometimes. One of our mails is at Vicksburg now. We will get it perhaps in a week or two. I have received every letter that you have written to me though sometimes they are two months old.

I sent you the necessary papers to draw my bounty before I left Mississippi. If you have not received them let me know and I will send again. Since I wrote you the last we have traveled from Miss. to Ky. Our stay in Miss. proved very disastrous to the health of our corps. We now have at least 2000 less for duty than when we left Kentucky last June. Some have died and many are in the hospitals. The principal diseases are Fever and Ague, Typhoid fever, and Diarrhea. Since we came back to Ky. a great many are being affected with pain in the head, caused by exposure to the hot sun. Andrew Lary has been unwell for several days from this cause. My health has been very good. I am now as well as ever I was. The climate about Vicksburgh is very unhealthy for persons not accustomed to it.

The organization of Negro troops is still going on along the Mississippi river. The Negroes make good soldiers and they fight well. There is quite a difference between the Negroes in Kentucky and further south. Here they are contented generally to remain with their masters but this is not the case further south. They are anxious to be free, and hate their masters intensely. They scorn the idea of not being able to support themselves if free. I am satisfied that the Negroes are the cause of this war and this war will free them. This opinion has gained very fast in the army during the past year.

I believe if the soldiers were now at home some of the copperheads would shortly cease to live. The feeling against them here is very bitter. We have heard a great deal about Union Leagues. Can you tell me their object and whether they are secret societies?

Our regiment will perhaps have a short rest here. The location is a very good one. John McElwain's health was middling good when I saw him last. I should be very glad if you would continue to write occasionally.

> Your affectionate son,
> Frederick Pettit"

Written to:
Brother, Evan Pettit.

> Camp Nelson, Ky.,   August 15th, 1863.

"Dear brother Evan,

I received a letter from you yesterday written July 1st. It was a good while coming. You wanted to know how I spent the 4th. Most of the day I lay in my tent. In the evening we marched about 6 miles. On that march we got half rations, that is half as much as common. This was when we went to Jackson.

We started on the 4th but peaches were getting ripe and the corn was in roasting ears and we had enough to eat. After we came back we got rations again. We get crackers, pork and beef, coffee, sugar, beans, and we now can buy potatoes, beans, apples, peaches, and all such stuff from the citizens. I have a lot of new potatoes to cook for dinner and must hurry and finish my letter.

I never ate so much corn in my life as I have this summer. It agrees with me better here than it did at home. I have eaten peaches by the peck.

The weather is not near so warm here as it was at Vicksburgh. The water we used in Miss. was not very good. We drank a great deal of water there out of frog ponds. The water is very good here but we have to carry it a long ways.

But I must stop and cook these potatoes for they look good. Write again soon.

> Your brother,
> Fred Pettit
> Co. C. 100th P.V.''

Written to:
Sister, Mary Ann

Camp Parke,[1] Ky.,   August 18th, 1863

''Dear sister Mary:

It is some time since I wrote you a letter. These long days drag slowly away and to while this one away I will write you a few scribbling lines. The day is bright and sunny like all August days. It would be called very hot but we [have] become so accustomed to the intense heat in Miss. that we are quite comfortable here.

Our camp is pleasantly located in a pasture field interspersed with shade trees. We have but little to do. From 7 o'clock in the morning until 5 in the evening there is scarcely anything occuring to break the monotony. With but little reading matter it is indeed wearisome.

Last Sunday I attended church about a mile from camp. The congregation is Methodist. There were two sermons preached, one by a Methodist preacher and the other by a Presbyterian. The Methodist's sermon was a funeral discourse upon the death of an old lady. The text was these words from the Revelation viz: There shall be no more curse. The great aim of the speaker was to get his hearers to stand as it were by death and look back upon his life and forward into eternity and see the infinite justice and mercy of God. The sermon was indeed good.

---

[1] The regiment moved from Camp Nelson to a new camp, Camp Parke, so named for the Ninth Corps commander, General John G. Parke. It was three miles closer to Nicholasville, Kentucky, than Camp Nelson and located in a drier and more convenient place in a beautiful piece of woodland. Colonel Daniel Leasure decided to situate here after his arrival on August 13 with the other three regiments of his brigade. From William G. Gavin, *Campaigning With The Roundheads*, Morningside Press, Dayton, Ohio, 1989, Chapter 11.

The second sermon was read by a very Presbyterianized minister. Between the sermons the congregation partook of a bountiful supply of refreshments. The soldiers were not forgotten at this time for we were supplied with an abundance of bread, meat, and pie. There were but four of us remained for the second sermon. The meeting was very much like those I used to attend at Slippery Rock [Butler County, Pennsylvania] Church. It was very pleasant to meet once more on the Sabbath with those who meet to worship the Almighty.

There is one thing that is painful for the Christians to reflect upon that is the small number who attend church or make any pretensions to even morality in this state. A person traversing any part of the south and even the southern border of the free states can not but notice the utter disregard of all morality and virtue. Why is this? What is it that causes this vice and immorality to be so widespread and universal in this bright and sunny southern land? It is idleness. And what has caused idleness to prevail more here than elsewhere? Slavery, undoubtedly. Slavery the great cause of all this wickedness is being fast done away by this war. After this war is over the whole south will be a ruined physically, intellectually, and morally. What a wide field it will open for those engaged in the education of the masses. There is much more that might be said upon the results of this war, but it is unnecessary. They will soon be upon us; and then action alone will be required. Let all be prepared for it.

The health of the regiment is *not* improving. Sickness still prevails to a fearful extent. The seeds of disease were sown in Miss. and are being fast developed here. This portion of the corps will be unfit for duty for some time.

The news from all points of the seat of war are most encouraging. A few years more will most probably wind up this rebellion.

F. Pettit.''

Written to:
Sister, Mary Ann

Camp Parke, Ky.,   August 20th 1863

"Dear Sister Mary,

I received your letter of July 30th and Aug. 7th last night. I was sorry to hear of your sickness but hope you will soon recover. I suppose the whole family will have the measles shortly. With proper care there is but little to fear from them. The accounts of the excitement produced by Morgan's raid causes much uneasiness here. It would have been rare fun for us to have seen the old farmers during the excitement.

The sickness still increases. Andrew Lary is quite low with an attack of intermittent fever. J.C. Stevenson has been sick for about a month.

I was greatly surprised by the news concerning the Normal. But I expected such would be the case when I left the school. Mr. Cooper was even then plotting against Mr. Thompson. You wished to know my candid opinion of Mr. C. as a man and as a teacher; and whether it would pay to expend time and money in attending a school under his direction. Morally I always considered Mr. C.'s character good. All men have their failings and his appeared to be a want of charity. He lacked even common Christian courtesy. His intellect is not of that class of which the great minds of our country are formed. He has not a mathematical mind, that is he cannot reason. His memory and will are very strong, but his reason and judgment very weak. As proof of his weakness of mind witness his blunt, boorish manners which I verily believe he considered the signs of a strong, original mind. Such a person should not be allowed to instill his principles into the mind of those who are expected to mold that of the persons who shall shortly form our society. Mr. Cooper knows enough but by his low bred, brutish manners he repels all who approach him to learn.

As to his faculty I would not consider myself (or you either) much benefited by reciting to them if they are all as well qualified as the representative from Lawrence Co. I would not expect to remain in the same class very long if they were my schoolmates. You now know my opinion of Mr. Cooper as a man and a teacher. It will not pay to attend the Normal if carried on as proposed. Mr. C. has had no experience and will shortly fail. Rest contented. Teach to the best advantage this winter and be ready to take advantage of affairs next spring.

Keep trace of Mr. Thompson if you can. I should be glad to write to him if I knew where to find him. Also try and find out how the school flourishes.

If the war is once over good schools will spring up, for there are many young men here who are determined to finish their education some day, if they reach home in safety. I do not consider it necessary to write more at present. If you wish to know more of my opinion write and I will answer.

Give my respects to all the friends. My health is very good.

> Your brother,
> Fred Pettit
> Co. C. 100th P. V."

Written to:
Sister, Mary Ann,

Camp Parke, Ky.,   August 25th 1863

"Dear Sister Mary:

I received your welcome letters of the 17th and 18th on the 20th inst. Nothing of importance has transpired since my last. We had some rain last night and this morning. Today is cloudy and quite cool.

The boys all have their blouses on and are hovering around the fire as though it was cold.

In my last letter I forgot to tell you that I sent twenty dollars home with Captain Critchlow. Father can get it by calling at his residence. I also sent my hymn book; it is of but little use to me here. I have a small book of soldiers' hymns give me by a member of the Christian Commission at Fredericksburgh. This is much lighter to carry.

I suppose our regiment will shortly be filled up again. There was a detail made last evening to go to Pittsburgh for the men to fill up. We need about 400 men. Just about one half the men who first enlisted are now in the regiment. The others have either died, been killed or discharged. None have been detailed [for the recruiting party] with who you are acquainted. I hope they will send us men from our own neighborhood.

The sick of our regiment are slowly recovering. A. Lary has been very low with an attack of the intermittent fever; but he is now slowly recovering. My health is good.

If we continue to be successful until winter, I think the war will be over by the time I serve my time out. Today makes one year since I left home. During that year I have seen an average of army life and find it no harder than I expected. My health is good and I am better contented than I was at home. I would not leave the army at present upon any considerations. It is just the place where every loyal able bodied man should be. The hardships of a soldier's life are half in imagination. If you must stand picket with the rain and snow freezing on you, thinking of your misery don't help it. And if at the same time you have nothing to eat but crackers and pork and sleep on the cold wet ground, complaining don't help it any.

Always keep cheerful and alls right. Those long, wet, cold nights we used to spend picketing on the Rappahannock last winter were some of the most fun provoking nights imaginable. For instance what better chance for a joke than when seated around a fire of green wood in an open field, the rain and snow coming down nicely and no shelter. The effect of smoke upon the eyes is exquisite. But upon the whole I like soldiering.

Tell Marg. to write if she has time. I have an old letter of hers not answered yet. Tell her to write again and I will try and reply. Tell Evan to write also. Letters of all kinds are quite welcome. I wish I had more of them.

> Your brother,
> Fred Pettit,
> Co. C. 100th P.V."

The Ninth Corps was now ordered to concentrate at Crab Orchard, Kentucky, prior to marching into East Tennessee. The 100th Pennsylvania left Camp Parke on August 28 and arrived at Crab Orchard on August 30 after a 30 mile march. The Ninth Corps remained here until September 10 preparing for the forthcoming campaign.

Written to:
Father, Nathaniel Pettit

Crab Orchard, Ky.   August 30th, 1863

"Dear father,

I received your letter of the 23rd inst. night before last at Camp Dick Robinson. We left Camp Parke near Nicholasville last Friday and arrived here today, having marched 30 miles in 3 days. This is very easy marching.

You told me how you spent last Sunday. Perhaps you would like to know how I spent this one. This morning we were waked up about 4 o'clock, ate our breakfast of hot coffee and crackers, packed up our blankets and tents and were on the march before sunup. We arrived here about 4 o'clock, put up our tents and have been sleeping, reading, and writing since. This evening we will perhaps have a short sermon by our Chaplain Mr. Browne.

You would be surprised to see the loads we carry. On this march I carried one woolen and one gum blanket, one piece shelter tent, pants, shirt, etc. all in my knapsack. My haversack weighed about 10 lbs. besides canteen, cartridge box, and gun. With this load I marched at the rate of 3 miles per hour.

The sick of the regiment are slowly recovering. A. Lary has been very sick but is getting better slowly. We left him in the hospital. I see John P. Wilson every few days. He is middling well. My own health still continues good.

What has become of all the drafted men? I am glad the Union League is so effectively organized. It is a thing very much needed. If this war is vigorously prosecuted I think it can be almost ended next summer. All depends upon the reinforcement of our armies. If the draft proves a failure our armies will fail to advance next spring. We must have men or fail.

Captain Critchlow is home on furlough. I sent $20 dollars with him which I suppose you have received by this time.

The country about our camp is quite hilly but middling good land. We are kept here as a reserve for a large force that has gone to eastern Tennessee. We may move soon and we may remain here for some time yet.

Your affectionate son,
F. Pettit.''

Written to:
Brother, Evan Pettit

Crab Orchard, [Ky.]   August 31st 1863

"Dear brother Evan,

I received your letter with father's and was glad to hear from you again. You must have worked pretty hard this summer. I suppose there will be no lack of linen (?) this year.

You wanted to know if I cooked my potatoes in my tin. We have half dozen camp kettles and three or four mess pans in our company. We do our cooking in these.

There are plenty of women around here of all kinds, big, little, ugly, pretty, good, bad, union, and rebel.

My boots are not quite worn out, but will be soon. The hot sun almost burned them up in Miss. They have been worn pretty well considering the hard usage. I should like to have another pair this winter but do not know whether I can get them or not.

Your brother,
Fred Pettit
Co. C., 100th P.V.''

Written to:
Sister, Mary Ann

Crab Orchard, Ky.,   September 6th 1863

"Dear sister Mary,

I received your welcome letter of the 31st ultimo today. It is Sunday and as I am at a loss for employment I will write you a few lines.

This morning we had inspection at nine o'clock. At these inspection we are required to have our brass, iron, steel, and leather all brightly polished. Our regiment is now in good condition in this respect. After inspection we had a short sermon by our chaplain Mr. Browne. The rest of the day we have to ourselves.

There is one thing observable in this part of the south as well as all other slaveholding parts, viz: the nonobservance of the Sabbath. I believe there are people here who do not know that the Sabbath is. The whole south is in this ignorant heathenish condition. It appears to me there was no other means of reaching the root of all this (Slavery) but through war and bloodshed. Slavery once rooted out (and it is now deadened) and this vast country will be opened to the influence of christianity. What a wide field will soon be opened for Christian labor. These masses of poor whites will need be to educated and christianized. The Negroes must be colonized sooner or later.

There is great danger of our armies being defeated this fall and next winter. The people of the North believe the war is almost over and are not reinforcing the army. The war is not over. The rebels have been whipped but not beaten and crushed. The only way to end the war soon is to reinforce the army and push the war forward. We must have 300,000 men by next spring or lose all we have gained.

The soldiers are all in good spirits. The health of the regiment is improving. A. Lary has come to the regiment [from the hospital] again. He is still getting better. John P. Wilson has the ague. My own health is good.

I am sorry to hear your picnic was disturbed.

Monday, Sept. 7th. There is nothing of importance to write. There are rumor of another move. I think we will move soon.

The school at Poland will no doubt be much better than normal now. If the war was over I should be glad to enjoy its advantages.

Do you intend to teach school this winter? I do not know anything more to write. If you have time I wish some of you would knit me a pair of army gloves and a pair of socks. You need not send them yet unless someone is coming out to the regiment. If no one is coming out I will find some other way to get them. Do not send anything until I tell you how and where to send it.

The days are quite hot but the nights are cool. Give my respects to all inquiring friends.

> Your brother,
> Fred Pettit
> Co. C. 100th P.V."

Written to:
Family

Laurel Co., Ky.,   Sept. 13th 1863

"Dear parents, brothers, and sisters,

I have received no letter from you since I wrote last, but as I may not have another opportunity soon I send you a few lines now. [SEE MAP #7]

We left Crab Orchard last Thursday the 10th for Knoxville, East Tenn. by way of Cumberland Gap. The first day we marched about 10 miles, and camped near Mount Vernon a small mountain hamlet. The second day we marched 15 miles camping at the foot of some lofty hills about 2 miles from Camp Wildcat. This is certainly one of the wildest places I ever saw.

The next day we marched about 10 miles and stopped about 11 a.m. 70 miles from Lexington and 45 from Richmond, Ky. We have lain over today Sunday to rest and sadly we needed it. We have not marched a great distance, only 35 miles in 3 days, but the road is the roughest and hilliest I ever saw. It is up the side of a mountain and down the side of a mountain etc.

Added to all this we carry eight days rations, or started with it, consisting of 8 pounds crackers, nearly 2 pounds sugar and coffee, and three days meat, say 3 pounds. I can tell you 5 lbs. crackers weighs down pretty heavy in a fellow's knapsack going up hill, and the hills are from 1 to 2 miles long in this country.

We move forward again in the morning. It is one hundred and fifteen miles to Knoxville yet and will take some time to go.

Write as usual. I will get your letters some day. In your next please send me some postage stamps.

We are paid today for 2 months. I will send some money as soon as I think it is safe. I am well and the rest are the same. We left A. Lary at Crab Orchard. He was getting better.

> Yours truly,
> Fred Pettit,
> Co. C 100th P. V."

The next letters describe the long and difficult march from Crab Orchard, Kentucky, to Knoxville, Tennessee. The journey started on September 10 with arrival in Knoxville on September 24.

Ambrose Burnside had long cherished his campaign into east Tennessee. During the Ninth Corps' absence in Mississippi, the newly formed Twenty-Third Army Corps was occupied with General John H. Morgan's raid into Kentucky and Ohio. After Morgan's repulse, Burnside decided to move without the Ninth Corps and by September 1 had occupied Kingston and then Knoxville, with movements in the direction of Loudon. The Federals then turned their attention to the Confederate forces at Cumberland Gap and were successful in capturing the Gap on September 9 along with 2500 Confederate prisoners. Thus, in a very short time, Burnside had succeeded in occupying most of east Tennessee and the important Cumberland Gap position. Efforts were now made by the Federals to move as far east as Abingdon, Virginia, while Burnside's cavalry would maintain contact with Rosecrans' cavalry as far west as Athens and Cleveland, Tennessee.[2]

---

[2] Major Henry S. Burrage, *Burnside's East Tennessee Campaign*, Military Historical Society of Massachusetts Papers, Boston, 1910, Volume 8. Burrage's paper fills the need for a well written, scholarly appraisal of the entire campaign.

Pettit's letters give a detailed account of the movements of the 100th Pennsylvania as they travelled on to Knoxville.[3]

Written to:
Family

Camp Near Cumberland River, Ky.,   Sept. 17th 1863.

"Dear parents, brothers, and sisters:

Last Monday we again resumed our journey and marched about 13 miles stopping about 1 P.M. We passed through New London the seat of Laurel Co. About noon we passed 2,000 rebel prisoners captured at Cumberland Gap. They were on their way north. They boasted much of being able to whip us yet they surrendered at the Gap without firing a gun.

Tuesday 15th we marched about 13 miles and camped near Barbourville on the Cumberland River. Wednesday we continued on up the Cumberland about 10 miles and reached our present stopping place about 10 o'clock A.M. We are about 5 miles from Cumberland ford and 19 from the Gap. Here the Cumberland is about the size of the Big Connoquenessing [Connoquenessing Creek is in Lawrence County and flows by Pettit's home, Hazel Dell]. Today we are lying over to rest our teams which are very much worn out.

During the last three days the road has not been so rough as it was before but from here to the Gap it is said to be very rough. Marching has not wearied me so much this week as it did last. I am becoming somewhat used to it and my load has become lighter being reduced from 8 to 3 days rations.

Our marching is much the same from day to day. We are roused at 3½ A.M., pack up, get our breakfast of coffee, crackers, and meat. At 5 o'clock we start our journey. We stop and rest about once an hour. If we have not reached our destination at noon we stop an hour or so to make coffee and then continue on.

It is said one brigade will stop at the Gap, one go to Kingston, and one to Knoxville so it is uncertain how far we will go yet.

Last Monday night we received another mail but it brought nothing for me. It brought word however of the marriage of E. E. Allison which greatly surprised me. May he and his betrothed live long and have much prosperity and happiness.

Last Tuesday a detail left this regiment to bring the conscripts to fill it up. A sergeant was sent from our company. I sent 20 dollars with him which he will send to father.

---

[3] For additional accounts and information on the 100th Regiment, see *Campaigning With The Roundheads*, Chapter 11. Morningside Press, 1989.

12 o'clock noon. I have an opportunity of sending this now. We will march again tomorrow I think. Write as usual.

F. Pettit
Co. C. 100th P.V."

Written to:
Family

Knoxville, Tennessee, September 25th, 1863.

"Dear parents, brothers, and sisters:

We left our camp on the Cumberland where I wrote last on the 19th [17th, previous letter]. On the 20th we reached Cumberland Gap, passed through it and camped 1 mile beyond. The Gap is a rough looking place. It is a low place in the mountains. On both sides the mountains rise very high and extend as far as I could see. The road leading up the mountain on the west is 1½ miles long. The one on the east is much shorter and steeper.

The next day we started at daylight and marched 18 miles almost east, crossed Powell's River and passed through Tazewell, the county seat of Clayborne Co. The next day 22nd we marched 21 miles waded Clinch and Holston rivers crossed Clinch mountain and a ridge of the Alleghenys and camped 1 mile from Morristown which is on the East Tenn. and Virginia railroad.

The next day 23rd we got on the cars and went to Greenville 35 miles north. We here found we were sent by mistake and should have gone to Knoxville 75 miles south. Stopped half an hour to make coffee and then started for Knoxville where we arrived the next morning about 4 o'clock. We remained at the station until about noon and marched about 1 mile above town and camped on the Holston river.

At last we are in Knoxville. Since the 10th of September we have marched 135 miles and [travelled] 110 by railroad [since leaving Crab Orchard]. This was a very important place to the rebels. It contains 3 car factories, foundries, etc. Burnside worked one month to make a road and get his army over the mountains south of Cumberland Gap. At least he succeeded and immediately dashed upon the railroad at Kingston away south of this, captured it, and then sent a mounted force away north of here and in that way captured 7 or 8 locomotives and a number of cars. These are now very useful to him in moving his troops.

We live mostly upon the country as there is plenty of grain, mills, and beef cattle here. We drew soft bread this morning baked in Knoxville. There is a large slaughter house near our camp, built for the rebels which is now run for our benefit. The mills, bakeries, and car factories are running for the government.

We are recruiting our army rapidly since we came here. At least 2,000 Tennesseans have enlisted in our army since Burnside came here. He bought arms and equipments to arm them as fast as they enlist. A large number of rebel prisoners and deserters have taken the oath and enlisted in our army. Everything works well and Burnside's great movement has been a great success so far.

The worst is when we get no news. We have plenty of rumors but nothing reliable. We are very anxious to hear from Meade. We hear he has been fighting.

I have had not letter from home since I left Crab Orchard. This is a very fertile country. My health is good. I have become so used to marching it tires me but little.

Fred Pettit''

With the Ninth and Twenty-Third Corps firmly established in east Tennessee, the Confederates were forced to consider measures to reopen the vital communication lines between Tennessee and Virginia. Bragg's army, reenforced by Longstreet's veteran corps from the Army of Northern Virginia, attacked Rosecrans and defeated him at Chickamauga on the 19th and 20th of September forcing the Federals into a siege situation in the city of Chattanooga. On September 27, Burnside was directed to hold his positions in east Tennessee, but send Rosecrans those troops he could spare. Accordingly Burnside sent White's division of the Twenty-Third Corps plus a cavalry force under Wolford to Loudon to strengthen communications with Rosecrans.

Burnside now began giving serious attention to arrangements for supplying his forces with food and clothing as the approach of winter was certain to increase the problems of logistics particularly with his long lines of communication from Kentucky through Cumberland Gap.

The Confederates did not remain idle but were determined to force Burnside out of Tennessee and with luck, destroy his somewhat isolated force. The results of this effort will be discussed in the following chapter.[4]

---

[4] Major Henry S. Burrage, *Burnside's East Tennessee Campaign*, Military Historical Society of Massachusetts papers, Boston, 1910, Volume 8.

CHAPTER EIGHT

THE EAST TENNESSEE CAMPAIGN

"I never felt more relieved in my life than when I found the rebel army gone."
December 5, 1863

General Braxton Bragg, commanding the Confederate forces besieging Chattanooga, decided to move against Burnside's forces in early November. Longstreet was ordered to push up the Tennessee River valley and attack Burnside. Longstreet protested this order, feeling that Bragg would be vulnerable in the event Grant moved against him and would have insufficient troops to successfully repel the Federals. Nevertheless, Bragg insisted the movement be made and Longstreet began it on November 4.

Longstreet had with him McLaws' and Hood's [under Jenkins] veteran divisions plus four brigades of Wheeler's cavalry. There were no finer infantry troops in the entire Confederate army than McLaws' and Hood's divisions. These consisted of several famous brigades who had assaulted the Army of the Potomac at the Peach Orchard and along the Emmitsburg, at Gettysburg on July 2nd, and moreover had successfully participated in the Battle of Chickamauga just a few weeks earlier in September.

Longstreet's orders were "to drive Burnside out of East Tennessee, first, or better, to capture or destroy him." Because transportation problems plagued Longstreet, it was not until November 12 that the last of his men were in Sweetwater. On that day, Burnside telegraphed Grant that he would endeavor to hold in check any Confederate troops moving against him until General George Thomas was ready to attack Bragg at Chattanooga.[1]

---

[1] William G. Gavin, *Campaigning With The Roundheads*, Morningside Press, Dayton, Ohio, 1989. Chapter 11.

Pettit continued writing home with frequency and his experiences are related in detail. [SEE MAP #8]

Written to:
Sister, Margaret

Near Knoxville, Tenn.   September 29th, 1863.

"Dear Sister Margaret,

I received your welcome letter of the 10th and 11th inst. last Sunday night and was very glad to hear from home once more. I was sorry to hear that father was so bad with the measles but hope he will soon be better. I sent a letter home last Saturday which would give you an account of our movements until our arrival at this place.

Last Sunday I attended church at the Baptist Church in Knoxville. The sermon was middling, the attendance small, one half soldiers. Knoxville is about as large as New Brighton [Pennsylvania town near Pettit's home in Hazel Dell] and Fallston.

Last Sunday evening we had orders to draw 5 days rations and be ready to march the next morning at 5 o'clock. The order was countermanded about midnight. At 3 o'clock that morning we were waked up very quietly and ordered to pack up and march without getting breakfast.[2] We immediately marched to the ferry on the Holston River on the east side of the town. Shortly after daylight we crossed the ferry, marched out one mile and took position on the brow of a hill with artillery in front. We remained in this position still.

We heard distant cannonading yesterday morning but all has been quiet since. A company of refugees from North Carolina came in this morning. They wish to enlist in our army. They report no enemy in the direction which they came.

My health is still good. I wish you could send me some papers. We get no news except by the mail. Send Pittsburgh papers and a *Star* or two.

Your brother,
Fred Pettit
Co. C 100th P.V."

[letter continued]

October 1st, 1863.

Shortly after writing the first part of this letter the regiment received orders to put up tents and make themselves comfortable. About the same time our company was sent on picket. I was on one of the

---

[2] This move was made to counter a Confederate force supposedly moving against Knoxville.

roads leading east from Knoxville. While we were on picket we sent in two squads of prisoners who were brought to our post by citizens. The first squad consisted of nine prisoners brought from Hook County by five citizens. They were mostly deserters from the rebel army and who had turned guerrillas against the union people of the state. The other squad was two deserters from Bragg's army who were on their way home. They were picked up by the home guards and sent in as prisoners. They said they were in the battle of Chattanooga [actually Chickamauga] about 10 days ago. They brought us the first reliable news from Rosecrans and Bragg. They say that there was 3 days hard fighting and that Rosecrans was driven back to Chattanooga. We get no news at all scarcely.

Everything from the north is hauled across the mountains from Nicholasville, Ky., a distance of 200 miles. There is no scarcity of provisions here. This is a very plentiful country. While we were on picket we had an abundance of biscuit, milk, and molasses. They raise a large quantity of cane in this country and they are just now manufacturing it into molasses.

Today it is raining and we have to stay in our houses. When we get used to it, it is not very hard for two persons to live in a shelter tent 4 feet high, 5 feet wide, and 6 ft. long.

My health is still good. The rest of the boys are all well. Write soon again. Address:

> Fred Pettit
> Co. C. 100th P.V.
> 1st Division, 9th Army
> Corps, Cincinnati, Ohio.''

Written to:
Sister, Mary Ann

Knoxville, Tennessee, October 17th, 1863.

"Dear sister Mary:

We have just returned from an expedition against the rebels in the northern part of the state, and I hasten to inform you of our safe arrival at this place again.

When I wrote to you on the 9th [letter not found] we were lying at the depot expecting to go north. We got on the cars a few minutes afterward and started. General Burnside accompanying us. We stopped at Rogersville Junction about 60 miles from Knoxville at dark. We here learned that the rebels were about 6 miles beyond and supposed to be from 10,000 to 15,000 strong. The cavalry and mounted infantry had several skirmishers but were repulsed.

The next morning the 10th we started at daylight. Four miles out we came up with the rest of our corps and a brigade of mounted men. The mounted men took the lead and soon came upon the enemy near Blue Springs. Skirmishing soon began and the enemy fell back on the hills beyond Blue Springs. The mounted men skirmished with them here until about 3 o'clock. Burnside then asked Gen. Shackleford[3] if his could not drive them. He said they could not. Burnside said he would soon send some men that could and ordered the 1st Division of the 9th Army Corps to move forward and drive the enemy from those hills.

We moved at once and formed line under fire of their skirmishers, the first and second brigades being in front and ours supporting at a distance of about 30 yds. In 15 minutes our lines were formed and we moved forward. The enemy were bold and defiant at first, daring our troops to move forward. The first and second brigades charged over the hill and into the woods and after a few volleys from their trusty rifles compelled the rebels to run in confusion. The gallant 1st division did not stop there but dashed on after them down into the hollow, over another ridge, into another hollow, and to the brow of the third hill.

Here they halted, being far in advance of either flank and immediately under the rebel cannon from which they were sheltered by a low hill. It was now sundown and the infantry firing ceased. The cannonading was kept up until dark. The rebel shell exploded very close to us and did some damage.

During all this time our brigade, the third, kept close behind the first and second. We were under fire all the time but were not engaged.

The rebels had about 5000 men mostly mounted and one battery. Several of our regiment were struck but none hurt seriously. I never saw them behave better under fire.

That night we lay in line of battle under the brow of the hill all night without any fires. Batteries were placed in position and every disposition made for a heavy battle on Sunday. In the morning everything being in readiness, skirmishers were sent out but to our surprise the enemy were gone. Not a man was to be found.

In about 15 minutes the cavalry were in hot pursuit and we followed rapidly. One brigade was sent several days before to get in their rear and prevent their escaping. They were in their rear but failed to stop them. Our cavalry overtook them about 12 miles out and skirmished with them all day. The rebels lost some wagons and a number of prisoners. Our loss in the fight was about 10 killed and 54 wounded. That of the enemy greater. We marched 20 miles on Sunday.''

---

3 James M. Shackleford, Brigadier General, commander of a cavalry division of the Twenty-Third Army Corps. Ezra J. Warner, *Generals in Blue,* Louisiana State University Press, 1964. Page 433.

[There is no signature block on this letter. This was the Battle of Blue Springs, Tennessee, fought October 10, 1863.]

Written to:
Brother, Evan

London [Loudon], Tenn.   October 25th 1863

"Dear brother Evan:

I received your welcome letter of the 10th and 12th last night and was glad to hear that you were all well again. I should be very glad to be at home to eat some of those apples and potatoes. They would be very acceptable now with our half rations of bread, coffee, and sugar.

Perhaps it would be very hard for you to appreciate the circumstances under which I received your letter. When I wrote last we were at Knoxville. We left that place last Tuesday and came to this place which is 29 miles almost south of Knoxville on the railroad. We marched it in two days stopping 4 miles above London [Loudon]. There was formerly a railroad bridge across the Holston River at this place but the rebels burned it. There is now a pontoon bridge here.

The rebels have threatened this place for some time. On Tuesday they surrounded Wolford's cavalry brigade 6 miles from here, captured 40 of his wagons, one battery, and about 200 prisoners.

Thursday evening we marched to the river, crossed on the pontoon and camped near the village. We found the troops here preparing for an attack. All remained quiet until yesterday when General Burnside came down early in the morning and we all expected something would be done soon. In the afternoon all our baggage, wagons, and some of the artillery were sent across the river and a large force of cavalry was sent to the front. We were ordered to pack up, stack arms and be ready to march at a moments notice.

About 4 o'clock cannonading was heard toward the front. We expected to be in a fight before night, but the cannonading came no nearer. The train continued to cross the river until long after dark reminding me very much of our retreat from Fredericksburg last winter. I fully expected to be back across the river this morning or to be engaged in a heavy battle. But neither of these things has happened yet.

It is now noon Sunday and we are still under marching orders. Report says the rebels have fallen back. I do not know how this is but we have heard no firing today.

Mr. Browne, our chaplain preached us a sermon this morning from Revelation 21:5.

Your brother,
Fred Pettit
Co. C. 100th P.V."

Written to:
Sister, Mary Ann

London, Tenn.   Oct. 25th 1863.

"Dear sister Mary,

I received your letter of the 12th inst. last night. I have written Evan nearly all the news. The weather has been very wet during the past week. The roads are muddy.

I hope you have received some letters from me from East Tenn. by this time. That money was necessarily delayed. It is all right now. Tell Mrs. Eliza Nye I see John Mcl. [McElwain?] every day or two. He is as well as usual. John P. Wilson has the ague again. I saw him yesterday. My own health is good.

I expect we will see enough soldiering if we stay in E. Tenn. this winter. Everything almost must be hauled nearly 200 miles over the mountains. The rebels keep us pretty busy.

Your brother,
Fred Pettit
Co. C. 100th P.V."

[letter continued]

November 10th, 1863.

"Captain Critchlow came back to the company the day before we left London [Loudon]. He brought me a pair of gloves and a pair of socks. They were much needed. The sender will accept my thanks for them.

Sergeant Bracken [Sergeant Elisha J. Bracken, Company C, killed in action at Spotsylvania, May 12, 1864] with whom I sent my money to Pittsburgh has returned to the company. On the way from us to Cincinnati he lost the book in which he had written father's address. He sent to the company for it but the letter had not reached him when he left home. He therefore left the money at home with orders to open the letter when it came and mail the money to the proper persons. I think it will reach its destination safely.

My health is good as usual. John P. Wilson is well. Bird [Phineas Bird] and Smiley [William Smiley] have been unwell but are better. John McElwain is well. I have not heard from Lary [Andrew Leary] for almost a month. He was then in the hospital at Crab Orchard. After we left that place he took the ague and was very low being delirious for some time. When the captain came through he was getting better. [All the soldiers mentioned in this paragraph were in Company C and were close friends of Pettit].[4]

---

[4] S. P. Bates, *History of Pennsylvania Volunteers*, Harrisburg, 1870, Volume 3, Pages 572-574.

The captain remained with us but two days and went back to Cincinnati on business.

Write regularly. Send some papers. News is very scarce from the north. Curtin's election and Vallandingham's defeat pleases us very much. We must have more soldiers. They must volunteer or be forced to come.

Fred Pettit
Co. C 100th P.V.''

Pettit's next letter, written December 6, 1863, gives details of the Battle of Fort Sanders, Knoxville, Tennessee, fought on November 29, 1863. In this attack, Longstreet's veterans of the brigades of Anderson, Wofford, Humphreys and Bryan were bloodily repulsed.

During the battle Pettit's 100th Regiment had only one company (A) in the fort. The balance of the regiment occupied an infantry trench leading from the left of Fort Sanders to the Kingston Pike.

His vivid first hand experiences and observations contribute to our knowledge of this segment of the Civil War history.

Written to:
Family

Knoxville, Tenn.   December 6th, 1863.

''Dear parents, brothers, and sisters,

We have just passed through the hardest experiences of a soldier's life. The siege of Knoxville which lasted eighteen days terminated yesterday. I suppose you have heard many rumors about the army in East Tenn. but I shall give you the facts as near as I can.

On the morning of the 14th of November the enemy were reported to be crossing the Tennessee river in large force on pontoons 4 miles below London. [Longstreet's offensive to drive Burnside from East Tennessee.] Everything was immediately in confusion and preparation made to leave for Knoxville immediately. Burnside came down early in the day and ordered the troops to face the enemy and the trains to start for Knoxville.

Seven companies of our regiment were detailed to guard the trains. Our company was one of them. Saturday the 14th was very wet and the roads very muddy and we only went 6 miles with the train. We reached Knoxville with the train on the 16th.

There was skirmishing with the enemy near Lenoir on both Saturday and Sunday. On Monday our forces commenced to fall back. The enemy pressed them closely and at Campbell's station 15 miles from here there was a sharp encounter. [In the Battle of Campbell's Station,

Companies A, D, and F, under Captain Thomas J. Hamilton, were the only companies of the 100th Pennsylvania involved in the combat[5].] Our troops held their ground until night and then fell back to this place. Our brigade here [Campbell's Station] lost 140 men. The rebels say their loss was 2000.

The next day Tuesday 17th we rejoined the brigade at the fort [Fort Sanders] west of the town. Everybody was soon busily engaged digging rifle pits. The enemy came in sight in the afternoon but were checked by Wolford's brigade one mile from the fort.

This hill was held during the night by Wolford's and Sanders' brigades of mounted troops.

The next day, the 18th, the enemy attempted to get possession of the hill which they did after three successive charges. The brave Colonel Sanders[6] was killed in this action. In consideration of his bravery the fort on the west of the town was called Fort Sanders. This is the only point the enemy have tried to carry and it was defended entirely by the 1st division of our corps.

The first brigade occupied the ridge between the fort and the river. The 3rd brigade, ours, was at the fort, our regiment on the left and the other regs. of the brigade on the right of it. The 2nd brigade was on the right of ours. The fort was garrisoned by the 79th N.Y. and Benjamin's battery, part of Buckley's Rhode Island, and part of battery L, 2nd N.Y. Artillery. [Company A, of the 100th Pennsylvania, was also stationed within the Fort as a part of the garrison.]

On the 19th the enemy's skirmishers came within gun shot of the fort and ours were about 400 yards from it. Things remained thus until Saturday Nov. 28th when our pickets were driven in. We lay on our arms all night. At daylight the enemy charged on the northwest corner of the fort with 11 regiments and was repulsed. They lost about 1000 men in this charge. We lost 46 men.

Things thus remained until yesterday when we found the enemy had gone. I have not time to write the particulars. Our company lost but one man, Phineas Bird, who was wounded in the head but is getting better.

I am well. I wish you would write soon. I will send you a full account of the siege as soon as I can. It is quite cold and we have suffered much but will soon be all right now.

The rebels have gone toward Virginia. They were commanded by Longstreet.

F. Pettit
Co. C 100th P.V.''

---

[5] William G. Gavin, *Campaigning With The Roundheads*, Morningside Press, Dayton, Ohio, 1989. Chapter 11.

[6] Brigadier General William Price Sanders graduated from West Point in 1856 and served in the U.S. Dragoons. He commanded the 1st Division of the Cavalry Corps under General Shackleford. He was mortally wounded on November 18 in checking Longstreet's advance on Knoxville. Ezra J. Warner, *Generals in Blue*, Louisiana State University, 1964, Pages 419 and 420.

Fred Pettit had time on Sunday, December 13, to compose a lengthy letter which gives a detailed account of his four weeks of activities around Fort Sanders at Knoxville. This letter was undoubtedly based on diary entries made during the period November 17 to December 15, 1863 based upon comparisons made with the surviving diary entries included as Appendix A.

Written to:
Family

Camp near Rutledge, Tenn.   Dec. 13th 1863.

"Dear parents, brothers, and sisters:

In my last I promised to give you some account of the siege of Knoxville. I will now try and do so.

We arrived at Knoxville about noon on the 16th [November] being train guards. We found everything in the greatest confusion. Everybody that could preparing to leave. Brownlow left the day before and his family were packing up. Government officials were all ready to leave at a moments notice. The wagon trains were all collected and prepared to be burned if necessary. The general impression was that everything would be destroyed and the troops fall back to the mountains.

On the night of the 16th the remainder of our division arrived and took position at the foot below town. During the day they had a heavy skirmish with the enemy about 15 miles below Concord. The loss on both sides was heavy.

Nov. 17th. Rejoined our brigade about noon. Negroes of the town and troops busy digging rifle pits. Great determination amongst the troops to hold the place. Enemy came in sight in the afternoon on the London road, but were checked by Wolford's and Saunder's brigades. I was sent out on picket at dark.

Wednesday 18th. Relieved from picket early. Enemy succeeded after three charges in driving in the cavalry. Col. Saunders was killed. Our troops fought well. The enemies loss was heavy. Their skirmishers came within gun shot of the fort in the evening. We lay on our arms all night.

Thursday 19th. Enemy drove in our pickets on the right. Lieutenant Reed [2nd Lieutenant Alvin M. Reed] of Co. D. wounded on the picket line. Two of the Mich. men wounded in the pits.

Friday 20th. Sent on picket before daylight. Brisk skirmishing between the pickets all day. Phineas Bird was wounded today. He was out as sharpshooter in a pit on the hill in the rear of the pickets. He was struck in the head wounding him seriously. In the evening a detachment of the 17th Mich. burned a house within the rebel lines.

Sat. 21st. Rained nearly all night and day. Relieved from picket before daylight. Wet, cold, and miserable. Our regiment moved to the left of the fort and put up tents. Enemies balls flew over the fort quite briskly. Two men wounded in front of it.

Sunday 22nd. Finished the rifle pit in our front. Two of the enemies shell burst over us but did no damage. Religious services by the Chaplain in the evening. Sent on picket at 9 p.m.

Mon. 23rd. On picket all day. Some firing as usual but nobody hurt. Pickets driven in on the right and a number of houses burned. Relieved from picket at 9 p.m. We afterwards learned that the enemy intended to attack us that night but did not on account of the light caused by the burning buildings.

Tuesday 24th. Rebels ran a rifle pit in front of our skirmishers last night. The 2nd Mich. charged on it and took it at daylight but could not hold it. They lost one half the men engaged. The enemy obtained a hold across the river today. Shackleford skirmished with them and took some prisoners.

Wed. 25th. A heavy skirmish across the river. Enemy driven some distance. Our fort was called Fort Saunders [Sanders]. Enemy fired two cannon shots at us but did no damage. Considerable cannonading from our side.

Thursday Nov. 26th. Ordered into the pits at daylight but nothing unusual took place. Thanksgiving service by the chaplain in the evening. Sent on picket at 8 P.M.

Friday Nov. 27th. Everything quiet on picket last night and today. Great commotion in the rebel lines this evening. Band playing and cheering. (Afterward learned that the rebels received reinforcements today.) Our rations were reduced to one quarter of a pound of bran bread and 1 lb. of meat daily to each man. No more coffee or sugar. Went on picket with nothing but some parched corn and a little meat.

Sat. 28th. Great activity amongst the rebels. Some cannonading last night. Enemy supposed to be planting a battery on the opposite side of the river.

Sunday, Nov. 29th. The rebels drove in our pickets about 10 o'clock last night. We tumbled into the ditches in a hurry. After waiting about 2 hours and no attack being made we were ordered out to drive the rebs back and reestablish our picket lines. We had scarcely formed when the pickets were driven in on the right and we were ordered back into the pits, where we remained until daylight.

Before daylight the enemy drove in the pickets on the left. At daylight our regiment was ordered out again to reestablish the picket lines, but we no sooner commended to form than they opened upon us with 6 guns at short range in front, 6 guns across the river, and 2 guns to the right of the fort. At the same time two brigades [actually

four brigades] of 11 [18] regiments charged upon the north west corner
of the fort. We of course tumbled back into the pits in a hurry.

The fort was manned by Benjamin's U.S. Battery 4 pieces 20
lb. parrotts, 2 pieces 10 lb rifled 2nd N.Y. Artillery, and 4 pieces 12
lb. smooth bore 1st Rhode Island Ar. and the 79th N.Y. reg., 4 cos.
29th Mass., 2 companies 20th Mich., 1 co. 2nd Mich., and 1 co. 100th
P.V. Co A of our regiment was in the fort and hotly engaged.

The enemy rushed up with great bravery. The cannoneers had
time to fire but one round until they were driven away. Lieutenant Benjamin picked up a shell in each hand, ordered one of his men to light
the fuses with matches and then threw them over into the ditch where
the rebels were crowded as thick as they could stand. This he did twice.
One rebel color sergeant climed up the parapet, stuck his flag and called
upon his comrades to come on. He was instantly shot down by an officer of Co. A. As fast as they climbed to the top of the parapet they
were shot down by our men. This lasted about 2 hours when the rebels
gave up the attempt. Many of them were afraid to go back and were
taken prisoners. All this time the shell flew like hail on our side of the
fort, but Providentially no one was hurt.

About noon a flag of truce was sent out for the purpose of carrying off the wounded. One hundred and fifteen dead were carried from
the corner of the fort, and a large number of wounded. Our loss in
killed and wounded and prisoners was 46 men. The enemies about 1000.
The prisoners said there were 50 artillerymen detailed to turn the guns
of the fort upon us when they drove us from it. We took 3 stand of
colors in the ditch of the fort. Thus ended the attempt to take Fort
Saunders by a charge.

Monday Nov. 30th. Sent on picket at 5 o'clock this morning.
Very cold. Rebel pickets about 150 yds from us. Had nothing to eat
but parched corn and meat. Relieved at 7 p.m. One third of the regiment in the pits all night.

Tuesday, December 1st. On watch in the pits last night from
3 A.M. to 6. Nine hearty cheers ordered by Burnside for Grant's victory [Chattanooga]. Wed. 2nd. on watch last night from 12 to 3. Rebels
seen moving up the river. Worked on the fort until midnight. Troops
up nearly all night expecting an attack, but none made. Reinforcements
reported coming from Grant.

Thurs. 3rd. Heard cannonading to the westward. Some cannonading here but no reply by the enemy. Warm and pleasant.

Friday, Dec. 4th. Roused twice last night by pickets firing. On
watch in the pits from 3 to 6. Rebels made a great show of force in
our front today. One brigade of cavalry arrived last night from Grant.
Report large reinforcements coming. Sent on picket at 7 P.M.

Saturday Dec. 5th. The Rebel Pickets were withdrawn from our
front at one o'clock this morning. Their position was reconnoitered

and the whole army found gone. I never felt more relieved in my life than when we found the rebel army gone. Thank God for this deliverance was the emotion of my mind.

We rested until Monday and then started in pursuit up the river marching 12 miles that day, 7 the next, and 12 the next, and camped near Rutledge where we are at present. We drew full rations of flour and meat yesterday for the first [sic], sugar and coffee have not yet arrived but we expect them soon. We need clothing very much. We have received no mail since Nov. 1st. My last letter is dated Oct. 31st. My health has been good. Bird was doing well last I heard.

F. Pettit

[letter continued]

Dec. 14th. We have seen hard time in East Tenn. Yet we do not complain. We believe it has all been necessary and for that reason we have been willing to endure it. This war is not over yet neither are its hardships. Are we to be compelled to bear them alone? We are willing to do our duty. But month by month disease thins our ranks and every skirmish or battle carries off some of our bravest men. Our ranks are becoming thin but we are not discouraged. Will the athletic sons of the north prefer the ease and comfort of home to their duty to their country? Shame, a burning shame I say rests on those who do. They can never look up manfully and say 'I did my duty.'

F.P.

[letter continued]

Tuesday Evening Dec. 15th 1863. We are now lying near Rutledge. I am well. A mail is in but this goes out before I get it. I expect a letter from home in it. John P. Wilson is well. I saw him today. Write as usual.

F. Pettit
Co. C. 100th P.V."

The Confederates under Longstreet left Knoxville on the night of December 4. With the realization that Grant was sending strong reinforcements from Chattanooga, they wisely moved up the Holston River valley to Blaine's Cross Roads. From there, they shortly moved on to Rogersville some 65 miles from Knoxville.

After a short rest, the 100th Regiment left Knoxville on Monday, December 7 and in three days' march were at Rutledge, Tennessee, 30 miles from Knoxville. Here the Ninth Corps assembled and awaited further moves from Longstreet.[7]

---

[7] William G. Gavin, *Campaigning With The Roundheads*, Morningside Press, Dayton, Ohio, 1989, Chapter 11. Details on the movements and locations of the 100th Pennsylvania in December 1863 are discussed in detail in this work.

Written to:
Family

Camp near Blanes [Blaine's] Cross Roads, Tenn.
Dec. 25th 1863.

"Dear parents, brothers, and sisters:

I suppose that you are busy today eating your Christmas cakes, Christmas dinner, and all the other good things which old Christmas is supposed to bring. Well, I hope you will have a good time and enjoy this Christmas very much.

Perhaps you would like to know how we are spending our Christmas in the army. Last night I was on picket and caught a bad cold and as you may suppose do not feel very funny. Last year I think I told you I had a mess of beans and pork for a Christmas dinner. This year I am not so fortunate. We have been furnished nothing but a small piece of boiled beef. But our sutler came up last night and we obtained a few crackers, a little cheese, and butter. But what do you think the price is? Crackers 50 cts. per lb., cheese 50 cts. per lb., and butter 80 cts. At these rates you can easily see what a dinner costs us.

Perhaps you say we need not buy them. Well, standing picket all night and making your breakfast and dinner on a small piece of boiled beef without any bread does not go well when you have money in your pocket. For the last month we have had but one fourth to one half rations of bread stuff. Last winter we thought it hard to live on full rations. If matters continue this I fear I cannot send you much more money. A soldier must live.

My clothing is the worst I ever had at this time of the year. My toes stick through both my shoes and everything else is in about the same condition.

Perhaps you think we are discouraged and complaining. Not at all. Far from it. This army is now in far better spirits than the Army of the Potomac was at this time last year with plenty of rations and good clothing. We have beaten the enemy and feel confident of being able to do so still.

We know that it is impossible to get supplies here fast enough for so large an army and therefore we do not complain.

There is much talk of reenlisting again. I think a number of our regiment will reenlist. This shows perhaps our opinion of the war better than I can express it.

Since I wrote last we have fallen back about 13 miles toward Knoxville where we are now encamped. I have received all letters sent me up to Dec. 1st.

We are all well. Write soon.

Fred Pettit
Co. C 100th P.V.

[letter continued]

December 27 1863

Well, Co. C have reenlisted and will no doubt be in Pa. within a month. The terms of enlistment are these:

All regiments having less than one year to serve may reenlist for 3 yrs., or the war, to date from Nov. 1st 1863. They will receive $100 bounty when mustered out and $402 when mustered in again, and also at least thirty days furlough. If a company reenlist, or three fourths of it, they may be sent to their state, get a furlough of at least 30 days and then remain in the state to recruit their full number.

We have about 30 men reenlisted which is more than ¾ of our company. The only ones from our neighborhood are Smiley [William], Weyman [Ernest Weyman], and Marshall [John C.]. [Editor's note: All three men survived the war.] I will reenlist if I can. Bird and Lary are in the hospital and of course cannot go. [Editor's note: Bird did not reenlist. Andrew Leary did.]

The reasons for reenlisting are that the war will be over in less than 3 yrs. and we wish to finish what we have begun. There but few in the company but will reenlist. The furlough promised within three months and perhaps immediately. Bird was doing well a few days ago. I have not heard from Lary for sometime.

[letter continued]

January 3rd 1864

The new year has been extremely cold thus far. Our regiment has reenlisted for three years. We will start for Cincinnati in 8 or 10 days. I think we will reach Pa. in a month. J.P. Wilson has reenlisted. J. McElwain has not.

We are all well. You need write no more letters to me until further orders. The last I received was dated Nov. 30th.

The weather is very cold. Provisions and clothing scarce as usual.

> Yours,
> Fred Pettit."

This was the last letter Pettit wrote home before going back to Pennsylvania with the regiment on veteran furlough. The reenlistment program was largely successful as only 27 men refused to sign for the additional three year term.[8] On December 28 the 100th Pennsylvania was sworn into Federal service for an additional term of three years. The men were now veteran volunteers and their regimental designation was the 100th Pennsylvania *Veteran* Volunteer Infantry.

---

8 Major James H. Cline, letter, "Bivouac near Blaine's Cross Roads, Tenn., December 21st 1863, 9 o'clock." Historical Collections and Labor Archives, McDowell Collection, Pennsylvania State University, University Park, Pennsylvania. For more details see Chapter 12, William G. Gavin's *Campaigning With The Roundheads*.

The regiment did not actually leave Tennessee for home until January 12, 1864. The time spent in December and January at Blaine's Cross Roads was considered by the soldiers as their "Valley Forge". Rations were almost non-existent, and local food supplies had been exhausted. Clothing was worn out and many of the Roundheads were without shoes. Nevertheless, they departed with a great deal of enthusiasm for the long march over the mountains and on to Pennsylvania on the 12th. The snow-covered roads over the mountains into Kentucky were extremely difficult at this time of year. On January 22, the regiment arrived at Camp Nelson where a short break was taken and new clothing and blankets were issued to replace the tattered outfits. After a delay of 11 days in Cincinnati, due to payroll administrative problems, the regiment proceeded to Pittsburgh where the long awaited furlough began on Sunday, February 7.[9]

The regiment was directed to reassemble at Camp Copeland, Pennsylvania [Pittsburgh area] beginning on March 8. Apparently the furlough policy was a liberal one for many of the veterans did not report to Copeland until March 22. By late February, many new recruits for the regiment were assembling there as the regiment was to be brought up to full strength before entering the spring campaigns of 1864.

There are no details on Pettit's activities while on furlough, but they undoubtedly were similar to most of the others in the regiment. Parties, visits with friends, perhaps a little hunting, and just plain eating and relaxing filled the time at home which passed all too quickly.

Pettit wrote one letter from Camp Copeland on March 15, just prior to the departure of the regiment for the Ninth Corps assembly point at Annapolis, Maryland.

Written to:
Family

Camp Copeland, Pa.   March 15th 1864.

"Dear parents, brothers, and sisters:

Well, we are still in camp Copeland in the midst of the mud, cold, and wet. The fact is we might as well have remained at home all this time. A great many of the regiment have been home again and are just getting back. Wm. Smiley just now came in. Our recruits have just been transferred to the regiment.

Last night an order was issued ordering every man to remain in camp, and that the recruits be drilled 4 hours daily. We are having as good a time as could be expected under the circumstances. Johnston Wilson came up yesterday and remains with us until tomorrow. He brought a great many things for John and David [his sons, John P. and David W. Wilson], amongst other things a fat chicken which we cooked for dinner and it was pronounced excellent.

---

9 William G. Gavin, *Campaigning With The Roundheads*, Morningside Press, Dayton, Ohio, 1989, Chapter 12.

We get plenty of good soft bread, pork, coffee, and sugar. We have what is called the wedge or A tent. We are messed 4 in a tent. Hege [James], Wilsons, and I are in one. David has not been well for a few days but is better.

It is very uncertain how long we will stay here. I think we would be better contented if we were farther from home. Do you miss us any at home? I believe we are just as fond of home as ever we were.

Quite a number of the boys employed an assistant to shave their joys and sorrows while they were at home, and a great many more formed an acquaintance that may lead to something more serious when this cruel war is over if we should be spared.

Write when convenient. Direct to Co. C. 100th P.V., Camp Copeland, Pa.

My health is very good and I was never better contented in my life.

> Fred Pettit
> Co. C. 100th P.V."

Rumors concerning the regiment's next destination were prevalent. Annapolis, Maryland, was the most discussed location, and for once the rumors were correct. The last of the regiment arrived in Camp Copeland on March 22 and the next day, the troops entrained for Baltimore, and then on to Annapolis, Maryland, the designated Ninth Corps rendezvous point on March 25.[10] From here, the Corps rejoined the Army of the Potomac for the momentous "Virginia Campaign of 1864".

---

[10] William G. Gavin, *Campaigning With The Roundheads*, Morningside Press, Dayton, Ohio, 1989, Chapter 12.

CHAPTER NINE

ANNAPOLIS TO COLD HARBOR
MARCH — JUNE 1864

"...and to fall back without orders was what we never did."
Spotsylvania assault, May 12, 1864.

The 100th Pennsylvania spent nearly one month in Annapolis as Burnside was organizing and rebuilding the Ninth Army Corps up to full strength. Preparations for the forthcoming campaign continued throughout the month and Pettit had ample leisure time to write several letters to various members of the family. On April 23, the regiment departed from Annapolis for Virginia and the front.

Written to:
Father

Camp of the 100th Annapolis, Md., March 31st '64

"Dear father:

It is now some time since I have heard from home but I hope your letters will soon be along. We left Camp Copeland on the 23rd of this month, on the cars going eastward. We arrived opposite Harrisburg the next day about 9 o'clock. We did not cross the river to the city, but after waiting a couple of hours we went on to Baltimore where we arrived in the evening. After marching to the other depot we stacked arms and went to supper in the Union Relief Association's rooms. This Association furnishes meals and lodgings to soldiers free of expense. It is now under control of a delegation from Massachusetts.

After supper we marched into the depot buildings and slept until morning. Took breakfast at the Relief rooms. About 10 o'clock we marched to the wharf and got aboard the steamboat *Columbia*. At 11 o'clock we started for Annapolis where we arrived about 3 P.M. After landing we marched out about 2 miles to Camp Parole and quartered for the night in the barracks. The next day being Sunday we still remained in the barracks.

This camp is where the paroled prisoners from Richmond are kept. There are quite a number here now and about 200 more came in day before yesterday.

The camp is a very good one and is kept in excellent order. It contains a chapel and reading room. The reading room is well supplied with books, pamphlets, and papers. It is a very pleasant place to spend a few hours.

Sunday morning I attended prayer meeting and in the afternoon heard two sermons in the chapel. Monday we marched out about 1 mile from Camp Parole and put up our camp. It is about 1 mile from Annapolis. The location is very good, the ground is sandy, and will never get muddy. We have what are called A tents. They are about 7 ft. square and the same height in the center. There are 5 men or boys in each tent.

We commenced drilling today — two hours in the fore and two hours in the afternoon. We now have 100 men in our company 69 of whom are present. P. Bird came up yesterday. His wound has healed up and he talks of reenlisting. David Wilson was sick but is well again. He is with us. We left Hege [Charles M. Hege] at Camp Copeland. By mismanagement he was not paid off and so was not turned over.

We are all well. There is a large force gathering here for the 9th Army Corps. There are several regiments of negroes amongst them and one company of indians.

I should be very glad if you would write to me soon. Direct to Co. C., 100th P.V. 9th A.C., Annapolis, Md.

Did you make payment of that note? Did you borrow how much? What do the people think of the new call for troops? Who were elected township officers in Wayne Tp.?

> Your affectionate son,
> Fred Pettit.''

Written to:
Sister, Margaret

> Camp of the 100th P.V. Annapolis, Md.   April 3, '64.

"Dear Sister Margaret:

I received your very kind letter last Friday. On the same day I mailed one to father. I was surprised to hear that Mary had gone to

Poland [Ohio]. I did not think she intended to go to school this spring. What are you doing? Still working at home, are you? Despise not the day of small things.

Has Evan selected any trade yet? Tell him to write to me. I am sorry to inform the girls of Hazel Dell that Hege is not with us yet. Through some neglect he was left in Camp Copeland. Our company is now full and I suppose he will be put in some other company.

[letter continues]

Monday, April 4th 1864.

Our new chaplain Mr. Dixon [Chaplain Robert Dickson replaced Chaplain R.A. Browne in March 1864 and then resigned in October 1864] preached us two very good discourses yesterday. He is a Presbyterian minister of the Old School and a Scotchman.

Yesterday afternoon John R. Evans and John McElwain came to the regiment. They are both well. J.R. Evans looks much better than when we saw him in Cincinnati. P. Bird has reenlisted. He thinks he can stand the service yet.

We are having a splendid time here. Our recruits are learning rapidly, though some of them are very awkward.

There is a large force gathering here that will be heard from some day. I do not know Mr. Hart [Sergeant John C. Hart, later 1st Lieutenant] of Co. D. Why do you inquire?

Give my respects to the friends.

> Your brother,
> Fred Pettit
> Co. C. 100th P.V."

Written to:
Sister, Mary

Camp of the 100th P.V., Annapolis, Md., April 7, 1864

"Dear sister Mary:

I received your letter of the 1st inst. yesterday and was very glad to hear from you. I was much surprised to hear from home that you had gone to Poland as I did not think you intended going to school this summer. Now I wish I could be with you but a more important duty than self interest prevents me. But still this army life is not all lost in the cultivation of the mind. A person cannot slide along here and have nominally a good character by keep aloof from vice; but he is compelled to see and hear of vice daily and hourly in its most hideous forms. Vice is not practiced in the army in secret but openly and discussed as an every day occurrence. Added to all this is the ennui and weariness caused by camp life which causes a person naturally to incline to vice. A person who withstands all these influences will certainly not come out of the contest weakened in moral principle.

I was very much pleased to receive your photograph. I shall preserve it carefully. There is no person in Co. D. by the name of J.C. Hart. [There is a John C. Hart, on the regimental roster in Company D.] There is a J. Sehart in Co. D. whom I know very well. He lives near Darlington, I think, and is now home recruiting. Why do you wish to know? I suppose the furloughs are stirring up some fun. I know some such cases already. Wonder if Minerva and her mother have found that J. P. W. [John P. Wilson?] is engaged yet? Does not Loo Wilson think a good deal of Hege? She writes some fun about him always.

We have a splendid camp about 1 mile from Annapolis. We are busy drilling. J.R. Evans and J. McElwain came here on Sunday. They look well. We are all well. The old 9th Corps will soon be on a war footing again. We have several negro regiments here. Recruits are coming daily.

P. Bird is with the regiment and has reenlisted. We are having a splendid time here.

Give my respects to Mr. Thompson and family and all other friends that may be there.

> Your brother,
> Fred Pettit
> Co. C 100th P.V."

Written to:
Family

Camp of the 100th P.V. Annapolis, Md.   Apr. 11 '64

"Dear parents, brothers, and sisters:

There is so little of importance going on here at present that I have but little to write. The weather which is always the first thing to talk about, is changeable. One or two days clear and warm and then the same number of rainy days. But we have one great advantage here in wet weather; the ground never gets muddy. The soil is nearly all sand and soon dries.

We have a beautiful drill ground in front of our camp. It is a dry level field containing about 12 acres. When it does not rain we drill four hours daily. We now have a very good tent having bought boards and put a floor in it. There are six in our tent. Two Wilsons, J.R. Evans, Samuel H. Cleeland (Mortally wounded at Spotsylvania), John Alexander (Mortally wounded at Cold Harbor) both from Portersville, and I. [Editor's note. Only three out of the six mentioned survived the war.] We are getting along finely.

Davy Wilson is beginning to look as hearty as ever I saw him and as full of mischief. We have another fellow (Cleeland) in our tent about his size. They are gay ones.

Last Saturday General Burnside stopped here a few hours and rode round to see the troops. We cheered him heartily and he seemed much pleased. All our corps is now here from Tennessee. I saw J. McElwain yesterday. He is well as usual. . He received one pair of socks his mother send him. A. Lary is still shaking with the ague once in awhile. The rest of us are all well.

Yesterday (Sunday) our chaplain preached us two short sermons: one in the forenoon and one in the evening. Our chaplain seems to be an excellent man and a good preacher.

I hear that Jordan C. Nye is in our country again. What is he doing there?

Poor Hege. I wonder what has become of him. He is not here.

I received a letter from Mary last week. She was well. How did Scott get along with his school? How are you getting along with your spring work? Are they talking of starting any Sabbath Schools about there this summer?

Some of you try and write soon if you have time.

> Fred Pettit
> Co. C. 100th P.V.''

Written to:
Brother, Evan

[No place given. Undoubtedly Annapolis, Md.] April 17, 1864.

"Dear brother Evan,

I was glad to see some of your writing at the end of father's letter. I think that foot of yours is very unfortunate or else you use that ax very carelessly. But I hope you will soon be able for duty again.

Mr. Hege came to us last Thursday but as our company was full he was obliged to go to Co. K of our regiment. [Charles M. Hege received a medical discharge on January 14, 1865.[1]] He is well. You can tell all the Hazel Dell girls if they wish to correspond with him letters will find him in Co. K of our regiment.

We get plenty of provisions now. Soft bread, pork, bacon, beef (salt and fresh) beans, rice, potatoes, sugar, and coffee.

Davy Wilson is getting along first rate. Hege can eat hard tack and pork I guess. We have the best time here we have ever had since I came to the army. We get very lonesome between drills and on wet days.

---

[1] Samuel P. Bates, *History of Pennsylvania Volunteers*, Harrisburg, 1870, Volume 3, Page 595.

I bought an Algebra the other day and John and I study it to pass the time away.

J. McElwain is well and J.R. Evans is the same. Write again when you have time.

> Your brother,
> Fred Pettit."

Written to:
Father.

Camp of the 100th P.V.   Annapolis, Md.   Apr. 18th '64

"Dear father,

I received your very kind letter of the 10th inst. yesterday and was glad to hear that you were well. I was surprised to hear that J.C. Nye was in your neighborhood though I heard it before you wrote. I think such ministers as Nye, Moffet, and some other do more harm than good. They have a zeal but not after knowledge. Some of their preaching is sound enough as far as it goes; but through their ignorance and bigotry they fail to produce that lasting effect which they should.

I suppose there is no hurry about that note so it is lifted when due.

The weather has been quite wet since we came here though not very cold.

We are busy drilling and getting ready for the field. There are about 900 men in our regiment and more coming. Our company has about 100 men about 80 of whom are present. We have no arms for our recruits yet. [Editor's note: The regiment was about to enter upon active campaigning, and the recruits, although with the regiment since February, were still unarmed and without marksmanship training. This inexcusable situation would result in disgraceful and needless losses in the weeks ahead.]

Last Wednesday Lieutenant General Grant and Major General Burnside reviewed all the troops at this place. Lieutenant Gen. Grant if not a good looking officer is a determined looking man.

Most of the colored regiments that were here have been sent to South Carolina.

It is very uncertain where we will go. Most probably to the Army of the Potomac. [This was an accurate guess.]

We are all well except J.P. Wilson who has the ague and mumps.

There is so little of importance taking place here now that I have but little to write. I should be glad to hear from you again when you have time to write.

> Your affectionate son,
> Frederick Pettit
> Co. C. 100th P.V."

Written to:
Sister, Margaret

   Camp of the 100th P.V. near Alexandria, Va.   April 26th, 1864.

"Dear sister Margaret:

   I received your welcome letter of the 17th last Saturday while
on the march. We left Annapolis last Saturday morning and reached
here last night, Monday. The distance is about 50 miles and considering
everything the march was a very hard one and we are all very tired.
   We were ordered to move again this morning at six o'clock but
it is now almost noon and we have not moved yet. We were obliged
to throw away our overcoats as they were too heavy to carry.
   The weather is quite warm. I sent a few books with some of J.R.
Evans's things by express. We are all well. The boys stood the march
as well as could be expected. There is a large force lying here now.
   We expect to leave today or tomorrow for the Army of the
Potomac. Tell Cyrus [brother, age 16] I was very glad to get his letter
and will answer it as soon as I have time.
   Direct your letters to Washington, D.C. I have not time to write
much now.

                              Your brother,
                              Fred Pettit
                              Co. C 100th P.V."

   The long awaited campaign was underway. There was little time for letter writing and the regiment was engaged in two major battles, Wilderness and
Spotsylvania, before Pettit had time to write home again.
   After leaving Alexandria, the 100th followed the railroad to Bealton Station, and then followed the army over the Rapidan River to the Wilderness.
On May 6, Leasure's brigade, of which the 100th was a part, were heavily
engaged in repulsing Lee's massive assault on Hancock's Brock Road position
on the afternoon of May 6. [SEE MAP #9][2]
   On May 12 the 100th Regiment received its worst casualties [135 killed,
wounded, or missing] of the entire war during their frontal assault on Confederate fortified lines at Spotsylvania. [SEE MAP #10] It was during this battle that Colonel Daniel Leasure, the founder of the regiment, was wounded and
was never active in field command again.
   Pettit's next letter is from the trenches in the Ninth Corps sector of the
Spotsylvania battlefield.

───────────────

   [2] William G. Gavin, *Campaigning With The Roundheads*, Morningside Press, Dayton, Ohio, 1989. Chapters 13
and 14 give detailed accounts of the 100th Pennsylvania regiment in both battles of the Wilderness and at Spotsylvania.

Written to:
Parents

                    Near Spottsylvania Court House   May 16th 1864.

"Dear parents,

        I have time to write but a few lines. We were in the heavy battle
of the Wilderness and at this place. We lost 26 men of our company.
None from our neighborhood. J.P. Wilson is sick at Fredericksburgh.
S.A. White was wounded. [Samuel A. White was transferred to the
Veterans Reserve Corps January 15, 1865.[3]]
        The rest of us are all well. Three of our company were killed
and 23 wounded. We are still in the front on the late battlefield. Do
not be uneasy about us.
        A kind hand guides us and watches over us. Our trust is in God.
        I will write as often as possible. Write as usual though we get no
mail now. D. Wilson, A. Lary, and J.K Evans are well. J. McElwain
was left at Alexandria sick.

                            Your son,
                            Fred Pettit
                            Co. C 100th P.V.

[P.S.] J. C. Stevenson was wounded. The battle was heavy."

        There was a slight break in the action when the 9th Corps was shifted
to the extreme left of the Federal line near the Quesenberry house on May 19.
They remained here for two days. Their stay gave the men the opportunity to
recuperate from the incessant fire endured in the front lines from the 12th until
the 19th. Pettit took the opportunity to write two letters. He gives accurate and
graphic descriptions of the last two battles.

Written to:
Parents

[Spotsylvania Court House, Va.] "Friday Evening, May 20th 1864.

"Dear parents:

        Supposing that you are anxious to hear from us I thought I
would write a few lines this evening. This is the first day of rest we
have had since we crossed the Rapidan which was on the 5th of May.

---

3 Samuel P. Bates, *History of Pennsylvania Volunteers,* Harrisburg, 1870, Volume 3, Page 572.

On the 6th we were engaged in the battle of the Wilderness. We had but one man wounded in our company but lost several in the regiment. Our brigade was sent in the morning to Hancock's assistance on the left and we helped to repulse the rebels last desperate charge on that part of the lines. [Editor's note: Four of the several Confederate brigades in this massive Confederate assault were ones involved on November 29th, 1863, in Longstreet's attack on Fort Sanders, Knoxville, Tennessee. All four brigades were veteran troops who had been fully engaged at Gettysburg the previous July. They were considered amongst the elite of the Army of Northern Virginia.]

The musketry was the most terrible I suppose ever heard. At least 30,000 muskets were being fired constantly for 1 hour and 40 minutes. We had three lines of breast works. The rebels charged with about 30,000 men and lost heavily. Our loss was small. But little artillery was used.

On the night of the 7th we marched to near Chancellorsville and remained in that vicinity until the morning of the 9th when we marched toward Spotsylvania Court House and were the supporting division in driving the enemy to that place. Here we remained until the 12th entrenching and skirmishing some all the time with the enemy. General Stevenson [Brigadier General Thomas G. Stevenson was killed in action before Spotsylvania Court House, May 10, 1864] commanding our division was killed here on the 9th [Morning of the 10th] by a stray shot.[4]

On the morning of the 12th at daylight our whole corps advanced against the enemy in front of Spotsylvania Court House. In a few hours we had driven the enemy to their rifle pits. Our lines were now so extended that we had but a single line of battle in front of their works. To attempt to carry those works with a single line was simply impossible.

Our regiment lay in a thick pine woods about 300 yards from the enemy's rifle pits losing heavily from their sharpshooters. About noon our regiment was ordered to advance. We did so driving the enemy's skirmishers before us. We soon came in sight of their rifle pits just over the crest of a ridge about 30 yards in front of us. [Editor's note: Actually this was a heavily entrenched defensive position covered in front with slashing and well manned. It was part of Heth's Salient in the Confederate defensive line. The front of the regiment's assault is estimated at 200 yards giving little depth to the attack. The slashing made the position practically impenetrable.] We immediately opened fire upon them and they did the same. We could see nothing but the flash of their guns while they could see us plainly as we had no protection at all. Men were being killed and wounded faster than you could count them. Yet no one flinched until we were ordered back.

---

[4] For more details on Stevenson's death, see *Campaigning With The Roundheads*, Chapter 14.

After falling back we formed again where we were [had been] before charging. All day we continued to lose heavily from the fire of their sharpshooters. That night we built breast works and remained in the same position until the morning of the 19th when we evacuated the position and moved about 3 miles to the left. [Vicinity of the Quesenberry house.]

Last night we were digging rifle pits until 11 o'clock and finished this morning at daylight. There was no enemy within gun shot of our front today and we rested.

We have lost 27 men of our company since the 5th of this month. Three killed and 24 wounded. S. A. White was wounded. He was the only one from our neighborhood. J. P. Wilson is sick and at the hospital. Lary, Wilson, Pence [William R. Pence], and Hege are well. My health is good.

I have not heard from you for a month or more. Our regiment has lost about 200 men killed and wounded since we came to Va.

> Your son,
> Fred Pettit
> Co. C. 100th P.V.

[P.S.]. Let us not be uneasy about what may happen to us here but put our trust in God. This fighting will last until the war is decided. As long as we live right we can do our duty without fear.

J. R. Evans is on cattle guard. He was well when I saw him last.

War is a sober thing and a soldier needs something more than mere courage to support him. Reading the Bible never seemed to afford me so much comfort as it does now. The only pleasant thing here is we have plenty to eat. There is fighting every day. Some of our recruits are *not* so brave here as they were at home!''

Written to:
Sister, Mary Ann, Poland, Ohio.

[Spotsylvania Court House, Va.] Saturday May 21st 1864.

"Dear sister:

Supposing that you have heard of the late movements in Virginia you are doubtless anxious to hear what part our regiment has taken in them.

We left Bealton Station on the 4th of May and marched to the Rapidan. The next day we crossed at Germania Ford [Germanna] and lay near it all day. On the morning of the 6th we marched to support Hancock on the left.

We reached him a little too late to save Birney's division [Second Corps] from being flanked. The 2nd Corps with part of the 6th and 9th were then massed on the left and commenced building breastworks. By 3 o'clock we had 3 lines of temporary breastworks, and six lines of battle. Our brigade was in the 4th line. About 3 A.M. [P.M.] the rebels charged with about 30,000 men on this part of the line. The musketry was fearful. The noise was so deafening that we could scarcely make each other hear at a few paces.

After fighting about 1 hour our first line gave way and our brigade [Leasure's, consisting of the 100th Pennsylvania, 21st Massachusetts, and the 3rd Maryland infantry regiments] advanced to the support of the second line. After firing a short time we charged on the rebels behind our first line and routed them. This ended the fight.

That night and the next day we lay on the field. On the 8th we marched to Chancellorsville and lay in that vicinity until the 9th when we moved toward Spottsylvania [sic] Court House and were the supporting division in driving the enemy to that place. We remained here skirmishing and fortifying until the 12th.

On the morning of the 12th our whole corps advanced against the enemy's works in our front. In a few hours we had driven them to their works and our line was so extended that we had no support for us at all. Our line now lay about 300 yards from the rebels rifle pits. Their sharpshooters were picking off our men rapidly.

About noon we advanced toward the enemy's pits. They were in a thick pine woods and we could not see them until we were within 30 yards. They then opened a murderous fire upon us from behind a rifle pit protected by a thick brush fence. [Editor's note: This was the heavy impenetrable slashing fronting the Confederate main defense line.] It was impossible to advance further and to fall back without orders was what we never did.

We sheltered ourselves as best we could and fired away. [Editor's note: Fortunately, there is a distinct ravine parallel about 60 yards away fronting the Confederate main line. This ravine gave some cover from the enemy fire. Without this protection the casualties would undoubtedly have been much higher.] In a short time we were ordered to fall back. This we did and formed a line where we were before advancing, and were ordered to hold our position. This we did though at great loss from the fire of the sharpshooters.

That night we built breastworks and remained in the same position skirmishing day and night until the morning of the 19th when we evacuated that position and moved to the left of our line. After reconnoitering and finding the enemy we were ordered to dig rifle pits and fortify. We worked on our fortifications until about midnight yesterday the 20th. The enemy did not approach within gun shot of our works and we rested.

The enemy's works are about 2 miles from ours and neither party appears disposed to attack the other.

Both armies have lost terribly since we cross the Rapidan. On the 12th our company lost 2 killed and 22 wounded, and since the 5th we have lost 3 killed and 25 wounded. The regiment has lost about 200 killed and wounded.

S. A. White and J.C. Stevenson [Company E] were wounded. J. P. Wilson is sick and in the hospital. The rest of us are well.

I have not heard from home for more than a month.

> Write soon,
> Fred Pettit
> Co. C. 100th P.V.

[P.S.] This is the great fight [campaign] of the war, one of the armies will be destroyed.''

Written to:
Sister, Mary Ann, Poland, Ohio.

Behind the breastworks 11 miles N.W. of Richmond, Va. June 1st 1864. [Editor's note: This position was astride the Shady Grove Road not far from Bethesda Church, Virginia.] [SEE MAP #11]

"Dear Sister:

I received your kind letter of May 20th yesterday and was very glad to hear from you. Since writing on the 2nd we have commenced one of the severest campaigns ever undertaken by any troops. For 25 days we had but one night's rest. The campaign is not over yet but is going on as vigorously as ever only we are becoming more accustomed to it.

I think I wrote to you after the battle of Spottsylvania though I am not sure [Pettit did write. See letter above.] as I can find no note of it in my diary. The battle at that place was one of the severest in which we were ever engaged. The regiment lost about 160 in killed and wounded. Our company lost 2 killed and 23 wounded, 2 of whom have since died. S.A. White was wounded in the shoulder. J. C. Stevenson in Co. E. was wounded slightly. Thus far Co. C. has lost 5 killed and 23 wounded since May 5th.

On the 21st ult. we left Spottsylvania and after marching 2 days and one whole night we came upon the enemy strongly posted upon the South Side of the North Anna River, 25 miles from Richmond. Considerable fighting took place on the 23rd, 24th, and 25th. A large force of our army crossed both above and below the enemy's main position. We crossed the river on the 24th just above the enemy's works and on the 25th we had a brisk skirmish losing 9 or 10 men wounded.

On the night of the 26th the whole army recrossed the river and marched rapidly down its north bank. Our corps was left in the rear and followed on the 27th. At the same time that our army moved down the river the rebel army moved up the river thinking we were moving in that direction. The advance of our army reached the intended crossing on the Pamunkey river and found nothing but cavalry and a small force of infantry to oppose them. They accordingly pushed forward and took up a strong position within 15 miles of Richmond.

Our corps marched from the morning of the 27th until the morning of the 29th day and night. We did not march so far but we were in the rear and moved very slowly but constantly. This was the most wearisome march we ever had. Since that time we have moved slowly forward skirmishing all the way.

Our present position is in the edge of a woods with a field in front. Our pickets are in the woods on the opposite side of the field 600 or 700 yards from our line. We have built a line of breastworks in our front and are lying behind it waiting for the rebels to attack us or an order to attack them.

The pickets keep up a constant pecking in our front. Occasionally a man is wounded but not often.

Quite a number of the reserves [Pennsylvania "Reserve" regiments] have gone home their time being out. The 9th Regiment P.R.C. [Pennsylvania Reserve Corps] went home on the 4th of May before the fighting commenced. Some of the other regiments started yesterday.

Ira Cunningham is in our regiment and is well. Hege, D.W.Wilson, Lary, Pence, and the rest of us are well. J. P. Wilson is in the hospital.

I can say nothing about the school at Hilltown as I know nothing about it. The subject of Baptism I must leave until another time.

The past month has been the busiest time with us I ever saw. Through the watchful care of Him who never sleepeth my life and health has been preserved. My trust is still in Him. I never knew the comfort there is in religion so well as during the past month. Nothing sustains me so much in danger as to know that there is one who ever watches over us.

Write soon again. What is the general opinion of the operations of this army?

Your brother,
Fred Pettit
Co. C. 100th P.V."

On June 2nd, 1864, Pettit's good fortune gave out at one of the many engagements known collectively as the Battle of Cold Harbor. The Ninth Corps was in the process of withdrawing down the Shady Grove Church Road to a new position to the rear. After moving about 1½ miles and before reaching their assigned location, they were assailed furiously by the pursuing Confederates. Caught in an exposed location and attacked from three sides, the regiment turned and fought off the enemy, but suffered severely in the effort.[5] In this fight, Pettit received a severe wound in the left arm between his elbow and wrist which necessitated his going to the rear for medical assistance and later for hospitalization.

The casualties in Pettit's regiment for the fight on June 2nd were heavy. The *Official Records* lists them as being 72 killed, wounded, and missing, but other estimates place them as high as 80.[6] For unknown reasons, the June 2nd engagement was never properly documented and the two short histories of the regiment by Samuel P. Bates as well as another by James C. Stevenson mentioned it but briefly.[7]

After being wounded, Pettit left the battlefield and walked to the 1st Division hospital. After spending two days there he was sent on to Washington, D.C. for further hospitalization.

---

[5] Two excellent accounts of the battle on June 2 are in the McDowell Collection, Historical Collections and Labor Archives, Pennsylvania State University. These are:

Lt. S. G. Leasure, letter, "Camp in the Field, June 6, 1864" and Private Hamilton Dunlap's "Diary" entries for June 2nd.

[6] Ibid.

[7] James C. Stevenson, *The Roundheads, A Condensed History of This Noted Regiment,* New Castle, Pennsylvania. Samuel P. Bates, *The One Hundredth Regiment Pennsylvania,* New Castle, Pennsylvania, 1884.

CHAPTER TEN

IN THE HOSPITAL

"Any person not with the army can form no idea of its hardships."

After being wounded and spending two days in his division's field hospital, Pettit along with others, walked to White House Landing and boarded the steamer *Connecticut* for the journey to Washington, D.C., for additional hospitalization. These details are covered in his letter of June 8, 1864.

Written to:
Family

Havewood Hospital, Washington, D.C., June 8th, 1864.

"Dear parents, brothers, and sisters,

From the date of this letter you need not suppose that the rebels have driven us back here. Far from it — the driving is all in the other direction. Nor need you think that I am sick, for my health is as good as usual; but it is simply because I have had my arm scratched a little with a bullet; and they must call me a wounded man and send me away here to the hospital. But I will endeavor to explain matters as well as I can.

On the afternoon of June 1st [it was June 2] we were lying behind rifle pits about two miles from Gaines Mill or Cold Harbor and about 10 miles from Richmond. [Along the Shady Grove Church Road near Bethesda Church] The rebel pickets and ours were about 50 yards apart. About 3 o'clock in the afternoon we were ordered to move back quietly and without any show. We had made such movements so often that we thought nothing of it but moved without any confusion.

141

After going a short distance we found the whole force gone and our division in the rear. After marching about one and a half miles we came upon the rest of the army. In a short time our pickets came running in and reported the rebels after them. At the same time a heavy thunder shower came on. In about half an hour after the pickets came in the enemy commenced firing close to our rear.

Our division immediately wheeled into line to check them until the rest of the corps with the artillery could get into position. Our brigade formed at a double quick in an open field and moved forward to the edge of a woods where the rebels came down upon us howling like wolves. First, they tried our right but we gave them a cross fire and sent them back like sheep. Next they tried our left and now they had a cross fire on us. Here our regiment lost heavily.

While preparing to load my gun I felt something strike my arm between the elbow and wrist. Upon looking at it I found a small cut across the leaders [tendons] which were much bruised about half way between the elbow and the wrist.

I went to the division hospital that night where I remained until Saturday. [Pettit was wounded, Thursday, June 2] At the hospital I found D.W. Wilson shot through the thumb, but not very bad. Smith Patterson [Company C] was killed. Our company had 8 wounded, one of whom [John Alexander] has since died.

On Sunday we started for White House landing. I and several others walked all the way. On Monday we got on the steamer Connecticut and arrived in Washington on Tuesday and were sent to Harewood Hospital. D.W. Wilson was kept at the Division Hospital.

I expect to go back to the regiment next week at the farthest as my wound will be well in a few days.

You need not write to me for a week or two. I will let you know when I start for the regiment and you can send my letters there.

Give my regards to all inquiring friends. My wound is in the left arm. D.W. Wilson is shot through the right thumb.

> Fred Pettit
> Co. C 100th P.V."

Written to:
Sister, Mary Ann

> Havewood Hospital, Washington, D.C., June 9th, 1864

"Dear sister Mary,

After writing to you on the 1st we attempted to move our lines forward a short distance. We built and occupied a part of our new line of works when the enemy made a sortie and drove us back to our old line. [This engagement occurred on the evening of June 1] In this action we lost a valuable officer killed, Lieut. Gilfillan of Co. F. [2nd Lieutenant David I. Gilfillan, Company F, who was on the brigade staff at the time and was killed while rallying the troops.]

Everything then remained quiet until the afternoon of the 2nd when we were ordered to leave our works quietly and without show. This we did about 3 o'clock in the afternoon. We moved about one and a half miles to the rear of our left when our pickets came running in and reported the rebels after them. At this time our whole corps was in the road marching toward the left. The wagons and artillery had stopped in front and the troops of course were obliged to stop also.

Our division was in the rear. Just after the pickets came in a heavy thundershower came on drenching us completely. In a few minutes the rebels commenced firing in our rear and our division immediately wheeled into line to meet them.

On they came howling like wolves. We were greatly exposed in our position as the rebels had a cross fire from our left. One of their balls happened to strike me on the arm inflicting a severe bruise. I now left the field to take care of my arm. I found the wound very slight, the cut not being over half an inch deep. I remained in or with the division hospital until Sunday morning the 5th when I started for White House landing with the rest of the wounded. I and several others walked all the way about 18 miles.

On Monday we got aboard the hospital steamer Connecticut. On Tuesday we arrived at Washington and were send to Havewood Hospital, Ward #9 where I now am.

I expect to go to the regiment again next week. You need not write to me here as I will probably be gone before it gets here. I will let you know when I leave for the regiment and you can write to me there.

Smith Patterson of our company was killed and D.W. Wilson shot through the thumb on the 2nd.

> Your brother,
> Fred Pettit
> Co. C. 100th P.V."

This letter was written to Pettit by his father and contains some interesting information about people and events in Hazel Dell.

Written to:
Private Fred Pettit

Hazel Dell   June 12th 1864

"Dear Frederick,

The last letter we received from thee was dated May 20. This gives us great satisfaction to know that thee was yet alive and well. We are all well as usual.

Grandfathers and James Hazens were all well yesterday. Evan came home from Middle Lancaster yesterday. Margaret was well and had plenty of work so far.

We received a letter from Mary Ann on last Monday. She expects to be home in two weeks from tomorrow.

We have been up to Center this forenoon to hear J.C. Nye. On last Sunday we went to Chewtown and heard Brother Harvey preach a good sermon on the duty of ministers. They held quarterly meeting there. Harvey, Kelty, and Nye were the preachers. I learned from Harvey and Kelty that Nye had brought the case of the North Sewickly Church before the quarterly meeting and wishes to get Farr's proceedings aside and reclaim the church. Harvey and Kelty are appointed as a committee to give them a hearing. They are to be here on the first Saturday in July.

The prospect for a wheat crop is not good in general. Many of our farmers will not have more than their seed. Fortunately for us ours looks well. If it fills well we will have a good crop. Oats and grass look well. Corn is short; the worms are very much complained of. The weather is cold for the time of year. Have had some frost but none to do harm as I have heard of.

Our stock and other affairs have been prosperous so far this summer. Our mares have each one a beautiful colt. We had a good increase of sheep. I sold 20 old sheep and 18 lambs for 100 dollars about six weeks ago. I have paid off all my debts without borrowing any money and have some little left. Have not sold any wheat; think it best to keep it till we secure the next crop.

Don't think it would be proper to undertake to make much improvements this summer as workmen are scarce and wages high. Will try to patch up our house and barn so as to shelter us through another winter.

The neighbors are all well so far as I know. Nothing more at present but remain as ever thy affectionate Father.

Nathaniel Pettit.''

Pettit's younger brother, Cyrus, age 16, also wrote Fred a short letter on June 12:

Written to:
Private Fred Pettit

Hazel Dell   June 12th, 1864

"Dear brother,

I again try to write you a few lines. We received a letter from you dated the 20th. There was a draft in Beaver County, three being drafted. Dick Johnston was drafted. He was at the furnace begging money to pay the $300 [For draft exemption].

Well, it is time for prayer meeting and I must go. I will finish
when I come back.

Monday morning. We received some books from you sent with
John Evans. We also received a jacket and necktie. Evan's foot has
not got well yet. He got a shoe on last Friday for the first time. He
was at Middle Lancaster last Friday. Maggie was well. Write soon.

Cyrus''

Written to:
Family

Havewood Hospital, Washington, D.C., June 13th 1864

"Dear parents, brothers, and sisters:

Well, I am still in the hospital, and my arm is healing slowly.
When I came here I supposed I would be ready to go to the regiment
by this time; but my arm is almost as sore as when I came. A person
having but a slight wound can spend the time here very pleasantly if
he can content himself.

We have cooked meals three times a day. For breakfast we
generally have hash of some kind, coffee, and bread. For dinner, meat,
soup, and potatoes. Supper, tea, bread, butter, or dried apples boiled.
There is a small library attached to the hospital where we can get books
to read.

I do not know how long it will be before I can go to the regiment but not long I hope. Tomorrow I expect to leave this place for
Philadelphia or some other point north. There are about 2000 wounded
here at present and some coming and going daily.

The weather for a few days past has been quite cool. I have heard
nothing from the regiment since I left it nor from any other place.

The hardships endured by the Army of the Potomac for the 30
days commencing May 4th were such as I supposed it impossible for
any set of men to endure. Any person not with the army can form no
idea of its hardships. For 25 days I did not sleep but a single night and
this was the average of the whole army. When we lay down to sleep
we could not take off anything nor unpack our blankets. We would
lie down upon the ground, wet or dry, with perhaps a gum blanket over
us with our cartridge boxes, haversacks, etc., canteens on, our knapsacks under our heads and our guns in our hands.

Perhaps we would not more than get to sleep until we would
be roused by the pickets being driven in or an order to move. Scarcely
a day passed without an exchange of shots with the enemy. From the
time we crossed the Rapidan until I left the regiment June 2nd we had
lost over 300 men killed and wounded.

My health is still very good. You need not write as I cannot tell you where to write to.

Frederick Pettit
Co. C. 100th P.V."

Written to:
Family

Summit House Hospital, Philadelphia, June 18th '64

"Dear parents, brothers, and sisters:

How much trouble a little thing sometimes causes! My wound, very slight at first has not entirely healed yet.

Yesterday in company with about 500 more wounded I was started from Washington for Philadelphia by railroad. We left Washington at one o'clock P.M. and arrived in Baltimore in the evening. Here the cars are drawn through the city by horses. We left Baltimore about 5 o'clock in the evening and arrived at Havre de Grace a small town at the mouth of the Susquehanna about dark. Here the cars are taken across the river on a boat, the water and mud being too deep to build a bridge. The boat is made very large and strong and will carry 21 cars at a load. A few years ago the ice was so thick here that the boat could not run and they laid railroad track across on the ice.

At midnight we arrived at Wilmington, Del. Here they told us that the news had come that Petersburg was captured with 13 cannon and 3000 prisoners.

About 2 o'clock this morning we arrived in Philadelphia. We got off the cars immediately and went to the Citizens Volunteers Hospital close to the depot. Here we had a good supper immediately of bread, meat, coffee, butter, and pickles. We then lay down and slept an hour or two. About 7 o'clock this morning we had a good breakfast of the same. These meals tasted excellent as we had nothing from the time we ate our breakfasts in Washington until we arrived here except what we bought; and as we have not been paid for almost six months our money is getting small.

This morning we were sent to the different hospitals in and about the city. I was sent to Summit House Hospital about 3 miles from the city. As I may remain here several days I wish you would write to me as soon as you receive this.

My wound heals slowly but I think it will be well in about a week. If am not here when your letter comes it will be sent to me. Direct to:

Fred Pettit
Ward 3
Summit House Hospital
Philadelphia, Pa."

Written to:
Family
                Summit House Hospital, Philadelphia, Pa.   June 27-'64.

"Dear parents, brothers, and sisters,

It is now more than a week since I came here and here I am yet. These troublesome wounds; how slowly they heal. Until I came to the hospital I do not know half the horrors of a battle. Even slight wounds require a long time to heal, especially those made by bullets. It is now almost four weeks since I was wounded and it is not quite healed yet, though it was but slight at first.

Perhaps you would like to know some of the treatment of wounds. When a man is wounded in battle he goes to the rear if able, if not he is carried by the stretcher bearers no man being allowed to leave ranks for that purpose. The regimental surgeon remains close in the rear of the regiment. The wounded of the regiment are first taken to him and are examined, bandaged, and sent to the division hospital still further in the rear. At the division hospital all necessary operations are performed, such as limbs amputated, bones set, balls extracted, etc. With each division hospital is a wagon loaded with Sanitary and Christian Commission stores and 2 or 3 delegates. These stores are of great value at the hospitals in front where the government supplies nothing but bread, coffee, and meat.

As fast as possible the wounded are sent away to permanent hospitals. Moving is very dangerous and many badly wounded die from it. There are none badly wounded at this hospital but there are some that will be a long time healing.

I have received no letter from home yet though I am looking for one every day. It is dreadful tiresome staying here. I have not been out since I came here because I cannot get out. We have no books to read, but few papers, and nothing to do but sit or lie day and night. Is it any wonder I am sick of it and wish to go to the regiment again? *I could get a furlough but do not want it. I think it would be a disgrace for me to go home on furlough now when soldiers are so much needed in the field.* [Editor's note: Emphasis added here as this is a clear indication of the intense devotion to duty that Fred Pettit displayed. There are few soldiers who would turn down the opportunity for a few days at home especially following the hardship of the recent campaign, and the trauma of being wounded in action.]

Most of the wounded men here think of nothing but staying away from the army until this fighting is over. I think their conduct disgraceful. I have asked the doctor to send me to my regiment again and he has promised to do so tomorrow or next day.

My arm is not quite well yet but I think it will be when I get to the regiment. I could have stayed in Washington as long as I wished and could stay here several weeks yet but I think it *is my duty* [Emphasis added] to return to the regiment as soon as I am fit for duty.

The next letter you write send it to the regiment as I will certainly start for it this week.

Fred Pettit"

Written to:
Father

Camp Distribution, Va., July 3rd 1864.

"Dear father:

I received your letter of June 25th on the 29th at Summit House Hospital, Philadelphia. On the same day I received my discharge from the hospital and reported to the Provost Marshal in the city. The same evening we were started for Washington where we arrived about 6 o'clock the next morning.

I was not sent away from the hospital but made application to the surgeon in charge to go to my regiment. *I could have remained several weeks yet as my arm was not entirely healed yet,* [Emphasis added] but it pains me very little and I can use it almost as well as ever. Besides, I am tired of this hospital life. At the present time I believe it to be the duty of every soldier, as soon as able, to return to his regiment and do his duty in the ranks. None but cowards and traitors will linger round hospitals and camps when able for duty at the present time.

I could have remained in Washington all summer and *was offered a position for three months and could have got a furlough home for a short time but did not want it.* [Emphasis added]

Every able bodied soldier is now needed in the front and I shall not remain away any longer than is necessary. It is a disgrace to see how many of our soldiers are here in easy positions, well and hearty, but too cowardly to go to the front. I have heard men declare they would never go to the front again if they did not get a furlough. And these same men have been in the service ever since last April, almost 60 days, and insisting on furloughs. Very few men who have served for 2 and 3 years act in this manner.

The same day we arrived in Washington we were sent over to Camp Distribution 3 or 4 miles from Alexandria where we are yet. We have orders to leave here tomorrow the 4th [July] at 8 o'clock for the front where will probably arrive on Tuesday.

J. McElwain is in the hospital at this place. He has been quite sick but is well as usual now. I think he will remain here until his term is out. My health is good and my arm has almost healed up.

Write soon directing your letters to the regiment.

Your son,
Frederick Pettit,
Co. C. 100th P.V.''

In a few days Pettit would be back at the front with his regiment positioned in the front lines before Petersburg. During his absence, after June 2nd, the 100th Pennsylvania was in the Cold Harbor trenches until June 12. Following this battle they joined the rest of the Army of the Potomac in its rapid move over the James River and on to Petersburg. On June 17 the regiment participated in a night assault against the Confederate defense lines at Petersburg. Here they lost 49 casualties including two valuable officers, the regimental commander, Lt. Colonel Mathew M. Dawson, mortally wounded, and Captain Leander C. Morrow, commander of Company H, killed in action.[1]

The regiment then took position with Ledlie's Division on the right flank of the Ninth Corps in the vicinity of Forts Haskell and Stedman. Here the opposing lines were extremely close, and musketry and sharpshooting were continued constantly. The lines were heavily fortified by both forces and trench warfare, which was to last for nine months, began in earnest.

One of the regimental historians, Private Silas Stevenson of Company K, wrote on June 23:

"Roundheads are entrenched in an open field in a very dangerous place supported by the 27th New York Battery. The least exposure of the body invites a shot from the enemy. Our position is altogether too hot for comfort, and I came very near being shot by one of the rebel sharpshooters who seemed to have an excellent range of the place."[2]

It was this dangerous situation that Fred Pettit confronted when he "returned to his regiment." Unfortunately he would not have the opportunity to learn the dangerous hazards present in this unfamiliar area, and that lack of knowledge would prove his undoing.

Upon his rejoining the regiment, Pettit was both surprised and pleased to learn of his promotion to corporal. This was unexpected but well earned advancement. Unfortunately, Pettit did not have many hours left to enjoy his new promotion.

---

[1] William G. Gavin, *Campaigning With The Roundheads*, Morningside Press, Dayton, Ohio, 1989, Chapter 16. This history contains detailed information on the operations of the 100th Pennsylvania in their attack on June 17th and of their activities in the front lines during June and July until the time of Pettit's return.

[2] Private Silas Stevenson, Manuscript "History", McDowell Collection, HCLA, Pennsylvania State University.

CHAPTER ELEVEN

THE END

"It becomes my painful duty to inform you that your noble son is no more."

Pettit is once again with his regiment and back on duty with the new rank of Corporal. It is July 9 and he has been back for just two days, having arrived in the front lines at the regimental position on July 7.

This is his final letter, written immediately before his untimely death.

Written to:
Sister, Mary Ann

In the trenches before Petersburg, Va., July 9th, 1864.

"Dear sister Mary:

I received your very kind letter of the 4th inst. today. I was very glad to get it indeed. It is only the second letter I have received since I was wounded. I wrote a letter home on Sunday from Camp Distribution [preceding letter].

The same night about 10 o'clock we left that place and went on board the steamer *Spaulding* at Alexandria bound for City Point. We remained at anchor in the river until about 8 o'clock on the morning of the fourth when we started down the river. The day was very fine and if we had been less crowded would have had a very pleasant time. A few miles below Alexandria we passed Mt. Vernon, the home of Washington, a spot dear to every loyal heart. The grounds and buildings are almost entirely concealed by the thick groves of shade trees which surround them. This is almost the only point of interest in passing up and down the Potomac.

About midnight we passed Fort Monroe and at 11 o'clock on the 5th we came in sight of City Point. This is quite a business place now, the wharf being crowded with steamers, schooners, and barges discharging their cargoes of commissary, quartermaster, and ordnance stores. The railroad is now in running order about 6 miles from the landing.

We went on shore about noon [July 6] (there was about a thousand of us) and in the afternoon we started for the front. It was quite warm and the dust was almost intolerable. We camped for the night about 2½ miles from the front. The next day we went on to Army Headquarters on the extreme left of the line and then back about 5 miles to the regiment where I arrived about 1 o'clock.

I found them in the front line about 2 miles from Petersburg and about 500 yds. from a rebel fort. [Probably Gracie's or Colquitt's salients] The pickets keep up an incessant firing along the line night and day which is relieved every 5 minutes by the mortars and siege guns throwing shell back and forth.

Our division is now divided into two brigades and we hold a line the length of a brigade, there being two lines of works. Each brigade remains in the front line 3 days and is then relieved by the other brigade. There is not much advantage in being in the rear line as both lines are equally exposed to the enemy's fire and it is necessary to keep under cover.

The boys here in front are much more cheerful and confident than in the rear about Washington and Philadelphia. The men are well satisfied with the campaign thus far and put great confidence in the government and General Grant. My health is good and I am getting along finely. D. [David] Wilson is now in the hospital sick. I have not seen him but understand he has been sent to City Point. J. R. Evans, Pence, and the rest are well.

Write again soon. Send me some papers and whatever reading matter you can. We get very lonesome lying in the ditches with nothing to do but watch the rebels.

The 76th P.V. are lying near us. I went to see them on Thursday. D. Shoemaker, D. Allen, and J. C. Grandy are with the regiment and are well. They say they never saw anything like this before. I saw C. M. McCoy at Philadelphia. He is slightly wounded in the arm. Andrew Lary is now guarding cattle. I have not seen him since I came back.

I think [if] Nye and Kelty try their missionary scheme on the old plan they may expect some success. There is indeed a wide field of Christian usefulness in that section. But Nye's ambition to establish a new society in that place will never succeed. Any established society in the neighborhood might find it a profitable field for missionary effort.

But I must close. The day is warm and cloudy and the usual amount of firing is going on. There has been no rain here for two months.

When I returned to the regiment I was quite surprised to find my name at the end of the list of corporals of Co. C. It was a thing I did not expect. I shall try to do my duty.

Write soon and send along those papers, magazines, or whatever you can find in the reading line.

> Your brother,
> Fred Pettit
> Co. C. 100th P.V."

The regimental adjutant, Lieutenant S. George Leasure, provides additional details on the regiment's activities on this fateful July 9th:

The Roundheads were: "in the old line of pits today, (July 9) having been relieved about midnight...Everything is quiet with the exception of sharpshooting and an occasional break-out among the pickets. We are steadily at work planting siege guns and mortar batteries. We will waken the "Johnnies" up some fine morning about daylight, I think...we have 19 officers and 285 enlisted men present for duty..."[1]

It must have been just a short time after Pettit completed his last letter to his sister Mary Ann when a sharpshooter's bullet struck him in the head bringing instant death. Captain Critchlow stated the time of death was about 7 o'clock in the evening. After his death he was buried behind the lines in the Ninth Corps cemetery at Meade's Station. Later reburial was in Poplar Grove National Cemetery near Petersburg.[2]

Corporal Pettit was probably not well informed nor accustomed to the exposed and dangerous portions of the trenches. Having been back with the regiment for only two days when they moved into position in the second lines, the territory was unfamiliar to him. As he mentioned, the enemy fire was just as dangerous in the secondary line as in the front line position. It is tragic that he received no "orientation" on the danger spots from his comrades, who having been in the neighborhood for over three weeks were aware of them. It is ironic that in his last letter, Pettit commented upon the necessity of "keeping under cover".

---

[1] Adjutant S. George Leasure, letter, "July 9th, 1864." McDowell Collection, Historical Collections and Labor Archives, Pennsylvania State University.

[2] Burial Site: Poplar Grove National Cemetery, near Petersburg, Virginia. Pettit's final resting place is in Division A, Section C, Grave 297. This grave is easily located today in this cemetery, there being a large grave site identification guide in the center of the cemetery. Adjacent to Pettit's grave site, is the grave of another hero of the 100th Pennsylvania, little "Johnnie March" who fell on March 15, 1865, defending Fort Haskell from the Confederate assault during the battle of Fort Stedman.

The company commander of Company C, David Critchlow, wrote Pettit's parents the following day:

Written to:
Father, Nathaniel Pettit

Near Petersburg, Va.,   July 10th 1864.

"Dear Sir:

It becomes my painful duty to inform you that your noble son is no more. He was killed yesterday about seven o'clock P.M. by a sharpshooter, the ball entering the left side of his neck and reaching the surface at the right cheek, producing instant death. He was sitting in his place reading at the time he was struck.

He had just returned to the regiment two days before. I can say but little to his afflicted and sorrowing parents, brothers, and sisters calculated to soothe their sorrow except that he died as he lived, a devoted and exemplary Christian and I trust and believe your loss is his eternal gain.

As a soldier, Fred was brave and always at his post. Everyone knew him in the Regiment as one of its best and bravest of men.

I have collected all his effects that I thought would be valuable to his friends as mementos and turned them over to the agent of the "Christian Commission" who will send them to Washington and thence by express to New Brighton where you can get them.

Among the articles you will find his bible, testament, hymn book, diary, [Pettit habitually kept a detailed diary. The only one surviving covers a brief period September 1863 to Sunday, January 24, 1864 and is copied in the Appendices of this book. None of the "mementos" mentioned by Captain Critchlow have apparently survived.] letters, etc.

I am, sir, with much sympathy.

Yours truly,
D. Critchlow"
[Captain, Company C.,
100th Pennsylvania Veteran
Volunteer Infantry Regiment.]

Unfortunately, the above letter from Captain Critchlow was missent to New Castle, and was promptly forwarded probably 20 or 21 July to Nathaniel Pettit with the following comment:

Written by:
Mrs. David Critchlow

[New Brighton, Pennsylvania]

"Mr. Pettit,

I wrote you a few lines on Monday [letter following, dated July 18, 1864] which I suppose you have received ere this. This letter [Captain Critchlow's above] was missent and came this evening from New Castle.

Yours respectfully,
C. Critchlow"
[Captain David Critchlow's wife]

[Editor's note: There is no date on Mrs. Critchlow's letter, and it is probable it was written two or three days later, July 20 or 21, 1864.]

The letter following was the one Mrs. David Critchlow wrote to Nathaniel Pettit on Monday, July 18, 1864, and because of the delay of Captain Critchlow's letter to the Pettits, this would have provided the initial shocking news the Pettit family received about Fred Pettit's death:

Written to:
Nathaniel Pettit

New Brighton, Pa., July 18th, 1864, Monday morning.

"Dear Sir:

I received a letter from Mr. [Captain] Critchlow on Saturday giving me the sad news of your son Fred's death. He was instantly killed by a sharpshooter on the evening of the 9th whilst sitting reading. He had him buried under a large pine tree and the grave distinctly marked.

Mr. C. wrote you a letter himself directing it to my care thinking you would get it sooner. As it did not come on Saturday I waited expecting certainly it would be here this morning but it did not come as I have written myself.

Mr. C. says he is extremely sorry to lose so good a man and soldier as Fred was, but the ways of Providence are not as our ways. You have my heartfelt sympathy in your bereavement. I feel as though any day may bring me sorrowful tidings as they are hourly exposed to the guns of the enemy.[3]

Yours respectfully,
C.P. Critchlow".

---

[3] Captain David Critchlow fortunately survived the war. He was promoted to Major October 8, 1864, but never mustered, as he was discharged October 14th. He served with the regiment for over three years, joining it upon its organization in August 1861. Samuel P. Bates, *History of Pennsylvania Volunteers*, Harrisburg, Penna., 1870, Volume 3, Page 572.

William Gilfillan Gavin

Undoubtedly the Pettit family was plunged into deep mourning. The Pettits were obviously a close knit family, and the loss of the oldest son must have caused them great remorse. There are no other Pettit family letters or other information known to the Editor to supplement the story of the Pettit family after Fred's death. Consequently, this is the end of the history of Corporal Fred Pettit in the American Civil War.

After Pettit's death, just three weeks later, on July 30th, the 100th Pennsylvania played a major role in the Battle of the Crater and suffered extremely heavy casualties. They participated in three more battles, Weldon Railroad, Pegram's Farm, and Fort Stedman before the war ended in April 1865.

This loyal and devoted human being was an excellent example of the kind of soldier who helped preserve the Union and gave "the last full measure of devotion."

APPENDIX A

CORPORAL FREDERICK PETTIT'S DIARY
1863-1864

Pettit's diary covers the period from September 18, 1863 until January 24, 1864 at the time the 100th Pennsylvania Regiment was involved in the East Tennessee campaign. This diary is the only one known to survive of those compiled by Pettit during his two years of service. It provides additional information on his service with the regiment while in East Tennessee.

Diary of Frederick Pettit
Co. C. 100th Pa. Vol.
1st Division, 9th Army Corps.

1863

I purchased this book Sept. 18th while on the march to East Tenna..At that time we were lying on the Cumberland river 6 miles below the ford. In the morning my tent burned up. Borrowed one of John McElwain. This day Friday, September 18th is wet and cool. We are waiting for the roads to dry so our teams may move. The country is mountainous and the people poor and ignorant. Very little can be bought to eat. All quiet. The evening cool and cloudy. We expect to move tomorrow early.

Saturday, September 19th 1863.

Awaked at daybreak. Cool and cloudy. Started at 6½ A.M. A little muddy but pleasant. Reached Cumberland ford about 8 o'clock. Marched on beyond the ford 4 miles and camped in a narrow valley. Marched about 9 miles today. Very pleasant marching. Battle of Chicamanga, Ga.

Sunday Sept. 20th 1863.

Reville at daybreak. Foggy and cold. Frost on the hills. Started early and traveled rapidly. Came in sight of the Gap about 9 oclock. Passed through it about 11 A.M. and camped 1 mile beyond. Scenery very romantic about the gap. Day warm and pleasant. Country looks more fertile. Was in three states today. Cumberland Gap. Second days fight at Chicamaga. Our loss 1800 killed, 9500 wounded and 2500 prisoners.

Monday Sept. 21st 1863.

Reville at 4 A.M. Started at daylight. Crossed Powels river 5 miles from the gap. Marched 12 miles and stopped at Tazowell two hours for dinner. Road and country improving. Fruit very abundant. Heavy frost. Marched 6 miles in afternoon. Stopped at 3 P.M. 18 miles today. Day warm and pleasant. First days march in East Tenn.

Tuesday Sept. 22nd 1863.

Started at daylight. Three miles out waded Clinch river. Crossed Clinch mountain and took dinner at its foot. From its top saw Cumberland mountains and Blue Ridge mountains in North Carolina. A.M. march 10 miles. P.M. passed Beans Station, waded Holston river, crossed a ridge of the Allegheny's. Camped about 8 P.M. Days march 21 miles. Saw four states today.

Wednesday Sept. 23rd 1863.

Remained in camp until afternoon then marched to Morristown 1½ miles, got on cars, went to Greenville 35 mi. then ordered to Knoxville 75 mi. south. Country very fine. Union people very glad to see us. Clear and warm.

Thursday, Sept. 24th 1863.

Arrived in Knoxville at 4 oclock A.M. and remained at the station until noon. Then marched 1 mile above town and camped near the Holston river. Very good camp. Water good and convenient. Day clear and warm.

Friday, Sept. 25th 1863.

Resting and washing today. Nothing going on. Teams and battery arrived in the evening. Day hot and cloudy. Evening cool, clear and windy.

Saturday, Sept. 26th 1863.

Nothing of importance transpired. Teams arrived. Orders to be in readiness to move. Drew a pair of new shoes. Day clear and warm. Sent a letter home.

Sunday, Sept. 27th 1863.

Pleasant day. Attended the Baptist Church in Knoxville. Heard a sermon read from Dan. 7:2 to 4 inclu. Good historical essay. Attendance small. Received a letter from Margaret dated Sept. 10 & 11. Orders to move at 5 tomorrow morning.

Monday, Sept. 28th 1863.

Waked up very quietly at 3 oclock and marched to the ferry without getting breakfast. Crossed the river and took position with artillery 1 mile beyond and remained during the night. Heard distant cannonading in the morning. All quiet in the afternoon. Day warm and pleasant.

Tuesday, Sept. 29th 1863.

Still remained in the position of yesterday. A company of refugees from N. Carolina came in this morning to enlist. Afternoon sent on picket. On post at crossroads 1 mile from Knoxville. At dark a squad of rebel prisoners in charge of armed citizens were sent in. Warm and pleasant.

Wednesday, Sept. 30th 1863.

Remained on picket all day. Two rebel prisoners brought in today by home guards. They were in three days fighting at Chattanooga. They report Rosecraus driven into his intrenchments. Privates 29th N.C. Relieved in the evening by Co. D.

Thursday, October 1st 1863.

A wet day. Commenced raining before daylight. Wrote a letter to Margaret today. Time passes very wearily. Rained almost all day and promises to be a wet night. No news from any quarter.

Friday, Oct. 2nd 1863.

Rained almost all night. Cleared up this morning. Day warm and pleasant. Went to the river and washed my clothes. No news. Nothing transpired worthy of notice.

Saturday, Oct. 3rd 1863.

Morning cool and foggy, day warm and pleasant. Baggage brought over. No news. Nothing of importance transpired.

Sunday, Oct. 4th 1863.

Company inspection at 9 P.M. Remained in camp during the day. No sermon today. Saw 3 rebel deserters today. Report Bragg falling back.

Monday, Oct. 5th 1863.

Nothing of importance transpired. Remained in camp all day. Slightly unwell. Quite at a loss for employment. Day cool. Night very cool. Some beginning to fix comfortable quarters for cold weather.

Tuesday, Oct. 6th 1863.

Another day passed in camp with nothing to do. Day warm and pleasant. Nothing transpired worthy of notice.

Wednesday, Oct. 7th 1863.

Cool and wet. Forenoon remained in camp. Afternoon sent on picket. Post on the river road. Evening cool but no rain.

Thursday, Oct. 8th 1863.

Last night passed very quietly on picket. At 8 A.M. was ordered to regiment. Went to camp, reg. gone. Joined them at the river. Marched to railroad depot. Remained at the depot all day.

Friday, Oct. 9th 1863.

Remained at the station last night. Got on the cars and left Knoxville at 10 A.M. Arrived at Morristown for coffee in the evening and at Bulls Gap about 8 o'clock P.M. Bivouaced near the railroad. Burnside came up on the same train with us. Mailed a letter home.

Saturday, Oct. 10th 1863.

Reveille at 5 A.M. Started at 6½ o'clock on the Greenville road. Came up with the enemy at Blue Springs. The mounted men drove them beyond the town. In the evening the ninth corps took the front and after a brisk fight drove them to their batteries and held the position during the night. Rebel force about 6000. Ours engaged about 3000. Our loss 6 killed and 54 wounded. Rebel loss unknown.

Sunday, Oct. 11th 1863.

All quiet last night. Made preparation for a heavy battle this morning. Sent out skirmishers about 7 A.M. but found no enemy. Mounted men went in pursuit and we followed. Mounted men skirmished in front and rear all afternoon but we did not overtake them. Marched 20 miles. Passed through Greenville and Rheatown.

Monday, Oct. 12 1863.

Remained in camp 1 mi. beyond Rheatown all day. Ordered to move at 6 and 2 but were countermanded. In the skirmish here yesterday a number were killed on both sides.

Tuesday, Oct. 13th 1863.

Reveille at 4½ A.M. Started at 6. Reached Greenville about noon. Stopped 1½ mi. out for dinner and then marched 5 mi. below to the railroad and camped. Days march 17 miles.

Wednesday, Oct. 14th 1863.

Reveille at 6. Started about 9 A.M. Reached Blue Springs at 10 and stopped 5 miles beyond for dinner. Then came to Bulls Gap and stopped for the night. Marched 14 mi. today. Received a letter from Mary of Sept. 17th and a package of Messengers. First account of the battle of Chicamauga.

Thursday, Oct. 15th 1863.

Reveille at 4½ oclock. Started at 6 A.M. Reached Russelville about 10 oclock and stopped 2 mi. beyond for dinner. Reached Morristown about 3 P.M. and camped for the night. Days march 13 miles.

Friday, Oct. 16th 1863.

Got on the cars about 7½ A.M. and started for Knoxville. Arrived about 11 oclock A.M. Remained at depot until afternoon and marched out and camped near the old one. Received a letter from Mary dated Sept. 28 and 29. Brownlow and Maynard returned to Knoxville.

Saturday, Oct. 17th 1863.

Remained in camp all day. Washing and cleaning up. Day cool, clear and pleasant. Wrote a letter to Mary. Three men detailed to go as wagon guarde. News of Curtins election. Chaplain Browne returned. Religious services in the evening.

Sunday, Oct. 18th 1863.

Wet and cool. Spent the day in camp. Afternoon heard a short sermon by Chaplain Browne. Day passed wearily. Did not feel the contentment I wish in spending the day thus. Had religious service in the evening by the chaplain.

Monday, Oct. 19, 1863.

Monday morning chilly and foggy. Boys busy fixing up their quarters. Fixed our tent quite comfortable. Received orders to move tomorrow morning. Drew two days bread to last us five. Attended prayermeeting in the evening.

Tuesday, Oct. 20th 1863.

Reville at 5½ A.M. Started at 7 toward London. Mess mate A.M. Akin detailed as teamster, 1st Sergeant Co. W. Fisher detailed to recruit. Marched about 9 miles and stopped 1¾ hrs. for dinner. Stopped at sundown for the night. Days march 15 mi. Road very muddy. Day warm and pleasant. Wolford surrounded at Philadelphia. Losses 200 prisoners, one battery, and 40 wagons.

Wednesday, Oct. 21st 1863.

Reveille at 3½ A.M. Started at 5. Thunder shower in the forenoon. Very muddy and wet marching. Marched rapidly. Stopped about 4 miles from London. Days march 10 miles. Do not feel contented. No one to tent with.

Thursday, Oct. 22nd 1863.

Remained in camp until afternoon. About 3 o'clock moved to London. Crossed the Holston river on a pontoon bridge. Camped about ½ mile from the river. Marched about 4 miles. Distance from Knoxville 29 miles. Day warm and pleasant.

Friday, Oct. 23rd 1863.

A thunder shower came on at daylight. Continued to rain all day. Wind from the north and quite cold. Did not move today but made ourselves as miserable as possible in the rain and mud. London is a poor miserable place. Could not get a bite to eat nor a place to warm myself.

Saturday, Oct. 24th 1863.

Rained nearly all night. Slept very comfortably on some sheaf wheat. Today windy and cool but no rain. General Burnside came down this morning. About 2 P.M. ordered to pack up, stack arms and await orders. Cavalry went on a reconnoisance. Heard cannonading from 4 o'clock until dark. Train all crossed the river. Evening very cool.

Sunday, Oct. 25th 1863.

Remained under marching orders all night. Morning very cool. All quiet. Sermon by Chaplain Browne from Rev. 31:5. Headquarter teams came back again. Put up camp again as usual. Religious services in the evening by the chaplain.

Monday, Oct. 26th 1863.

On picket today. On post today in the front. Rebels captured 1 wagon 1 mile from our post. Cavalry and artillery sent out and drove them back. Skirmish near Philadelphia. All quiet along the picket lines during the day. Cavalry returned during the evening. Clear and pleasant.

Tuesday, Oct. 27th 1863.

Rebel cavalry made a dash on our pickets last night about 2 A.M. Captured 2 of the 20th Michigan. No further disturbance. Relieved by 45th P.V. Some of detail for conscripts returned and Cap. Critchlow and L. C. Greves. Day cloudy and wet.

Wednesday, Oct. 28th 1863.

Awaked, ordered to pack up and fall in without noise about 3 o'clock A.M. Crossed the river at daylight and found the place was being evacuated. Stopped about 1 mile from the river for breakfast and remained until almost noon. Then marched 5 miles and camped at Lenoir station for the night. Day cloudy and wet.

Thursday, Oct. 29th 1863.

Remained in camp until afternoon, then marched about 1 mile above the station and camped in the woods. Ordered to put up winter quarters as we would perhaps remain a month. Captain Critchlow started for Cincinnati. Warm and pleasant.

Friday, Oct. 30th 1863.

Co. C. commenced cutting timber for quarters. Had an ax but a short time. Rained in the evening. Detail made of carpenters for building pontoons. H. N Kelly and R. M. Eckles detailed. Great activity prevails in putting up quarters.

Saturday, Oct. 31st 1863.

All is activity in creating quarters. Co. C. drew an ax and cut most of timber for huts. Day fine and warm. No messmate yet.

Sunday, Nov. 1st. 1863.

All at work on quarters. Co. C. commenced to build. Recall at 10. Ceased work until 12 o'clock for church. Sermon by chaplain of 20th Mich. Text Rom. 14:12. Theme personal responsibility. At work again in afternoon. Found a messmate W. J. Redick. Religious services in the evening by Chaplain.

Monday, Nov. 2nd 1863.

Commenced building our hut. Worked hard. Got the logs up ready for roof. Religious service by Chaplain in the evening. Day warm and pleasant.

Tuesday, Nov. 3rd 1863.

Finished our house all but a chimney to it. Think it will be very comfortable. Quite tired. Religious services in evening.

Wednesday, Nov. 4th 1863.

Built a chimney to our house of mud and sticks. Houses getting finished rapidly.

Thursday, Nov. 5th 1863.

Detailed on forage party today for 3 days. Went out in wagons and found forage in the evening. Loaded wagons partly. Had headache.

Friday, Nov. 6th 1863.

Loaded remainder of the wagons and started for camp 8 miles. Arrived about 2 P.M. Day clear and warm. Grand skedaddle of 7th Ohio cavalry from Rogersville.

Saturday, Nov. 7th 1863.

Roused about 11 oclock last night and ordered to pack up immediately. Got on the cars about 3 A.M. Arrived in Knoxville about 8 o'clock. Remained in and about the cars until night then got off and bivouacked. Men on detail to recruit in Tennessee returned to regiment.

Sunday, Nov. 8th 1863.

Last night was quite cold. Still remained near the station. Sermon by chaplain. Day cool and cloudy.

Monday, Nov. 9th 1863.

Last night very cold. Still remaining near the station at Knoxville. About 2 o'clock got on the cars and started for Lenoir. Arrived before dark. Marched to camp, put up tents and were all right again. Day cold and cloudy.

Tuesday, Nov. 10th 1863.

Morning coldest of the season. Wrote a letter and mailed it home today. Engaged getting wood, fixing tents, etc. Day cool and windy.

Wednesday, Nov. 11th 1863.

Ordered to stack arms at daylight, remain in camp, and be ready to move. Morning clear and frosty. Bought first no. Brownlows paper. Received a letter from Mary and Margaret dated Oct. 19 & 22 and one from Mary and Evan of Oct. 31st.

Thursday, Nov. 12th 1863.

Ordered to stack arms again at daylight. Cleaned up quarters. Detailed at 11 A.M. to dig road to pontoons on river. Day warm and pleasant.

Friday, Nov. 13th 1863.

Ordered to prepare for inspection. Engaged cleaning guns and accoutrements, writing etc. Day warm and pleasant. Mailed Brownlow's "Rebel Ventilator" to father.

Saturday, Nov. 14th 1863.

Ordered to pack up at daylight and be ready to move at a moments notice. Commenced to rain as we commenced to pack up and rained almost all day. Reg. guarding wagon train. Moved about 6 miles.

Sunday, Nov. 15th 1863.

Stopped last night beside the road. Started early and kept along with the train. Cos. H, C, & M under command of the major. Marched about 7 miles. Cool and cloudy.

Monday, Nov. 16th 1863.

Roused at 2 A.M. Started at daybreak. Train moved rapidly. Reached Knoxville about 11 A.M. Marched about 1 mile beyond and camped with the train. Day cool and cloudy. Our division had a heavy skirmish near Concord. Loss total 148.

Tuesday, Nov. 17th 1863.

Remained with the train until about 10 A.M. then ordered to join the brigade which we did at the fort west of town. Negroes and soldiers busy preparing for defending it. Enemy advanced in sight about 12 M. On picket at 7 P.M. Cool and cloudy.

Wednesday, Nov. 18th 1863.

Relieved from picket early in the morning. Remained at the rifle pits all day. Enemy approached close to our pickets in the evening. Ordered into the pits. Warm and clear. Our advance driven from their last position outside the pits.

Thursday, Nov. 19th 1863.

Remained at the pits all day. Enemy drove in our skirmishers on the right. Opened on them with a new battery. Two houses burned in front of our rifle pits. Balls commenced to fly over us. Lieu. Reed wounded on picket line. Two wounded in the works. Clear and warm.

Friday, Nov. 20th 1863.

Sent on picket before daylight in the morning. Skirmishing quite brisk all day. P. Bird wounded in the head in the sharpshooters pits. Brisk cannonading in the evening. 17th Mich. burned a house within the rebel lines. Day warm and cloudy.

Saturday, Nov. 21st 1863.

Relieved from picket before day. Rained most of the night and day. Everybody wet and miserable. Our regiment moved from the pits to rear of the fort. Two men wounded in front of the fort. Rain ceased about 3 P.M. One or two shots fired from our battery above town. Evening cool.

Sunday, Nov. 22nd 1863.

Moved our camp to rear of rifle pits on left of the fort. Finished the pit in our front. Some cannonading. Two shells burst over us. No one hurt. Cavalry made a reconnoisance 5 miles on the Gap road and found no enemy. Religious services in the evening by the chaplain. Sent on picket at 9 P.M.

Monday, Nov. 23rd 1863

On picket all day in front of the fort. Nothing in interest took place. Some firing as usual. A few cannon shots fired from the fort. An old arsenal and some other buildings burned on the right. Attack on the pickets at the same time. Relieved at 9 P.M. Warm and pleasant.

Tuesday, Nov. 24th 1863.

Rebels ran a rifle pit in front of our skirmishers last night. The 2nd Mich. charged on it and took it in the morning but were obliged to leave it. No engaged 160. Loss 86. Rebels obtained a hold on opposite side of the river. Shackelford skirmished with them and took 200 prisoners. Wet and cloudy.

Wednesday, Nov. 25th 1863.

A heavy skirmish took place on the opposite side of the river. Our forces drove the enemy some distance. Considerable cannonading on our side. The enemy fired but two shots at Fort Saunders. One passed over us and the other struck on the opposite side.

Thursday, Nov. 26th 1863.

Ordered into the pits at daylight, but nothing unusual took place. A number of shots were fired at the enemy but they did not reply. Thanksgiving service in the evening by the chaplain. Sent on picket at 8 P.M. Clear and cool.

Friday, Nov. 27th 1863.

Everything quiet as usual on the picket lines last night. Several shots fired at the enemys works on the right today from Fort Saunders but no reply. Great commotion in the rebel lines. Band playing and cheering. Clear and cool.

Saturday, Nov. 28th 1863.

Pickets kept up a scattering fire all night. Great activity amongst the enemy. Chopping on the hill across the river. A shot or two fired from our batteries at them but no reply. Heavy cannonading in the afternoon but no response by the enemy. Very active all round. Wet, cool and cloudy.

Sunday, Nov. 29th 1863.

Roused at 11 last night by our pickets being driven in. Enemy charged on our pickets all round and drove them almost to the fort. Lay in the trenches all night expecting an attack. Enemy charged in mass on north west corner of the fort. 11 regiments Mclaws division Georgia troops charged and were repulsed. Loss heavy. Flag of truce sent out to carry off the dead and wounded until 7 P.M. Enemys loss 240, prisoners 200 and 300 wounded. Our loss about 100.

Monday, Nov. 30th 1863.

Sent on picket at 5 P.M. Very cold. Rebel pickets within 50 yards. Kept very quiet. A few shells thrown at them from our batteries. Relieved at 7 P.M. On watch last night in the pit from 9 P.M. to 12 M.

Tuesday, December 1st 1863.

Co. C. was on watch last night in the pits from 3 A.M. to 6 A.M. Everything quiet. Nine hearty cheers ordered by Gen. Burnside for Grouts victory. Our batteries fired a number of shells at the rebs but no reply. Clear and cool.

Wednesday, Dec. 2nd 1863.

Co. C. on watch from 12 to 3 last night. All quiet. Rebel waggon train seen passing up the river with cavalry. Enemy massing troops on the right. Much cannonading, but one shot by the enemy in reply. Detailed at 8 P.M. to work on the fort. Worked until 12 M. Cannonading during the night. Expecting an attack. Clear and cold.

Dec. 3rd. 1863. Thursday.

Heard cannonading to the westward. Some cannonading here but no reply by the enemy. All quiet as usual. Day warm and pleasant. Evening frosty.

Friday, Dec. 4th 1863.

Roused twice last night by pickets firing. On watch in the trenches from 3 to 6 A.M. Rebels observed moving to the right. Made a great show of force in the afternoon. Heavy shelling from our batteries. On picket at 7 P.M. Warm and pleasant.

Saturday, Dec. 5th 1863.

Rebel pickets withdrawn from our front at 1 oclock this morning. Position reconnoitered and whole army found gone. Signed pay roll in afternoon. A large number of prisoners taken. Cool and cloudy.

Sunday, Dec. 6th 1863.

Prisoners continue to come in. Morning very cold. Sent a letter home. Chaplain Brown preached a short sermon in the evening. Afternoon more pleasant.

Monday, Dec. 7th 1863.

Roused at 5 A.M. by light marching orders. Started at 7 on the road to Strawberry Plains. Marched 12 miles and stopped for the night. Cool but pleasant.

Tuesday, Dec. 8th 1863.

Remained at last nights camp until 1 P.M. today, then marched 7 miles and camped where the rebels were yesterday. Cool and cloudy. One mile from Blains X Roads.

Wednesday, Dec. 9th 1863.

Reveille at 5½ A.M. Started at 7. Marched rapidly and stopped near Rutlege. Days March 12 miles. Saw the smoke of rebel camps on the mountains. Warm and pleasant.

Thursday, Dec. 10th 1863.

Remained at our camp near Rutledge until night. Our regiment was then sent to guard a mill near the Holston river. Started at dark and reached the mill at 10 P.M. and went on picket. Distance marched 9 miles. Warm and pleasant.

Friday, Dec. 11th 1863.

Remained on picket near the mill until 1 oclock P.M. Was then ordered back to the brigade where we arrived at dark. People along the river very friendly. Warm and pleasant.

Saturday, Dec. 12th 1863.

Remained in camp all day. Drew full rations of flour and beef. Ordered to remain in camp. Roll call every hour. Warm and cloudy in evening.

Sunday, Dec. 13th 1863.

Everything quiet as usual. Train arrived from the Gap with supplies. Had a short sermon by the chaplain in the afternoon and service in the evening. Wet and cloudy.

Monday, Dec. 14th, 1863.

Roused at 2 this morning to draw rations. Reveille at 3. Started at 5 and marched rapidly to Holston river 9 miles. Our brigade guarding fords. Rebel cavalry appeared on opposite bank in the evening and opened upon us with artillery wounding two of 2nd Mich. About midnight moved back 5¼ miles. Morning wet. Day cool and windy.

Tuesday, Dec. 15th 1863.

Remained at last nights bivouac until 9 o'clock. Then started for the ford again. 2 miles out drove in the enemys pickets. Were then ordered back to old position where we remained until 9 p.m. then joined the division and marched back 6 miles and bivouaced. Received 4 letters from home, 2nd one from H. J. P., dates Nov. 8, 15, 23, 30th and Nov. 28. Mailed a letter home.

Wednesday, Dec. 16th 1863.

Remained at last nights bivouac until 8 A.M. Then marched to Blaine Cross Roads, took dinner and formed line of battle in which position we remained all night. Warm and pleasant. Received a letter from Erskine E. Allison dated Nov. 28th.

Thursday, Dec. 17th 1863.

Remained in position all day. Rained last night. Cannonading on the right in afternoon. Received 2 months pay in the evening up to Nov. 1st. Cold and windy.

Friday, Dec. 18th 1863.

Still in our old position. Cold and windy. On fatigue a few hours blockading a road in the mountains. Everything quiet.

Saturday, Dec. 19th 1863.

Very cold. Requisition sent in for clothing. Mr. Francis came to visit us. Talk of reinlistment in veteran corps. Night very cold. Saw Maj. Gen. Foster for first time.

Sunday, Dec. 20th 1863.

Very cold. Mr. Francis made us a short address. Baggage came up in the afternoon. Short sermon by the chaplain in the evening.

Monday, Dec. 21st 1863.

Still at our mountain bivouac. All quiet as usual. Weather more moderate. Washed my clothes.

Tuesday, Dec. 22nd 1863.

Nothing of importance occured. Wrote a letter to H. J. P. Weather more moderate.

Wednesday, Dec. 23rd 1863.

Nothing of importance occured. Still in our mountain camp. Still talk over enlistment. Service in the evening by the chaplain. Quite cold.

Thursday, Dec. 24th 1863.

Sent on picket at 9 A.M. Nothing unusual. Warm.

Friday, Dec. 25th 1863.

Relieved from picket at 9 A.M. Christmas dinner very light. Nothing important. Service in the evening by the chaplain.

Saturday, Dec. 26th 1863.

Twenty three of Co. C. reinlisted for three years. Wet and cloudy.

Sunday, Dec. 27th 1863.

Chaplain delivered a short sermon in the forenoon. Reinlistments still continue. Wet and cloudy.

Monday, Dec. 28th 1863.

Reinlistments still going on. Co. C. has 32 names reinlisted today. Sworn by Captain Hamilton. The regiment will go. Cool and windy.

Tuesday, Dec. 29th 1863.
    Reinlistment still goes on. Quite cold. Chaplain Brown having resigned, delivered his farewell address. Subscribed for "History of Roundheads" 1 copy.

Wednesday, Dec. 30th 1863.
    Nine co's mustered in for 3 years more, 33 of Co. C.

Thursday, Dec. 31st 1863.
    Wet and cloudy. Mailed a letter to A. Lary. Some convalescents arrived.

Friday, Jan'y 1st 1864.
    The old year went out with rain and wind and the new year came in with a bitter cold wind. Day very cold. Nothing important has transpired in camp all day.

Saturday, Jan. 2nd 1864.
    Still very cold. Did nothing but get wood for the fire. Not so uncomfortable as yesterday.

Sunday, Jan. 3rd 1864.
    Everything quiet as usual. Mailed a letter home. Did not appear much like Sunday. Not so cold as usual today.

Monday, Jan. 4th 1864.
    A wet day. Nothing of importance transpired. Received a letter from father in the evening dated Dec. 21st 1863.

Tuesday, Jan. 5th 1864.
    Cold and windy again. Detailed for guard at 3 P.M. On post at brigade quartermasters on corn pile.

Wednesday, Jan. 6th 1864.
    Relieved at 3 P.M. Very cold. Nothing of importance transpired today.

Thursday, Jan. 7th 1864.
    The 21st Mass. started home with 160 prisoners. Cold with some snow in the evening.

Friday, Jan. 8th 1864.
    Ground covered with snow this morning. The 8th Mich. started home this morning.

Saturday, Jan. 9th 1864.
    Ordered to make moccasins last night. Busy at it all day. Made a pair over my shoes. Very cold.

Sunday, Jan. 10th 1864.
          A very cold morning. Ordered to leave next Tuesday. Those not enlisting assigned to duty in the 45th P.V.

Monday, Jan. 11th 1864.
          Busy preparing for tomorrows journey. Drew rations in the evening 1¼ lbs. of bread and 3 lbs. of pork.

Tuesday, Jan. 12th 1864.
          Roused at 5 A.M. Started at daylight and marched rapidly. Very cold in the morning. Muddy in the afternoon. Stopped 1½ miles from the river. Marched 17 miles.

Wednesday, Jan. 13th 1864.
          Started at daylight and crossed the river in a ferry. Reached Tazewell at noon. Marched 3 miles beyond. Days march 16 miles.

Thursday, Jan. 14th 1864.
          Roused at 3½ A.M. Started at 5. Reached Powels river at daylight and the Gap at noon. Drew 1 days rations and marched 7 miles beyond. Days march 17 miles. Threw away my moccasins and got a pair of old shoes.

Friday, Jan. 15th 1864.
          Started shortly after daylight and reached C. ford at noon. Drew 2 days rations from the train and marched 6 miles farther and camped at wet hollow. Days march 16 miles.

Saturday, Jan. 16th 1864.
          Started at daylight. Reached Barbersville at noon and took dinner then marched 9 miles and camped for the night. Days march 19 miles. Morning cold. Afternoon muddy.

Sunday, Jan. 17th 1864.
          Drew all the crackers we wanted and 3 days of coffee and sugar. Stopped 1 mile from Pitmans. Days march 17 miles.

Monday, Jan. 18th 1864.
          Started shortly after daylight. Rained nearly all day. Crossed Wild Cat mountain and camped, from there to Mt. Vernon. Stopped with Wilson 4½ miles from Mt. Vernon. Days march 19 miles.

Tuesday, Jan. 19th 1864.
          Snowy and cold. Started early. Overtook the Co. at Mt. Vernon. Marched rapidly and reached Crab Orchard before sundown. Quartered in an old building. Days march 18 miles.

Wednesday, Jan. 20th 1864.

Remained in Crab Orchard all day. Had a good time generally. 50th P.V. continued on to C. Nelson.

Thursday, Jan. 21st 1864.

Left Crab Orchard at daylight. Took dinner near Lancaster. Stopped 1 mile from C.D.R. for the night. Days march 19 miles.

Friday, Jan. 22nd 1864.

Started at daylight. Reached C.N. at noon. Drew clothing, marched on 2 miles and camped near Camp Park.

Saturday, Jan. 23rd 1864.

Went to Nicholasville, got on the cars at 4 P.M.

Sunday, Jan. 24th 1864.

Arrived at Covington at 4 A.M. this morning. Went to the barracks.

APPENDIX B

ROSTER OF COMPANY C
100TH PENNSYLVANIA VETERAN VOLUNTEER INFANTRY
1861-1865

This roster is taken from Samuel P. Bates' *History of Pennsylvania Volunteers 1861-1865* which was published in 1870. It contains some errors and must be used with caution. However, it does provide basic information on the officers and men who served with Pettit during his period of service from 1862 to 1864.

ONE HUNDREDTH REGIMENT,

COMPANY C.

RECRUITED IN BUTLER COUNTY.

NAME	RANK	DATE OF MUSTER INTO SERVICE	TERM-YRS	REMARKS
James E. Cornelius	Capt. .	Aug. 31, '61,	3	Wounded at Chantilly, Va., Sept. 1, 1862—resigned March 4, 1863.
David Critchlow	.. do ..	Aug. 31, '61,	3	Pr. fr. Sgt. Maj. to 2d Lt., Nov. 1, '61—to 1st Lt., Oct. 5, 1862—to Capt., Mar. 4, 1863—com. Maj., Oct. 8, 1864—not mus.—discharged Oct. 15. '64.
George W. Fisher	.. do ..	Aug. 31, '61,	3	Pr. to 1st Sgt., Nov. 1, 1862—to 2d Lt., June 28, 1864—to Captain, Nov. 26, 1864—mustered out with company, July 24, 1865—Vet.
Philo S. Morton	1st Lt.	Aug. 31, '61,	3	Resigned October 4, 1862.
Robert W. Weller	.. do ..	Aug. 31, '61,	3	Pr. fr. 1st Sgt. to 2d Lt., Oct. 5, 1862—to 1st Lt., March 4, 1863—mustered out, Oct. 15, 1864.
Matthew Stewart	.. do ..	Aug. 31, '61,	3	Pr. to Cor., Nov. 13. '62—to Sgt., April 15, '63—to 1st Sgt., June 28, '64—to 1st Lt., Nov. 26, '64—mustered out with company, July 24, '65—Vet.
Isaac W. Cornelius ..	2d Lt .	Aug. 31, '61,	3	Pr. from Sgt. Maj., march 4, 1863—died June 6, of wounds received at Cold Harbor, Va., June 2, 1864—buried at New Kent C. H.
William Smiley	.. do ..	Aug. 31, '61,	3	Pr. from Cor. to Sgt., Feb. 15, 1863—to 1st Sgt., Dec., 1, 1864—to 2d Lieut., May 12, 1865—mustered out with company, July 24, 1865—Vet.
Joseph A. Craig	1st Sgt.	Dec. 20, '61,	3	Promoted to Corporal, Feb. 15, 1863—to Sgt.—to 1st Sergeant, May 12, 1865—mustered out with company, July 24, 1865—Vet.
Henry W. Watson ...	Serg't .	Aug. 31, '61,	3	Promoted to Corporal, May 1, 1864—to Sgt., Sept. 1, 1864—mus. out with Co., July 24, 1865—Vet.
Henry Ribb	.. do ..	Aug. 31, '61,	3	Mustered out with company, July 24, '65—Vet.
Hiram Gill	.. do ..	Dec. 7, '61,	3	Promoted from Corporal, Arpil 1, 1865—mustered out with company, July 24, 1865—Vet.
Oliver Tebay	.. do ..	Aug. 31, '61,	3	Promoted from Corporal, May 12, 1865—mustered out with company, July 24, 1865—Vet.
Hiram N. Kelly	.. do ..	Aug. 31, '61,	3	Mustered out, Aug. 30, 1864—expiration of term.
John P. Wilson	.. do ..	Aug. 31, '61	3	Promoted to Corporal, Nov. 13, 1862—to Sergeant—discharged March 20, 1865—Vet.
Phineas Bird	.. do ..	Aug. 31, '61,	3	Mustered out, Aug. 30, 1864—expiration of term.
Elisha J. Bracken	.. do ..	Aug. 31, '61,	3	Promoted to Sergeant, Nov. 13, 1862—killed at Spottsylvania C. II, Va., May 12, 1864—Vet.

NAME	RANK	DATE OF MUSTER INTO SERVICE	TERMS-YRS	REMARKS
Samuel L. Moore	.. do ..	Oct. 18, '61,	3	Pr. to Sgt., May 12, 1864—killed at Petersburg, Va., June 22, 1864—buried in Poplar Grove Nat. Cem., div. A. sec. C, grave, 180—Vet.
James M'Casky	.. do ..	Aug. 31, '61,	3	Killed at James' Island, S.C., June 16, 1862.
Hugh Morrison	.. do ..	Aug. 31, '61,	3	Promoted to Sergeant, May 15, 1862—discharged Dec. 27, 1862, for wounds received in action.
William F. Monroe ...	.. do ..	Aug. 31, '61,	3	Deserted August 10, 1862.
Addison Cleland	.. do ..	Aug. 31, '61,	3	Promoted to Sgt., Nov. 13, '62—died Feb. 5, '63.
William J. Redick ...	Corp .	Dec. 7, '61,	3	Mustered out with company, July 24, 1865—Vet.
Robert J. Brown	.. do ..	Dec. 7, '61,	3	Mustered out with company, July 24, 1865—Vet.
John C. Marshall	.. do ..	Aug. 31, '61,	3	Mustered out with company, July 24, 1865—Vet.
Charles Schwing	.. do ..	July 9, '64,	3	Promoted to Corporal, April 1, 1865—mustered out with company, July 24, 1865.
Andrew Leary	.. do ..	Aug. 31, '61	3	Promoted to Corporal, April 1, 1865—mustered out with company, July 24, 1865—Vet.
John Glenn	.. do ..	Oct. 18, '61,	3	Promoted to Corporal, April 1, 1865—mustered out with company, July 24, 1865—Vet.
Wm. W. M'Quiston .	.. do ..	Dec. 7, '61	3	Promoted to Corporal, April 1, 1865—mustered out with company, July 24, 1865—Vet.
Samuel F. Miller	.. do ..	Dec. 20, '61,	3	Promoted to Corporal, May 12, 1865—mustered out with company, July 24, 1865—Vet.
Samuel A. White	.. do ..	Dec. 28, '61,	3	Transferred to V.R.C., January 15, 1865—Vet.
Loyal C. Greares	.. do ..	Aug. 31, '61,	3	Transferred to V.R.C., January 15, 1865—Vet.
John C. Moore	.. do ..	Aug. 31, '61,	3	Promoted to Sergeant Major, Sept., 1864—Vet.
Frederick Pettit	.. do ..	Aug. 10, '62,	3	Killed near Petersburg, Va., July 9, 1864—buried in Poplar Grove National Cemetery, division A, section C, grave, 207.
John J. Hogue	.. do ..	Dec. 16, '61,	3	Died at Annapolis, Md., March 13, 1865—Vet.
Jacob Ake	.. do ..	Aug. 31, '61,	3	Discharged on Surgeon's certificate, Dec. 1, 1861.
Findley Brandon	.. do ..	Aug. 31, '61,	3	Discharged on Surgeon's certificate, Aug. 18, '62.
John S. Watson	.. do ..	Aug. 31, '61,	3	Killed at James' Island, S.C., June 16, 1862.
Akin, Alexander W. .	Private	Aug. 31, '61,	3	Mustered out with company, July 24, 1865—Vet.
Auberry, William P. .	Private	Mar. 25, '64,	3	Mustered out with company, July 24, 1865.
Aikin, James W.	.. do ..	Feb. 27, '64,	3	Mustered out with company, July 24, 1865.
Ashbaugh, James	.. do ..	Mar. 1, '65,	1	Substitute—mustered out with Co., July 24, '65.
Aikin, Erskine E.	.. do ..	Aug. 31, '61,	3	Mustered out, Aug 30, '64—expiration of term.
Aikin, David S.	.. do ..	Dec. 28, '63,	3	Discharged by General Order, May 17, 1865.
Armstrong, Thos.	.. do ..	Feb. 27, '64,	3	Killed at Spottsylvania C.H., Va., May, 13, '64.
Alexander, John	.. do ..	Dec. 28, '63,	3	Died June 4, of wounds received at Cold Harbor, Virginia, June 2, 1864.
Anderson, Wm. A. ..	.. do ..	Dec. 2, '61,	3	Killed at James' Island, S.C., June 16, 1862.
Boyer, Edward	.. do ..	Mar. 9, '65,	1	Substitute—mustered out with Co., July 24, '65.
Burtner, John E.	.. do ..	Mar. 31, '64,	3	Discharged by General Order, June 10, 1865.
Baker, Ellis	.. do ..	Mar. 6, '65,	1	Substitute—discharged by G.O., June 20, 1865.

NAME	RANK	DATE OF MUSTER INTO SERVICE	TERM-YRS	REMARKS
Bauder, (?) Frederick	.. do ..	Sept. 9, '61,	3	Transferred to Vet. Res. Corps, Jan. 15, '65—Vet.
Banes, Thomas	.. do ..	Feb. 29, '64,	3	Transferred to Vet. Reserve Corps, Jan. 15, 1865.
Brown, William K. ..	.. do ..	Aug. 31, '61,	3	Discharged on Surgeon's certificate, Oct. 27, '62.
Brown, James R.	.. do ..	Oct. 18, '61,	3	Died Sept. 20, of wds. received at South Mountain, Md., Sept. 14, 1862—bu. in Nat. Cemetery, Antietam, sec. 26, lot C, grave, 338.
Braden, William L. ..	.. do ..	Aug. 31, '61,	3	Deserted August 4, 1862.
Brandon, John H. ...	.. do ..	Feb. 27, '64,	3	Not on muster-out roll.
Coombs, John W. ...	.. do ..	Jan. 10, '65,	1	Substitute—mustered out with Co., July 24, '65.
Cohenan, Isaiah	.. do ..	Mar. 2, '65,	1	Substitute—mustered out with Co., July 24, '65.
Curran, Richard	.. do ..	Mar. 9, '65,	1	Substitute—mustered out with Co., July 24, '65.
Christman, John	.. do ..	Mar. 8, '65,	1	Substitute—mustered out with Co., July 24, '65.
Campbell, James F. ...	.. do ..	Aug. 31, '61,	3	Mustered out, Aug. 30, '64—expiration of term.
Christy, Marquis C. ..	.. do ..	Dec. 7, '61,	3	Discharged on Surgeon's certificate, Oct. 11, '62.
Campbell, James C. ..	.. do ..	Aug. 13, '61,	3	Transferred to Vet. Reserve Corps. June 5, 1864.
Campbell, Joseph E. .	.. do ..	Mar. 2, '64,	3	Died May 20, of wounds received at Spottsylvania C.H., Va., May 13, 1864.
Cleeland, Samuel H. .	.. do ..	Feb. 20, '64,	3	Died June 2 of wds. rec. at Spottsylvania C.H., Va., May 12, '64—bu. in Nat. Cem., Arlington.
Campbell, Henry S. ...	.. do ..	Aug. 31, '61,	3	Killed at Bull Run, Va., August 29, 1862.
Devictor, Joel H.	.. do ..	Mar. 4, '65,	1	Substitute—mustered out with Co., July 24, '65.
Daisey, Daniel	.. do ..	Mar. 8, '65,	1	Substitute—mustered out with Co., July 24, '65.
Deitrick, Delorma ...	.. do ..	Mar. 6, '65,	1	Substitute—discharged by G.O., June 2, 1865.
Dalton, James	.. do ..	Mar. 24, '64,	3	Killed at Spottsylvania C.H., Va., May 18, 1864.
Dunwoody, Rob't C. .	.. do ..	Oct. 18, '61,	3	Died Aug. 19, of wds. rec. at Petersburg, July 30, 1864—buried in Nat. Cem., City Point, Va., division 1, section B, grave, 139—Vet.
Doutt, Reuben	.. do ..	Jan. 26, '64,	3	Died at Washington, D.C. Aug. 18, 1864—buried in Nat. Cemetery, Arlington, Va.
Duncan, George W. ..	.. do ..	Dec. 28, '63,	3	Killed at Petersburg, Va., December 6, 1864.
Dillaman, Henry	.. do ..	Dec. 7, '61,	3	Discharged on Surgeon's certificate, Feb. 23, '63.
Durham, Francis J. ..	.. do ..	Feb. 9, '64,	3	Not on muster-out roll.
Elder, John N.	.. do ..	Feb. 29, '65,	3	Absent, sick, at muster out.
Evans, John R.	.. do ..	Aug. 31, '61,	3	Mustered out, Aug. 30, 1864—expiration of term.
Eckels, Robert M.	.. do ..	Aug. 31, '61,	3	Mustered out, Aug. 30, 1864—expiration of term.
Evans, George	.. do ..	Mar. 21, '64,	3	Not on muster-out roll.
Evans, Russell	.. do ..	Feb. 8, '64,	3	Not on muster-out roll.
Eakin, James M.	.. do ..	Feb. 27, '64,	3	Not on muster-out roll.
Fuller, Jacob	.. do ..	Feb. 27, '64,	3	Mustered out with company, July 24, 1865.
Forquer, James	.. do ..	Mar. 24, '64,	3	Mustered out with company, July 24, 1865.
Freed, Henry C.	.. do ..	Aug. 31, '61,	3	Discharged on Surgeon's certificate, Mar. 10, '63.
French, Stiles	.. do ..	Jan. 14, '62,	3	Not on muster-out roll.
Fry, John	.. do ..	Feb. 19, '64,	3	Not on muster-out roll.

NAME	RANK	DATE OF MUSTER INTO SERVICE	TERM-YRS	REMARKS
Franklin, Benjamin ..	.. do ..	Mar. 19, '64,	3	Not on muster-out roll.
Gorman, Robert J. ...	.. do ..	Feb. 29, '64,	3	Mustered out with company, July 24, 1865.
Gibson, James	.. do ..	Jan. 5, '62,	3	Mustered out, Jan. 4, 1865—expiration of term.
Gibson, William W. .	.. do ..	Aug. 31, '61,	3	Discharged on Surg. certificate, June 7, '65—Vet.
Gray, Jacob	.. do ..	Aug. 31, '61,	3	Transferred to Vet. Reserve Corps, Jan. 5, 1864.
Guy, Henry S.	.. do ..	Aug. 31, '61,	3	Wd. in action—disch. on Surg. cert., Mar. 27, '63.
Gibb, Alexander	.. do ..	July 30, '64,	1	Not on muster-out roll.
Hatch, John P.	.. do ..	Feb. 29, '64,	3	Mustered out with company, July 24, 1865.
Hatch, David	.. do ..	Feb. 29, '64,	3	Mustered out with company, July 24, 1865.
Hudson, Orando	.. do ..	Mar. 6, '65,	1	Substitute—mustered out with Co., July 24, '65.
Holmes, Orange	.. do ..	Mar. 6, '65,	1	Substitute—mustered out with Co., July 24, '65.
Holmes, Richard D. .	.. do ..	Oct. 18, '61,	3	Promoted to Quartermaster Sgt., Nov. 13, 1862.
Hastings, Thomas ...	.. do ..	Jan. 31, '65,	1	Substitute—died May 28, 1865—buried in National Cemetery, Arlington, Va.
Heliker, Elias R.	.. do ..	Feb. 29, '64,	3	Died July 17, '64—bu. in Cypress Hill Cem., L.I.
Hanaghan, James	.. do ..	Feb. 28. '65,	3	Substitute—deserted May 15, 1865.
Hoge, James	.. do ..	Aug. 31, '61,	3	Not on muster-out roll.
Irvin, James	.. do ..	Feb. 3, '65,	1	Substitute—mustered out with Co., July 24, 1865.
Jamison, Ewell	.. do ..	Jan. 5, '62,	3	Mustered out, Jan. 4, 1865—expiration of term.
Jones, Thomas	.. do ..	Feb. 3, '65	1	Substitute—discharged by G.O., June 17, 1865.
James, William	Private	Dec. 20, '61,	3	Absent on detached service, at muster out.
Kirker, Silas W.	.. do ..	Feb. 26, '64,	3	Mustered out with company, July 24, 1865.
Kirker, Nesly	.. do ..	Mar. 27, '64,	3	Mustered out with company, July 24, 1865.
Knapp, Lorenzo K. ..	.. do ..	Jan. 30, '65,	1	Substitute—mustered out with Co., July 24, 1865.
Kennedy, Thomas ...	.. do ..	Feb. 28, '65,	1	Substitute—mustered out with Co., July 24, 1865.
Kirker, Francis H. ...	.. do ..	Aug. 31, '61,	3	Wounded—disch. on Surg. cert., March 20, '63.
Kelly, Martin	.. do ..	Feb. 9, '64,	3	Not on muster-out roll.
Lintz, John W.	.. do ..	Feb. 26, '64,	3	Mustered out with company, July 24, 1865.
Leach, Hugh	.. do ..	Jan. 11, '65,	1	Drafted—mustered out with Co., July 24, 1865.
Logue, Willard	.. do ..	Mar. 6, '65,	1	Substitute—mustered out with Co., July 24, 1865.
Leary, Jacob	.. do ..	Aug. 31, '61,	3	Killed at James' Island, S.C., June 16, 1862.
Logan, Robert	.. do ..	Dec. 20, '61,	3	Died at Newport News, Va., Sept. 18, 1862.
Murray, John T.	.. do ..	Feb. 29, '64,	3	Mustered out with company, July 24, 1865.
Murray, James T. ...	.. do ..	Feb. 29, '64,	3	Mustered out with company, July 24, 1865.
Malaby, Benjamin ...	.. do ..	Mar. 8, '65,	1	Substitute—discharged by G.O., July 19, 1865.
Meanes, Jacob	.. do ..	Mar. 9, '65,	1	Substitute—mustered out with Co., July 24, 1865.
Moore, Joseph	.. do ..	Jan. 5, '62,	3	Mustered out, July 12, '65—to date exp. of term.
Moore, John N.	.. do ..	Oct. 18, '61,	3	Discharged on Surg. cert., Jan 6, 1865—Vet.
Masker, Warren	.. do ..	Mar. 6, '65,	1	Substitute—discharged by G.O., May 30, 1865.
Moore, Samuel A. ...	.. do ..	Feb. 18, '64,	3	Discharged by General Order, June 27, 1865.
Meanor, George W. ..	.. do ..	Aug. 10, '64,	1	Discharged by General Order, June 24, 1865.

NAME	RANK	DATE OF MUSTER INTO SERVICE	TERM-YRS	REMARKS
Murray, Samuel	.. do ..	Aug. 31, '61,	3	Wd. in action—disch. on Surg. cert., Aug. 29, '63.
Miles, Thomas N.	.. do ..	Dec. 7, '61,	3	Discharged February 14, 1863.
Miller, Thomas M. ..	.. do ..	Aug. 31, '61,	3	Killed at Petersburg, Va., July 29, 1864.
Miller, John C.	.. do ..	Dec. 20, '61,	3	Killed at South Mountain, Md., Sept. 14, '62—bu. in Antietam Nat. Cem. sec. 26, lot C, grave, 303.
Miles, John F.	.. do ..	Dec. 7, '61,	3	Died at Beaufort, S.C., June 12, 1862.
M'Combs, Hugh	.. do ..	Jan. 16, '65,	1	Drafted—mustered out with Co., July 24, 1865.
M'Elwain, John	.. do ..	Aug. 31, '61,	3	Mustered out, Aug. 30, 1864—expiration of term.
M'Clymonds, T. G. ...	.. do ..	Aug. 31, '61,	3	Mustered out, Aug. 30, 1864—expiration of term.
M'Connell, Henry	.. do ..	Oct. 18, '61,	3	Discharged April 28, 1863.
M'Clure, Hiram W. ...	.. do ..	Dec. 7, '61,	3	Discharged January 10, 1863.
M'Cune, H. H.	.. do ..	Oct. 18, '61,	3	Killed at Petersburg, Va., July 30, 1864—Vet.
M'Kissick, Robert	.. do ..	Feb. 29, '64,	3	Killed at Petersburg, Va., July 30, 1864.
M'Gowan, William ...	.. do ..	Oct. 18, '61,	3	Died December 21, 1861.
M'Kain, John	.. do ..	Dec. 20, '61,	3	Died October 15, 1862—burial record, died at Alexandria, Va., April 23, 1864—grave, 1,827.
M'Ginnis, John	.. do ..	Jan. 30, '65,	3	Substitute—deserted May 15, 1865.
Ogden, John M.	.. do ..	Jan. 11, '65,	1	Drafted—died June 12, 1865—buried in National Cemetery, Arlington, Va.
Pence, William R.	.. do ..	Feb. 23, '64,	3	Mustered out with company, July 24, 1865.
Phillips, Ely B.	.. do ..	Jan. 5, '62,	3	Mustered out, Jan. 4, 1865—expiration of term.
Pisor, John	.. do ..	Aug. 31, '61,	3	Discharged on Surg. cert., Nov. 4, 1864—Vet.
Patterson, Gimsy S. ..	.. do ..	Aug. 31, '61,	3	Discharged March 19, 1863.
Patterson, Smith	.. do ..	Aug. 31, '61,	3	Killed at Cold Harbor, Va., June 2, 1864.
Rutter, Joseph	.. do ..	Aug. 31, '61,	3	Mustered out with company, July 24, 1865—Vet.
Rutter, James	.. do ..	Sept. 29, '64,	3	Mustered out with company, July 24, 1865.
Rhodes, Benjamin	.. do ..	Sept. 23, '64,	3	Mustered out with company July 24, 1865.
Rothmire, George	.. do ..	Sept. 18, '64,	3	Mustered out with company, July 24, 1865—Vet.
Russel, William	.. do ..	Mar. 6, '65,	1	Substitute—mustered out with Co., July 24, 1865.
Reckard, Adam J.	.. do ..	Mar. 7, '65,	1	Substitute—mustered out with Co., July 24, 1865.
Rutter, Alexander	.. do ..	Feb. 29, '64,	3	Discharged on Surgeon's certificate, May 4, '65.
Rowe, John K.	.. do ..	Mar. 23, '64,	3	Died at City Point, Va., July 8, 1864.
Rutter, William	.. do ..	Aug. 31, '61,	3	Discharged November 12, 1862.
Riley, George	.. do ..	Feb. 3, '65,	3	Substitute—deserted March 23, 1865.
Rose, John C.	.. do ..	Aug. 31, '61,	3	Not on muster-out roll.
Shafer, Lafayette	.. do ..	Feb. 23, '64,	3	Mustered out with company, July 24, 1865.
Stewart, Joseph	.. do ..	Dec. 28, '63,	3	Mustered out with company, July 24, 1865.
Suber, Frederick	.. do ..	Feb. 27, '64,	3	Mustered out with company, July 24, 1865.
Shields, Levi	.. do ..	Feb. 23, '64,	3	Mustered out with company, July 24, 1865.
Sullivan, James	.. do ..	Aug. 31, '61,	3	Deserted—ret.—mus. out with Co., July 24, '65.
Shultz, John	.. do ..	Mar. 6, '65,	1	Substitute—mustered out with Co., July 24, 1865.
Straub, Summerf'd ..	.. do ..	Mar. 17, '65,	1	Substitute—discharged by G.O., June 7, 1865.

NAME	RANK	DATE OF MUSTER INTO SERVICE	TERM-YRS	REMARKS
Sweitzer, Daniel	.. do ..	Aug. 13, '63,	3	Drafted—discharged by G.O., July 10, 1865.
Spear, David	.. do ..	Mar. 23, '64,	3	Died at Philadelphia, Pa., September 6, 1864.
Spear, Alexander	.. do ..	Mar. 23, '64,	3	Killed at Petersburg, Va., July 30, 1864.
Sharp, William	.. do ..	Aug. 31, '61,	3	Discharged September 6, 1862.
Sterling, Hiram	.. do ..	Dec. 7, '61,	3	Discharged October 15, 1862.
Stewart, Calvin	.. do ..	Mar. 22, '64,	3	Died at Washington, D.C., March 1, 1865.
Shaffer, John	.. do ..	Sept. 22, '64,	1	Drafted—died May 27, 1865—buried in National Cemetery, Arlington, Va.
Schmitt, John	.. do ..	Mar. 7, '65,	1	Substitute—died June 20, 1865—buried in National Cemetery, Arlington, Va.
Stickle, Simp	.. do ..	Aug. 31, '61,	3	Died at Alexandria, Va., September 23, 1862, of wounds received in action—grave, 316.
Scott, David M.	Private	Aug. 31, '61,	3	Died August 12, 1862.
Slater, Archibald G. .	.. do ..	Aug. 31, '61,	3	Killed at South Mountain, Md., Sept. 14, 1862.
Smith, Solomon W. ...	.. do ..	Aug. 31, '61,	3	Died November 29, 1861.
Smith, John	.. do ..	Feb. 2, '65,	3	Substitute—deserted June 10, 1865.
Silk, Henry	.. do ..	Dec. 7, '61,	3	Not on muster-out roll.
Thomburg, Chas. C. .	.. do ..	Feb. 29, '64,	3	Mustered out with company, July 24, 1865.
Trusdle, Robert	.. do ..	Mar. 7, '65,	1	Substitute—mustered out with Co., July 24, '65.
Ullery, Andrew	.. do ..	Feb. 26, '64,	3	Killed at Petersburg, June 28, 1864—buried in National Cemetery, Meade Station, Va.
Vogan, John A.	.. do ..	Dec. 7, '61,	3	Mustered out with company, July 24, 1865—Vet.
Weyman, Ernest	.. do ..	Aug. 31, '61,	3	Mustered out with company, July 24, 1865—Vet.
White, William	.. do ..	Dec. 24, '61,	3	Mustered out with company, July 24, 1865—Vet.
White, James W.	.. do ..	Aug. 31, '61,	3	Mustered out with company, July 24, 1865—Vet.
Wimer, Adam	.. do ..	Feb. 26, '64,	3	Mustered out with company, July 24, 1865.
Wilson, David W. ...	.. do ..	Feb. 29, '64,	3	Absent, sick, at muster out.
Wier, Thomas	.. do ..	Feb. 29, '64,	3	Mustered out with company, July 24, 1865—Vet.
Watson, Clark	.. do ..	Feb. 20, '64,	3	Wounded at Spottsylvania C.H., Va., May 12, 1864—absent, sick, at muster out—Vet.
Wilson, Milo	.. do ..	Feb. 27, '64,	3	Mustered out with company, July 24, 1865.
Wingert, William	.. do ..	Jan. 11, '65,	1	Drafted—discharged by G.O., Aug. 9, 1865.
Willhelm, John W. ...	.. do ..	Nov. 24, '64,	1	Drafted—mustered out with Co., July 24, 1865.
Winters, George	.. do ..	Feb. 2, '65,	1	Substitute—mustered out with Co., July 24, '65.
Wilson, James	.. do ..	Mar. 10, '65,	1	Substitute—absent, sick, at muster out.
White, Richard R. ...	.. do ..	Mar. 7, '65,	1	Substitute—mustered out with Co., July 24, '65.
Weaber, Adam	.. do ..	Jan. 11, '65,	1	Drafted—mustered out with Co., July 24, 1865.
Wright, Samuel S. ...	.. do ..	Feb. 20, '64,	3	Drafted—mustered out with Co., July 24, 1865.
Wick, Alfred N.	.. do ..	Aug. 31, '61,	3	Mustered out, Aug. 30, 1864—expiration of term.
Williamson, John	.. do ..	Mar. 9, '65,	1	Substitute—discharged by G.O., June 13, 1865.
Walton, John E.	.. do ..	Aug. 31, '61,	3	Mustered out, Aug. 30, 1864—expiration of term.
Watson, Winans	.. do ..	Aug. 31, '61,	3	Transferred to Vet. Reserve Corps, Jan. 5, 1864.

NAME	RANK	DATE OF MUSTER INTO SERVICE	TERM-YRS	REMARKS
Watson, Winans	Private	Sept. 10, '64,	1	Killed at Poplar Spring Church, Va., Oct. 2, '64.
Wright, William	.. do ..	Feb. 27, '64,	3	Died in Lawrence county, Pa., Dec. 18, 1864.
Wimer, Robert	.. do ..	Aug. 31, '61,	3	Died May 30, '63—buried in National Cemetery, Camp Nelson, Ky., section D, grave, 87.
Wright, Miller	.. do ..	Aug. 31, '61,	3	Discharged Dec. 1, 1862, for wds. rec. in action.
Wilson, Eli H.	.. do ..	Aug. 31, '61,	3	Killed at Bull Run, Va., Aug. 29, 1862.
Wilson, Hugh	.. do ..	Aug. 31, '61,	3	Disch.—date unknown—for wds. rec. in action.
Williams, John C.	.. do ..	Aug. 31, '61,	3	Not on muster-out roll.
White, Addison S.	.. do ..	Aug. 31, '61,	3	Not on muster-out roll.
Winner, William C. ..	.. do ..	Feb. 26, '64,	3	Not on muster-out roll.
Wixson, Alfred	.. do ..	Mar. 21, '64,	3	Not on muster-out roll.
Weber, John	.. do ..	Aug. 8, '64,	3	Not on muster-out roll.

APPENDIX C

THE 100TH PENNSYLVANIA VETERAN
VOLUNTEER INFANTRY REGIMENT

"A FIGHTING REGIMENT"

This extract on the service of Pettit's regiment, the 100th Pennsylvania, is taken from William F. Fox's *Regimental Losses in the American Civil War* which was printed in Albany, N.Y., in 1889. It provides an excellent summary of the regiment and includes the various battles in which the regiment participated. The 100th was in service for 47 months and ranks amongst the highest of all Pennsylvania regiments in casualties suffered.

ONE HUNDREDTH PENNSYLVANIA INFANTRY—"ROUNDHEADS."

LEASURE'S BRIGADE—STEVENSON'S DIVISION—NINTH CORPS.

(1) COL. DANIEL LEASURE; BVT. BRIG. GEN.   (2) COL. NORMAN J. MAXWELL; BVT. BRIG. GEN.

COMPANIES.	Killed and Died Of Wounds.			Died Of Disease, Accidents, In Prison, &c.			Total Enrollment.
	Officers.	Men.	Total.	Officers.	Men.	Total.	
Field and Staff	4	..	4	·	1	1	18
Company A	1	18	19	·	22	22	184
B	2	13	15	·	17	17	184
C	1	27	28	·	20	20	198
D	·	21	21	·	15	15	192
E	·	30	30	·	21	21	191
F	1	22	23	2	21	23	201
G	2	20	22	·	16	16	202
H	1	12	13	·	12	12	181
I	1	6	7	·	8	8	82
K	3	19	22	·	17	17	186
M	·	20	20	·	13	13	195
Totals	16	208	224	2	183	185	2,014

224 Killed — 11.1 per cent.
Total of killed and wounded, 887; died in Confederate prisons (previously included), 29.

BATTLES.	K. & M. W.	BATTLES.	K. & M. W.
Legare's Point, S.C.	3	North Anna, Va.	2
James Island, S.C.	13	Bethesda Church, Va.	2
Manassas, Va.	27	Cold Harbor, Va.	18
Chantilly, Va.	7	Siege of Petersburg, Va.	21
South Mountain, Md.	12	Petersburg, Mine, Va.	23
Antietam, Md.	2	Weldon Railroad, Va.	7
Jackson, Miss.	1	Poplar Spring Church, Va.	5
Blue Springs, Tenn.	1	Boydton Road, Va.	1
Campbell's Station, Tenn.	1	Picket, Va., Dec. 13, 1864	1
Siege of Knoxville, Tenn.	5	Fort Stedman, Va.	22
Wilderness, Va.	4	Fall of Petersburg, Va.	2
Spotsylvania, Va.	44		

Present, also, at Port Royal, S.C.; Coosaw River, S.C.; Fredericksburg, Va.; Vicksburg, Miss.

NOTES.—The Pennsylvania Roundheads proved on many a hard fought field that they were worthy of their *nom de guerre,* and their ancestral namesakes. Bates, the historian, says that they were recruited in a part of the State which was settled by English Roundheads and Scotch-Irish Covenanters. Be that as it may, there was no stancher stuff in Cromwell's regiments than in the blue-coated line that dressed on the colors of the Hundredth Pennsylvania. They were well officered, Colonel Leasure being a man of remarkable soldierly ability, and although in command of the brigade most of the time, the regiment was always ably handled. Lieut.-Col. Dawson fell, mortally wounded, in the assault on Petersburg; Lieut.-Col. Pentecost was killed at Fort Stedman; Major Hamilton and Adjutant Leasure fell in the fighting at the Petersburg Mine. Five line-officers fell at Manassas, the casualties in that battle amounting to 15 killed, 117 wounded, and 8 missing. At Spotsylvania it sustained a loss of 23 killed, 110 wounded, and 2 missing; total, 135. Like all the Ninth Corps regiments its service was a varied one; it made long journeys by sea and land, and fought its battles in many and widely separated States.

BIBLIOGRAPHY

This bibliography consists of a comprehensive listing of sources relative to the history of the 100th Pennsylvania Volunteer Infantry Regiment. It includes manuscripts, books, and publications utilized in the preparation of this work plus many others which should prove useful in researching the history of the 100th Pennsylvania Volunteer Infantry Regiment.

BIBLIOGRAPHY

MANUSCRIPTS

PENNSYLVANIA STATE UNIVERSITY, UNIVERSITY PARK, PENNA.

Historical Collections and Labor Archives, Pattee Library.

Doctor M. Gyla McDowell Collection. Referred to as McDowell, HCLA.
The McDowell Collection has been the primary manuscript source for
this work. Dr. McDowell was designated the regimental historian in the veterans'
organization of the "Society of the Roundheads" and in this position was able
to collect a large quantity of manuscript material over a period of many years.
The collection is an extensive one necessitating six archival file boxes to house
it. Both Dr. McDowell, and Dr. Silas Stevenson, a veteran of Company K, were
untiring in their efforts to collect any and all material pertaining to the regiment from the regimental survivors. They were eminently successful in their
effort as judged by the quantity and quality of the material comprising the
McDowell Collection.

The collection has been inventoried and files have been created which
facilitate access to the material. The following annotated list includes the important files within the McDowell Collection which have been utilized in the
writing of this book.

1. *Doctor M. Gyla McDowell, "Stories of the Roundheads."* This is the
   manuscript history of the 100th Pennsylvania Regiment which was written over a period of several years by Dr. McDowell. It contains a total
   of nineteen chapters covering the activities of the Roundheads in their 47
   months of service from 1861 to 1865. This history was never published.
   It does contain a vast amount of eyewitness accounts by members of the
   regiment which is not to be found elsewhere. This history has been of great
   value in the preparation of "Campaigning with the Roundheads."

   Dr. McDowell's objective was to let the "boys tell their story in their
   own words." It was to be a "reflection of the life of the boys of '61 in
   camp, at the front, in battle, prison, at home on furlough." Unfortunately,
   Dr. McDowell's history is somewhat disconnected and does not give the
   reader an understanding of the tactics and strategy of the various campaigns in which the regiment was involved. There were no maps included,
   but there are photographs and illustrations, some of the latter being
   original sketches of wartime scenes by a member of the regiment. Despite
   the shortcomings of "Stories of the Roundheads," this work has an invaluable source of information and guidance in preparing "Campaigning with the Roundheads."

2. *Reverend Robert Audley Browne, "letters" written 1861-1863.* This collection of Dr. Browne's wartime letters written when he was the regimental chaplain have been transcribed. Dr. Browne wrote his wife on an almost daily basis during his tour of duty with the regiment from September of 1861 until his resignation in December of 1863. Browne wrote well and his description of the environment, the personalities of men in the regiment, and the everyday life and activities of the Roundheads is superb. There are several hundred letters in the collection and some thought should be given to publishing them as a separate entity. Reverend Browne submitted news stories from the field to New York newspapers as a sort of unofficial war correspondent. There are some unexplained gaps in the period in which the letters cover, but these are of limited consequence. The U.S. Army Military History Institute, Carlisle Barracks, Pennsylvania, has a great number of the originals of the Browne letters.

3. *James C. Stevenson, "The Roundheads, A Condensed History of this Noted Regiment, etc."* James Stevenson served in the regiment for four years in Company E. After the war he became the very active secretary of the "Society of the Roundheads." His history was published in New Castle in Stevenson's publication entitled the "Volunteer." A copy of this brief, but concise, history of 18 pages is in the McDowell Collection. It was never published for general distribution elsewhere. An 1861 diary kept by Stevenson is in the McDowell Collection and has fine details on the early experiences of the Roundheads.

   In the McDowell Collection is a bound scrap book of 140 pages which Stevenson compiled. In it are extracts of New Castle newspaper articles on the regiment including Captain Joseph T. Carter's account of the 1864-1865 campaigns, articles on prisoners of war, and Stevenson's own "Condensed History" quoted above. There are 140 pages of excellent information in this scrap book.

4. *Doctor Silas Stevenson, History of the Roundheads.* Dr. Stevenson compiled a history of the regiment which was used extensively in Dr. McDowell's "Stories of the Roundheads." Unfortunately, a complete copy of Stevenson's work is not in existence and exists in the McDowell Collection in "bits and pieces." It appears that Stevenson's work was mostly in diary format. Apparently it was never published. The portions of Stevenson's history that have been studied give much important and useful information of the activities of the Roundheads. Dr. Silas Stevenson served in the regiment during the last years of the war and later lived in Ellwood City, Pennsylvania, where he remained active in veteran affairs of the regiment. A fifteen page pamphlet which Stevenson wrote is entitled "The Epitomized History of the Roundheads." A large number of manuscript pages of Stevenson's history can be found in File Box Number Four in the McDowell Collection.

5. *Lieutenant William Taylor, Company G.* Taylor kept a journal and was an excellent writer. Portions of his writings appear in Dr. McDowell's "Stories of the Roundheads." His account of the Vicksburg Campaign is excellent and has been incorporated into the text of "Campaigning with the Roundheads."

6. *Sergeant G. L. Preston, Company B.* Transcribed diaries for January to December of 1864.

7. *Private Hamilton R. Dunlap, Company K, Letters and diaries for 1861-1865.* Hamilton's letters home are filled with humor and are a delight to read. There is a vast amount of detailed information on the Roundheads in the Dunlap collection.

8. *Colonel Daniel Leasure.* Leasure was the regimental commander. There are transcribed copies of many of his letters to his family for the period 1861-1865. There is also an extensive number of handwritten letters by Leasure for the same period. Leasure wrote portions of the history of the regiment, but there was never a complete history done by him. His account of Pope's Campaign in Virginia in 1862 is well written and was published by the Minnesota Commandery of the Military Order of the Loyal Legion.

9. *Adjutant (Lieutenant S. George Leasure).* A series of transcribed letters by Adjutant Leasure to his family give excellent details of the campaigning during the period May to July of 1864. Adjutant Leasure was killed in action on July 30, 1864.

10. *Private Marius K. McDowell,* "A Private's Story." McDowell served in Company F of the Roundheads until wounded in September 1862 at Antietam. His story, written fifty years after, exists in handwritten manuscript form in the McDowell collection. It contains excellent information on South Mountain and Antietam as well as a detailed account of the miseries of a wounded Civil War soldier. Marius McDowell was the father of Dr. M. Gyla McDowell.

11. *Major Thomas Jefferson Hamilton.* Hamilton was serving as regimental commander at the time of his death in 1864. There is a collection of transcribed letters written by and also some about him for the period 1861 to 1865. Some of the latter give details of his death and burial in Petersburg after the Battle of the Crater.

12. *Lieutenant John W. Morrison, Company E.* Morrison wrote several articles after the close of the war. One of these, "The Mine Explosion,"

was used by Dr. McDowell on the Battle of the Crater. It was Morrison's intention to write a history of the regiment, but he deferred in doing this after learning that others were preparing such a work. There are other writing and reminiscences by Morrison in the files of the McDowell Collection.

13. *Captain Joseph T. Carter, 3rd Maryland Infantry Regiment.* This regiment served with the 100th Pennsylvania during the Virginia Campaign of 1864 and 1865. Carter wrote an excellent account of the history of the 3rd Brigade, of which the Roundheads and 3rd Maryland were a part. His history was published by the New Castle "Courant" newspaper but, apparently, no place else. A copy of this brief history is in the McDowell Collection and contains excellent and detailed original information on the Battles of the Wilderness and Fort Stedman.

14. *Lieutenant John H. Stevenson, Company K, pamphlet, "Company K, Leasure Guards."* Stevenson is another member of the Roundheads who had intented to write a history of the regiment. An 1884 advertisement for this "forthcoming book" mentions that it will be "a large illustrated history." Unfortunately, this was the last heard of it. Stevenson died in 1904.

The McDowell Collection is a vast one. The sources above comprise some of the more significant files in the Collection.

U.S. ARMY MILITARY HISTORY INSTITUTE, CARLISLE BARRACKS, PENNSYLVANIA.

Archives

1. *Corporal Frederick Pettit, Company C.* Pettit served with the Roundheads from 1862 until his death at Petersburg on July 9, 1864. Young Pettit was a prolific writer and left behind a large collection of letters giving details of the movements of the regiment during the period. The letters are well written and quite accurate in their description of the terrain and the battles in which the Roundheads participated. There are details in them which are not available elsewhere. In some of the letters, he relates minutia of soldier life with comments on the food, uniforms, and camp life. The Pettit letters comprise one of the important sources on the Roundheads. Pettit's letters are in the *Civil War Times Illustrated* collection at the archives in Carlisle. A complete copy was kindly furnished the writer by Mr. T. C. Williams of New Castle, Pennsylvania.

2. *Lieutenant Henry Applegate, Company H.* Letter pertaining to the "mutiny" in the regiment. Beaufort, South Carolina, March 7, 1862.

3. *Private Robert W. Rodgers, Company E, Diary.* January to 31 December, 1863.

4. *Sergeant Elisha Bracken, Company C, letter, July 1862 to January 1863.*

5. *The "Camp Kettle."* Eleven issues of the regimental newspaper.

6. *Reverend Robert Audley Browne, a collection of original Civil War letters written by the regimental chaplain.* Another collection of Browne's original letters is in private hands. These letters cover the period May 23 to November 11, 1863.

7. *Photographs.* The Photographic Branch of the Archives of the Army Military History Institute had an excellent collection of photographs of members of the 100th Pennsylvania regiment, many of which have been utilized in "Campaigning with the Roundheads."

LAWRENCE COUNTY HISTORICAL SOCIETY, NEW CASTLE, PENNSYLVANIA.

1. *Captain Robert F. Moffatt, Company F.* Moffatt served throughout the War with the Roundheads. His original diary is in the Lawrence County Collection. It covers the period August 28, 1861, the day his service began, until November 25, 1863. The diary was transcribed by Mr. T. C. Williams, New Castle, Pennsylvania, who graciously provided the author with a copy.

2. *Photographs.* There is an extensive collection of photographs of soldiers of the Roundhead regiment in printing block form in the collection of the Historical Society.

THE HISTORICAL SOCIETY OF WESTERN PENNSYLVANIA, PITTSBURGH, PENNSYLVANIA.

1. *Corporal Alexander Adams, Company A, letters, "Civil War Letters of Alexander Adams" compiled by John A. Adams, grandson.* These letters cover the period January 30th, 1862 until June 10, 1865. They were written by an enlisted man and contain many valuable comments on life in the Roundhead Regiment for over three and one half years.

AUTHOR'S COLLECTION.

1. *Lieutenant David I. Gilfillan, Company F, letters written in 1863.*

NEWSPAPERS

Harper's Weekly.
Camp Kettle, Regimental Newspaper, 100th Pennsylvania Vols.
Courant, New Castle, Pennsylvania.
New York Herald.
New York Times.

OFFICIAL DOCUMENTS

1. *The War of the Rebellion: A Compilation of the Official Records of the Union and Confederate Armies.* Washington, D.C. U.S. Government Printing Office, 1880-1901.

2. *Atlas to accompany the Official Records of the Union and Confederate Armies.* Washington, U.S. Government Printing Office, 1891-1896.

3. *Cold Harbor, A Study of the Operations of the Army of Northern Virginia and the Army of the Potomac from May 26 to June 13, 1864.* Major Charles J. Calrow, Manuscript form. U.S. Dept. of the Interior, National Park Service. Written in 1933, Norfolk, Virginia.

4. Civil War Atlas to accompany Steele's *American Campaigns*, U.S.M.A., West Point, New York. Colonel T. D. Stamps, Department of Military History and Engineering, 1941.

5. *Historical Report on the Troop Movements for the Second Battle of Manassas, August 28 through August 30, 1862.* John Hennessy. U.S. Department of the Interior, National Park Service, 1985.

AUTOBIOGRAPHIES, BIOGRAPHIES, DIARIES, LETTERS, MEMOIRS, AND PERSONAL NARRATIVES

Bates, Samuel P., *Martial Deeds of Pennsylvania.* Phila., 1876.

Fox, William F., *Regimental Losses in the American Civil War, 1861-1865.* Albany, New York, 1889.

Jones, Vigil Carrington, *The Civil War at Sea.* New York, N.Y., 1960-1962.

Longstreet, James, *From Manassas to Appomattox.* Phila., 1896.

Merrill, James M., *DuPont, The Making Of An Admiral.* New York, 1986.

Stevens, Hazard, *The Life of Isaac Ingalls Stevens.* Boston and New York, 1900.

Warner, Ezra J., *Generals in Blue*. Baton Rouge, Louisiana State University Press, 1964.

Weld, Stephen Minot, *War Diary and Letters of Stephen Minot Weld*. Cambridge, Massachusetts, 1912.

Young, Victor, *The Major*. (Major James Harvey Cline) Privately Printed, Pittsburgh, Pennsylvania, No date.

CAMPAIGN AND BATTLE NARRATIVES

Atkinson, C. F., *Grant's Campaign of 1864-1865*. London, 1908.

Bearss, Edwin C., *The Siege of Vicksburg*. Dayton, Press of Morningside, 1987.

Bearss, Edwin C., *The Siege of Jackson*. Baltimore, 1981.

Bigelow, John, *The Campaign of Chancellorsville*. New Haven, 1910.

Buel, Clarence, Clough, and Johnson etc., *Battles and Leaders of the Civil War*. New York, Yoseloff, 1956.

Carter, Joseph T., *History of the Third Brigade, First Division, Ninth Army Corps*. New Castle, Penna., "Courant," N.D.

Hodgkins, William H., *The Battle of Fort Stedman*. Boston, 1889.

Humphreys, Andrew Atkinson, *The Virginia Campaign of 1864 and 1865*. New York, Scribner's, 1883.

Johnson, John, *The Defense of Charleston Harbor 1863-1865*. Charleston, S.C., Evans and Cogswell, 1890.

Merrill, Frank L., *Poplar Spring Church*. National Tribune, 1894.

Military Order of the Loyal Legion, Minnesota Commander, *Glimpses of the Nation's Struggle*. St. Paul, Minn., 1887-1909.

Papers of the Military Historical Society of Massachusetts, Multi Volumes, Boston, 1895-1918.

Sears, Stephen W., *Landscape Turned Red*. New York, Ticknor and Fields, 1983.

Seymour, Digby Gordon, *Divided Loyalties*. Dayton, Ohio, Morningside House, Inc., 1982.

Sommers, Richard J., *Richmond Redeemed*. New York, Doubleday, 1981.

Southern Historical Society Papers, Richmond, Virginia, 1876-1919.

Stackpole, Edward James, *Drama on the Rappahannock*. Harrisburg, Penna., Military Service Pub. Co., 1957.

Steele, Mathew Forney, *American Campaigns*. Washington, U.S. Infantry Association, 1922.

Steere, Edward, *The Wilderness Campaign*. Harrisburg, Penna., Stackpole, 1960.

UNIT HISTORIES

Albert, Allen D., *History of the Forty-Fifth Regiment, Pennsylvania Veteran Volunteer Infantry, 1861-1865*. Williamsport, Penna., Grit Pub. Co., 1912.

Anderson, John, *The Fifty-Seventh Regiment of Massachusetts Volunteers in the War of the Rebellion*. Boston, Stillings, 1896.

Bates, Samuel P., *History of the Pennsylvania Volunteers*. Harrisburg, B. Singerly, 1871.

Bosbyshell, Oliver C., *The 48th in the War, Being a Narrative of the Campaigns on the 48th Regiment, Pennsylvania Veteran Volunteers*. Philadelphia, Avil Printing, 1895.

Burrage, Henry, *History of the Thirty-Sixth Regiment, Massachusetts Volunteers*. Boston, Rockwell and Churchill, 1884.

Caldwell, James F. J., *The History of a Brigade of South Carolinians...McGowan's Brigade*. Phila., King and Baird, 1866.

Carruth, Sumner, *History of the Thirty-Fifth Regiment Massachusetts Volunteers, 1862-1865*. Boston, Mills Knight, 1884.

Cogswell, Leander, *A History of the Eleventh New Hampshire Regiment Volunteer Infantry*. Concord, Republican Press, 1891.

Cuffell, Charles A., *Durell's Battery in the Civil War*. Phila., Craig, Finley and Co., 1900.

Cutcheon, Byron, M., *The Story of the Twentieth Michigan Infantry*. Lansing, Robert Smith Printing, 1904.

Dyer, Frederick A., *A Compendium of the War of the Rebellion*. New York, Yoseloff, 1959.

Ely, Ralph, *The Diary of Captain Ralph Ely, of the Eighth Michigan Infantry*. Mount Pleasant, Central Mich. Univ. Press, 1965.

Embick, Milton, *Military History of the Third Division, Ninth Corps*. Harrisburg, Aughinbaugh, 1913.

Gould, Joseph, *The Story of the Forty Eighth Regiment Pennsylvania Veteran Volunteer Infantry*. Phila., Slocum and Company, 1908.

Hinckley, *The 58th Mass*. National Tribune. May 1915.

192

William Gilfillan Gavin

Jackman, Lyman, *History of the Sixth New Hampshire Regiment in the War for the Union*. Concord, Republican Press, 1891.

Livermore, Thomas L., *History of the Eighteenth New Hampshire Volunteers, 1864-1865*. Boston, Fort Hill Press, 1904.

Lord, Edward O., *History of the Ninth Regiment New Hampshire Volunteers in the War of the Rebellion*. Concord, Republican Press, 1896.

Osborne, William H., *The History of the Twenty Ninth Regiment of Massachusetts Volunteer Infantry*. Boston, Wright, 1877.

Parker, Thomas H., *History of the 51st Regiment of P.V. and V.V.* Phila., King and Baird, 1869.

Pierce, S. W., *Battlefields and Camp Fires of the Thirty-Eighth Wisconsin Volunteer Infantry*. Milwaukee, Daily Wisconsin Printing House, 1866.

Seventeenth Michigan Volunteer Infantry Regiment, *The Stonewall Regiment*. Published by the 17th Michigan Volunteer Infantry Regiment, Detroit, 1986.

Shaw, Charles A., *A History of the 14th Regiment, New York Heavy Artillery in the Civil War*. Mt. Kisco, North Westchester Publishing Company, 1918.

Robertson, *Michigan in the War*. Lansing, George and Co., 1882.

Swinton, William, *Campaigns of the Army of the Potomac*. New York, Richardson, 1866.

Thompson, Gilbert, *The Engineer Battalion in the Civil War*. The Engineer School, U.S. Army, 1910.

Todd, William, *The Seventy-Ninth Highlander, New York Volunteers in the War of the Rebellion*. Albany, N.Y., Brandow, Barton, and Company, 1886.

Walcott, Charles F., *History of the Twenty-First Massachusetts Volunteers... 1861-1865*. Boston, Houghton Mifflin, 1882.

Walkley, Stephen W., *History of the Seventh Connecticut Volunteer Infantry, 1861-1865*. Harford, 1905.

Woodburg, Augustus, *Major General Ambrose E. Burnside and the Ninth Army Corps...* Providence, Sidney S. Rider and Brother, 1867.

PHOTOGRAPHS

U.S. Army Military History Institute, Carlisle Barracks, Pennsylvania.

INDEX

A

Alexander, John (Co. C, 100th PA), 130
Alexandria, VA, 133, 151
Allison, Erskine E., 58, 168
Annapolis, MD, 125, 126, 127, 128, 130, 131, 132, 133
Antietam, Battle of, 10, 11, 16, 27
Antietam Creek, 16
Antietam Furnace/Iron Works, 14, 18, 20, 22, 26
Army Corps:
    2nd, 137
    9th, 27, 31, 52, 60, 66, 80, 86, 98, 104, 107, 110, 114, 122, 125, 127, 130, 133, 134, 149, 153
    23rd, 86, 98, 107, 110, 114
Army of Northern Virginia, 20, 27, 31, 110, 135
Army of the Potomac, 20, 27, 31, 35, 43, 44, 78-79, 111, 126, 132, 145, 149

B

Baltimore, MD, 6, 7, 19, 63, 64-65, 67, 126, 127, 146
Batteries:
    Benjamin's (Buckley's Rhode Island), 118, 121
    2nd New York Artillery, 118, 121
    27th New York, 149
Bealton Station, VA, 136
Bell Plain (Belle Plain), Landing, VA, 33, 35
Berlin (Brunswick), MD, 27, 29, 30, 31
Bethesda Church, VA (Cold Harbor), 138, 141
Big Black River, MS, 90, 91, 93
Bird, Phineas (Co. C, 100th PA), 17, 18, 95, 116, 118, 119, 124, 128, 129, 130
Blaine's (Blanes) Cross Roads, TN, x, 122, 123, 124, 125, 168
Blue Springs, TN (Battle of Oct. 10, 1863), 114, 115, 160
Bracken, Elisha O. (Sergeant, Co. C, 100th PA), 116

Bragg, Braxton (C.S.A.), 73, 110, 111, 113, 160
Browne, Robert Audley (Chaplain of the 100th PA), 17, 43, 60, 74, 78, 79, 104, 105, 115, 120, 129, 161, 162, 163, 166, 169, 170, 185, 188
Burns, William Wallace, 37
Burnside, Ambrose (Commander, 9th Corps), 8, 18, 44-45, 49, 52, 64, 66, 72, 73, 75, 76, 86, 97, 98, 107, 109, 110, 111, 113, 114, 115, 117, 121, 131, 132, 162

C

Cairo, IL, 87, 95, 96, 97
Camp Copeland, PA (near Pittsburgh), 125, 126, 127, 128
Camp Curtin, PA, 3, 4, 5, 19
Camp Dick Robinson, KY, 70, 71, 72, 73, 75, 76, 77, 97, 104
Camp Distribution, VA, 148, 151
Camp Israel (Pleasant Valley, MD), 20, 21, 23, 24, 25, 27
Camp Nelson, KY, 97, 98, 125
Camp Parke, KY, 100, 101, 103, 104
Camp Parole, MD (near Annapolis), 128
Campbell's Station, TN, Battle of, 117-118
Carters Run, VA, 32, 34
Cavalry:
    Sanders', 118, 119
    Wheeler's, 111
    Wolford's, 110, 115, 118, 119
Chambersburg, PA, 90
Chancellorsville, VA, 135, 137
Chattanooga, TN, 110, 111, 113, 121, 159
Chickamauga, Battle of, 110, 111, 113, 158, 161
Chickasaw Bluffs, MS, 88, 89
Cincinnati, OH, 52, 65, 66, 68, 76, 95, 96, 97, 98, 117, 125
City Point, VA, 151, 152
Clay, Henry, 68, 69
Cleeland, Samuel H. (Co. C, 100th PA), 130